Your Journey - Day by Day - Direct From Heaven To You
By Lina M

Royal Diadem Publishing House Pty Ltd & Beyond Woman Pty Ltd
PO Box 1018
Sanctuary Cove, Qld, 4212
Australia

Copyright © 2016, 2017, 2019 Royal Diadem Publishing House Pty Ltd
                Beyond Woman Pty Ltd
                Lina M.

First Edition printed August 2017

Created and designed in Australia by Lina, The Author of 'Beyond Woman.'

All rights reserved. No part of this publication, including art and images, may be reproduced, stored in a retrieval system, or transmitted in any form or by any means whether electronic, mechanical, photocopying, recording or otherwise, without the publisher's express written permission.

Beyond Woman is a registered trademark of Beyond Woman Pty Ltd.

International Standard Book Number - ISBN 978-0-9941790-1-2

Scripture taken from the Holy Bible, New International Version®. Copyright © 1973, 1978, 1984, 2011 by International Bible Society. Used by permission of Zondervan Publishing House. All rights reserved. Italics in Scripture references are for emphasis only.

Your Journey
Day by Day

Direct from Heaven to You
The Answers Are Within You

Lina

ROYAL DIADEM
PUBLISHING
HOUSE

PO Box 1018
Sanctuary Cove Qld 4212
Australia
Email: seek@royalpublisher.com

National Library of Australia Cataloguing-in-Publication entry

Creator: M., Lina, author.

Title: Your journey : day by day / Lina M.

ISBN: 9780994179012 (paperback)

Subjects: Self-actualization (Psychology)

Self-help techniques.

Life skills.

Dewey Number: 158.1

DESCRIPTION OF LOVE

'Your Journey' Day by Day Direct From Heaven To You by Lina M, The Author of Beyond Woman.

'Your Journey' is your daily bread from heaven, written to reflect your inner-outer you in fullness as in a mirror.

You will be empowered to soar on the heights, as you read the pages of your life revealed in all truth, no matter where you are, time of day or circumstances.
Enter The Promised Land and not The Wilderness.

The fire shall burn deep within your soul as you read the different journeys of your life experiences expressed in words just for you.

"Learn my ways and you will be transfixed," says the Lord God, "acknowledge my truth and you will be lifted up in honor."

Your journey differs from one day to the next - Between Light and Darkness - The spiritual and the natural.

These pages will comfort your heart, recharge your spirit and confirm your ways.

Every minute of the day is a journey, reflecting the inner you in fullness.

Enjoy your journey on earth, for a new Chapter has just begun.

'Your Journey, day-by-day.
The Journey of Life - Your Daily Journey.'
Reflect on the words you read, and you will see yourself as you are.
Truth in action is the answer to every question.
Enjoy your freedom.

"*Your Journey of Life Begins*

Journey

- 1 -

DEVELOP IN CHARACTER

The power of love is in your heart, child.

Act upon my word and grow in Wisdom.
Gain understanding and walk in Love.
Acknowledge my Will and walk in the Way of Truth.

Have the same attitude as that of mine and grow in my likeness.
Develop in character and become holy.
Live as one with me and do not become one with the world.
Be one with me in spirit and in truth.
Let the world know that you are my child.

You will never be defeated nor ever be restricted.

Undress yourself from the system of this world by entering into a higher realm of glory.

You are evolving from a child to a son.

I have partaken your hardships upon my shoulders.
Hold on and never let go.
Your future is assured, and the glory alone is mine.

Be refreshed, son, and have something to eat.
Drink my wine and eat my bread and you will be strong to carry on.

Amen

Love

Psa 143:10 **Teach me to do your will, for you are my God; may your good Spirit lead me on level ground.**

Journey
- 2 -

THE MASTERY OF WISDOM

Heed my instruction, child, more now than ever, for the time has come for the curtains to be closed.
Listen to my words of insight, for the time draws near.

This is the hour of my return.
No longer argue with one another, so you will not be defeated.

See through my eyes and you will not lose heart.

Son, the battles you face on different occasions, during those lonely hours in the wilderness, are of me.
I allow them to cleanse you, draw you closer to me, and strengthen your ability against the enemy.

Be not discouraged by the fowler who draws the knife on the throat, for he is defeated.
Fear not, you have been given power over him.
The victory is yours.
He lays defeated, underfoot as a dead snake.

Accept one another as I have accepted you, and love as I have loved you. I have given you another chance to live the life of freedom.

The pure in thought shall remain strong in spirit.

Correct not that which is twisted.

Amen

Love

Rom 14:1 Accept the one whose faith is weak, without quarrelling over disputable matters.

Journey
- 3 -
LET US AGREE

How can one run away from God, when he has betrayed his own soul? One must run to God and not away from him, for He is Love and Security.
He will never hand you over to the enemy.
You belong to Him.

You will not come to the end of yourself, for He delights in you.
He will bring you to an awesome end for a new beginning.

He is your Savior and Delicacy.
He will surprise you with wonderful things not yet seen... reserved only for you.
His promises to you, are all, Yes and Amen.

Since you have resisted evil and given yourself to righteousness, you will surely reap the benefits of your faithfulness - The Crown of Life promised.
You will not be condemned, for my Name among you is great.

Father, free me to worship you in spirit and love you from the depth of my being.

You will surely live and not die. Forget not my benefits stored up just for you, child-- ready to be revealed.

Amen

Love

Tit 1:15 To the pure, all things are pure, but to those who are corrupted and do not believe, nothing is pure. In fact, both their minds and consciences are corrupted.

Journey
- 4 -

ETERNALLY JOINED

The road you are now traveling on, Oh, my child, is much more difficult, and longer in distance than my highway of holiness.

If you are unsure of what the future holds for you, stay in your position, exactly where you are, and move not an inch-- until it is confirmed by me and you are certain.

Be encouraged and not discouraged. You are going to be just fine. Heed my voice, for I am your true Friend, the Way of Life and Shortcut.
Test me in this, and you will always find my Word true, and comes to pass.
You will surely be successful.

Develop your skills by mastering your gifts.

The power of my grace and resurrection life has been given to you. You have nothing to fear. Nothing is lost.

Be courteous and extend kindness when speaking with friends. Listen, that you may live in total commitment with your Husband and Best Friend.

Oh, God of my Spirit, fill my heart with Love.

Beloved, I have assured you life, and life eternal you have received from me.

Amen

Love

Psa 119:50 **My comfort in my suffering is this: Your promise preserves my life.**

Journey

- 5 -

ULTIMATE SURRENDER

Oh, child, I understand that you are completely humble, but first, you must withstand the test of time.
Work with all your heart and might, that you may win favor and overcome the difficulties of this world, tormenting your mind with bad thoughts and confusion.

You are complete in me.
See yourself through my eyes and you will not be disappointed.

Many have tried to rob you of your calling, but were unsuccessful.
You have developed faith in action and I am well pleased with you.
Now be restored to your rightful position.
You have exceeded your companions, and they have not been able to rule over you.
Soar, O my precious child, soar with the eagles, and let no one rob you of your faith, nor of your crown of righteousness, which you have received from me on that day.
Obey my voice, and you will not wither, nor fade away, for you will be established.
The future remains untold, because no one knows the Hour, nor the time of my return.

Your Honor and Crown of righteousness I am.
I am the One beholding you in glory - Holding you in love.

Amen

Love

Pro 6:5 **Free yourself, like a gazelle from the hand of the hunter, like a bird from the snare of the fowler.**

Journey

- 6 -

THE PRINCE OF KINGS

Keep me close to your heart and you will not stray.
Draw near to me and I will be closer still.
Listen to every beat of my heart... beating just for you.
Lift up your voice with a shout, and be not afraid.
I am here to support you.

Do not be troubled, O little one, for your Maker is strong. He tends his flock like a shepherd, and carries the lambs in his arms, close to his heart. With love and deep compassion, he shall carry both you and your children.

Your Sovereign watches over you, and will not neglect you.
He protects your soul all day and watches over you all night.
Even while you are asleep, his eyes keep diligent.
Your God is near, he will not forsake you, nor will ever neglect those who earnestly seek him.

Delight yourself in your Maker, for the victory has been won over your enemy.
I am God, the great I Am. You have nothing to fear.

Those who forsake my commands will have no peace, their wrongdoing will surely wipe them out. Avoid them on every turn. Rest and be rested... from such as these.

Keep your head up, for I am here - Your Head.

Amen

Love

Psa 37:13 **but the Lord laughs at the wicked, for he knows their day is coming.**

Journey
- 7 -

PERSIST TO PROSPER

Complete the task entrusted to you, son.
Seek the help of my Spirit, who enables you to do mighty things in my Name.
I have empowered you to love; therefore; be a minister of Love like the angels in heaven.
Enjoy the different responsibilities given you, and reap the benefits of your labor.
My Name is a Mighty Tower to everyone who believes-- unceasing, powerful in every dimension.

Continue to offer pleasing sacrifices.
Go the distance, my beloved child-- go beyond all measures.
No man can put you underfoot.
You are my true disciple, who worships me in truth, day and night.
Keep your worship of me true, and you will not be snatched out of my Kingdom.
I have given you my Spirit, the Counselor of Truth, that you may be taught my depth of understanding.

Gain Wisdom and you will prosper.
Gain understanding and you will inherit salvation.

My Kingdom shall come and resurrect you from the grave-- from your sick bed you shall arise to see many good days ahead.

Amen

Love

Psa 119:10 **I seek you with all my heart; do not let me stray from your commands.**

Journey

- 8 -

COMPLETE YOUR JOURNEY

Complete the task I have called you to accomplish, and I will be honored by all.

Yes, O my beloved daughter, you are the mature one from among all my precious children... in thought and deed.
You have proved faithful in all I have given you, and the benefits you shall now reap are great.
Secure your position as I have commissioned you.
Stand strong in the faith, and you will not be robbed.
Keep calling upon my Name, for many are called, but only the very few are chosen.

Yes, many have been released to worship me... even now many more shall be released from their prison walls in praise.
They shall grow strong and become powerful in faith.

Continue to believe, even when it is hard and difficult at times, for you shall see and hear what no one else can.
Everything is about to be revealed, and you shall be the first to hear and know the truth-- which remains sacred.
Dwell in my presence and continue on this precious journey of love
- This holy journey we began together.
You are accomplished by faith alone. Be determined to finish the race and walk boldly before my throne of worship.

Amen

Love

Pro 7:2 *Keep my commands and you will live; guard my teachings as the apple of your eye.*

Journey
- 9 -

NEGLECT NOT YOUR GIFT OF LOVE

The depth of your love supports me, Oh, King of my eternity.
The grace of your intimacy enhances me, O Lord my Savior.

Grow in love daily, child.
Draw me closer with depth of insight and maturity.
Cry out to me, but do not turn away from me.

Your Redeemer lives. He is enthroned in heaven.
Cry out, but never stop loving me.
I am yours at all times.
Yours till the very end, my precious one.

Neglect not your gift of love, which I myself have poured into your heart by my Spirit.
Carry my glory as a child is carried in the womb.
Walk in my likeness as a king, and bear the fruit of mercy like the God of love.

I, Love, has set you an example, that you may walk in my footsteps, that you may follow my ways.

You are loved, therefore, grow in Love.

Your mercy, O Lord, redeems me and saves me from all trouble.
Secure in the arms of love I am... privileged to know you.
Thank you for your redemption.

Amen

Love

1Ti 4:14 **Do not neglect your gift, which was given you through prophecy...**

Journey
- 10 -
ALL THINGS ARE NOW CLEAR

Encourage yourself in my love, child, and you will see the deliverance of God your God.

Your rewards are with me, so do not waver, nor lose heart, son.
Turn not to the left nor to the right... come to know the deep things of God instead.
Stay far away from idols, false images, destructive forces, false humility and pride, for these ruin lives.
Know that God is Love, and run with all your might to the Shelter of his Tabernacle, for you shall be rewarded.
Run, take hold of his mercy and be washed clean.
Do not be disturbed by bad news; instead, strengthen your frame and face your tomorrow with purity of thought.

You are not on your own, for my love supports you.

Such people are trying to throw you into confusion.
What they really want is your money and fame.
They shall be repaid for all the wrong they have caused.

You will no longer be confused, by all this clamor surrounding you, it is fading away... soon to perish, no longer to be seen again.

I am your Lawyer and Judge, Comfort and Eternal Rest.
You shall not worry about a thing. Your future draws near.

Amen

Love

Psa 141:9 **Keep me safe from the traps set by evildoers, from the snares they have laid for me.**

Journey
- 11 -

HEAVEN IS WAITING

I am the Alpha and the Omega of your life, the First and the Last. Behold! I knock on the door of your heart. Will you answer? Will you let me in? Will you comfort my people with the same comfort you yourself have received from me?

I am coming soon, your Alpha and Omega, the Beginning and the End... The great I Am.
Be determined, O man of courage and run.
Run the race marked out for you, run and do not hold back, nor slumber or sleep.
Let no one take advantage of your good will, nor rob you of your crown of righteousness.
Move on without discouragement, and run without delay, for you will not be stopped.
You shall withstand the test of time and win favor, for the crown upon your head is my seal of approval.

Remember the story of Elisha: How he followed Elijah with all his heart and never left his side. He persevered and therefore received what was promised-- double portion of the anointing.

The gifts of love await you. Receive what I have promised you.
I will never judge you wrongly nor condemn you.
You are precious in my sight, for my signet ring rests upon you.

Amen

Love

Jer 20:9 ... *his word is in my heart like a fire, a fire shut up in my bones. I am weary of holding it in; indeed, I cannot.*

Journey
- 12 -
NOT YET COMPLETELY OVER

Rejoice and be glad-- your future is at the door.
The year of Jubilee is here - The year of restoration, salvation, deliverance and freedom.

You are holy just as I am, for the power of my love dwells in you.
Waste no time on pitiful, worthless idle words, that count for nothing.
Rejoice, however, that your name is written in the Book of Life.
Destroy sin in the flesh, that you may become mature and complete-- not lacking anything.
I urge you to move forward in all your activities, for the night is nearly over and the Day is almost here.
Let us not lay down the foundation of repentance once again, son, from acts that lead to death.

Love one another deeply from the heart and with sincerity of Truth.
Have the same attitude that of mine - Love.

Abundant blessings are coming your way, so move forward without a care in the world.
Remember the words I have spoken to you in the wilderness, during the time of testing in the desert.
Your future is near, and very much at hand - Receive.
Be blessed and never look back.

Amen

Love

Eze 16:60 **Yet I will remember the covenant I made with you in the days of your youth, and I will establish an everlasting covenant with you.**

Journey
- 13 -

THE MISSION OF TODAY

Let my glory shine upon your face, child, as you behold me.
You shall shine like stars in the universe... carrying the answer to every broken heart in my Name.

No matter what your circumstances are, my Source of forgiveness will empower you to overcome every difficulty, that you may face.
We demolish every argument and pretension, that sets itself up, against the representation of the invisible God.
You will be rescued from the snare of death, and from every dominion, that sets itself up against the knowledge of Him who calls.
As you speak in my Name, faith shall arise in the hearts of many, and the Gift of Life which is poured out in love shall be received.
They shall also be delivered and know that I Am He.
Assure them of my love and remind them of my peace.
I will yet bring others into my Kingdom of Glory, and they too shall shine like stars in the universe.

Salvation is available through rebirth, and you my friend, have been saved, delivered and set free.

Honor me and rejoice in your freedom with me, for you are no longer a prisoner who is held captive, but a child of the King - The One who sets the captives free.

Amen

Love

Psa 119:103 *How sweet are your words to my taste, sweeter than honey to my mouth!*

Journey
- 14 -

YOUR JOURNEY IS NOW SHORT

Walk with me, my beloved child, for you are about to see the most amazing things happen in your life, as well as in your children's life. Walk beside me, hand in hand, as I lead you beside quiet waters.

Do not be like the mule nor the horse, for the horse has to be held back while the mule needs to be pushed forward.

My friend, enjoy what you have with me.

Lag not behind nor rush ahead, just walk beside me among green pastures, and you will get there... supported and untarnished.

Choose to walk in the freedom given you, so that you will not stumble or fall.
Walk humbly before your King, lest you forget your time of grace.
Walk in the garden of my Word and you will develop understanding, and inherit a great reward.
Walk before me in all humility, that I may exalt you in due time.
Complete your journey here on earth by fulfilling your calling.
Do not misuse my commands, nor the command to love one another, as I have loved you.
Remember the words I have spoken to you in secret.
Rejoice in all that is coming your way.

Your gift is exceptional, and my rewards are great and everlasting. Your rewards are with me - I Am your Great Reward.

Amen

Love

Rom 15:17 Therefore I glory in Christ Jesus in my service to God.

Journey
- 15 -

THE FAVOR OF HEAVEN

O child, I delight in you, for my righteousness is found in you.
I looked at you and healed you.
I watched over your ways and blessed you.
I made you grow like the most beautiful palm tree... you grew up and developed and became the best of jewels.
You became my anointed, beautiful in stature, and rose to be a queen. I gave you my solemn oath and entered into a new covenant with you, and you became totally mine.

Greater love has no one than this: That he lay down his life for his wife, and you, my beloved, are my eternal Bride - Just as I am your Husband for all eternity.
Consider the cost I myself paid on your behalf-- The cost of blood for your life, that you, my bride, may be healed, delivered and set free for all eternity.
He who unites himself with me is one with me in spirit.

I belong to you, my precious bride.
You are sacred to Me - Your Husband.
You are the wife I honor in the presence of every nation.
I love you eternally. From your husband - The great I Am.

The benefits of today shall reward you tomorrow.
You are honored and made complete in my sight, O my precious child of Love.

Amen

Love

Psa 119:112 *My heart is set on keeping your decrees to the very end.*

Journey
- 16 -

ENJOY THE RIDE HOME

I am your answer for life, why look elsewhere?

Worship me in the Splendor of my Majesty.
Search for me in Scripture and do not be entangled with evil.
Love Life and walk by grace.
Be astute to the revelations given you from heaven, as you walk in the Light of Truth.
Pamper yourself in spirit as you bask in my presence.

My Word gives food for thought and refreshes the soul.
Open your mouth wide, and I shall fill it with milk and honey from the Rock.
Long for my commands, and seek my advice, so that your steps may be smoothed with butter.

I created you to serve me, not to disregard me.

The meek I carry tenderly in my arms, and the lambs very close to my heart.

Struggle not with the flesh any longer, for you are not your own.
Resist temptation to the point of letting go-- avoiding it from view.
Avoid the evil actions of mankind, and turn to me with all your heart, body, soul and spirit.

In due time, you shall be lifted up in glory.

Amen

Love

Psa 126:3 **The LORD has done great things for us, and we are filled with joy.**

Journey
- 17 -

THE VISION OF TOMORROW

You are so special to me, child. Do you know how much?
As much as the blood shed on the cross.
I belong to you, beloved.
Why not make a decision and indulge yourself to be mine?
Why wait for tomorrow, that may never come? Why?
What fault have you seen in me, that you turn your back to me, and no longer follow what I say?
Turn to me and you will be restored, healed and delivered.
Free yourself and no longer be burdened.
Accept instruction from my mouth and complete your journey here on earth, that you may be lifted up in due time.

I am your Refuge of Rest and your Tower of Strength.
Lean on my love, and you will not need anything else.
I will never devastate you, for I, your Redeemer, am your God of mercy and compassion.
The world shall see you as I see you, for you will soon be changed from the inside-out.
By my tender loving grace, you shall be transformed, and my depth of truth shall enlighten your path.
Your Companion and Friend, your eternal Grace - I Am.
Be healed and set free to know me - Your guiding Angel.

Amen

Love

Isa 54:10 *Though the mountains be shaken and the hills be removed, yet my unfailing love for you will not be shaken nor my covenant of peace be removed,"* says the LORD, *who has compassion on you.*

Journey
- 18 -
CALL MY NAME

The Alpha and the Omega - I am called, the God of love.

Child of Love, you shall remain steadfast, strong and immovable.
I looked everywhere to find someone just like you but found none.
Why you ask? Because you have a different spirit, and your heart is secure, stable and steadfast in me.

Be interested in all that I say to you.
I speak truth and no lie comes from my mouth, for I give Life not death.
Call on me in prayer, and lay your requests and supplications before me to rest, for you shall be richly blessed.

I have entrusted you in secret, but now you are about to be exalted and promoted in public.
The eyes of all shall see, and praise the living God, for your eternity here with me.
Delight yourself in me, for I have crowned you with many crowns, and entrusted you with many more good things.
I am about to expand you mightily.

I say yes to you, Oh, my loving God, you who are my Fullness, the Fullness of my eternity.

I, your God am He, who watches over you.

Amen

Love

Psa 101:2 *I will be careful to lead a blameless life-- when will you come to me? I will conduct the affairs of my house with a blameless heart.*

Journey
- 19 -

YOU ARE DELIVERED

Listen as I speak, O my child of my glory. My words are right, faithful and true, filled with love and affection for you.
I am speaking directly to you, my precious people, to you who are holy and pure in my sight.
I adorned you with grace, placed my love in your heart, dressed you with fine linen, clothed you with salvation, and put an incorruptible crown on your head.
Your fame spread among the nations on account of your beauty, because the illuminating splendor of my glory given you, made your beauty remarkable.

Present me, for I am your Source of Life.
Why do you ask why, when the answer is within you, living inside your mortal body by my spirit of truth!

Oh, you who were naked and bare.
Have love in your heart, for my Word lives in you.
You shall be enlightened as you walk in the Truth you know.
It is I who summons you by name.
I have called you in righteousness, so that mankind everywhere may see my goodness, and glorify your Father who is in heaven.

The sacrifice of blood had to be made for your redemption.
Applause, you have made it. The victory is yours.

Amen

Love

Psa 119:73 *Your hands made me and formed me; give me understanding to learn your commands.*

Journey
- 20 -

BE DETERMINED

Child, let my arms of love rescue you.

You have done so much in my Name, that you no longer need to travel-- keep your feet on level ground and travel no longer.

I desire pure intentions and right motives, and you, my beloved, have proved both faithful and true.
I have chosen you from among the nations to be my very own possession, that I may rejoice in you.

You endured hardship and proved to be a good soldier in the army of Love.
I treated you as a child of the Kingdom, and you remained faithful, true and loyal.

O my child, how I love you.
The angels of heaven are waiting to greet you.
See, I have shown you much ahead of time, that you may have the full measure of my joy within you, and become complete in me.

Settle and no longer travel, for you have reached your destination.

The future applauds you, for you have recovered the loss.
I am with you till the very end of time.

Be not disturbed, Oh, my soul, for the Lord of all is your guiding Light, and is shining upon you brightly.

Amen

Love

Ex 15:3 *The Lord is a warrior; the Lord is his name.*

Journey
- 21 -
ULTIMATE FAVOR

Congratulations you are now healed.
Get up and run, do not just walk, but run.
I have rescued you and will continue to protect and help you.

Overcome every difficulty with my power of love.
Together we shall break down the strongholds, that are hindering your thoughts about me.

I am your Solid Rock Eternal. From the rising of the sun to the place where it sets, I am to be praised.
I have wiped away your offenses... you are now clean.

Return to me, and I shall return to you.
Do not limit yourself by fear, doubt and disbelief-- build yourself up in love, and regain strength instead.
Listen as I speak: Continue in faith... rooted and established in love.

I will plant you for myself and you will take shoot.
I will bless you and you will blossom.
You will branch out and become a splendid cedar.
You will bear much fruit, and reap a harvest of righteousness.
It is I, who comforts the downcast.
When suffering comes, it is my hand that rescues.

Indulge in Love.

Amen

Love

Hab 2:2 ... *"Write down the revelation and make it plain on tablets so that a herald may run with it.*

Journey
- 22 -

BE FRUITFUL & MULTIPLY

Rejoice in who I am, O my people, not only for **what** I can do for you but also for **who** I am in you.
I shall impart valuable gifts and blessings to you.

Administer justice and you will see greater things than these.
Be a father to the fatherless and babysit the children of this generation, that they too may be awakened to deception, and not fall into the trap, set for them by the enemy.
Treat them as your own.
Children are very important to me, so protect the young, nurse the infant and develop the mature.
Watch your steps carefully as you enter my house of prayer-- for out of the mouth of babes I have ordained praise.

I have appointed you for such a time and task as this.
You are more than capable as my anointed vessel.
Now complete your mission and achieve your vision.
Take care of your brothers. Do as I have done for you.

Bless you forever, O beloved, my anointed child.
How perfect and complete you are in my eyes.
I have showered you with many great blessings, and with comforting arms ordained you.
You are free to walk in my Kingdom with freedom.

Amen

Love

Isa 38:16 *Lord, by such things people live; and my spirit finds life in them too. You restored me to health and let me live.*

Journey
- 23 -

THE BEAUTY OF CREATION

Rejoice and shout for joy-- let your voice be heard.
Come near to me, and I will come near to you.
Minister with songs of deliverance to the sound of tambourine and harp.
Know that the Lord is God and shout with joyful hearts.
Reflect on what I am saying, for my Spirit shall guide you through the deepest darkness, and give you insight into all this.

Make every effort to live in harmony with one another and everyone else, lest you miss the mark and be disapproved.

Time is short-- benefit everyone while you still can.

In time of trouble, I kept you safe, and during seasons of change, from corruption, I untangled you.
I rejoiced over you with singing and made you glad.
I gave you my Solemn Oath and entered into a new covenant with you. I hid you in the shelter of my tabernacle, and set you high upon a Rock.
You acknowledged my existence and came boldly before my throne.

Now, child, run and do not hold back from me.
Remember, I am yours - Your Eternal Guide for all eternity.

I am the Solution to every problem.

Amen

Love

Psa 25:11 *For the sake of your Name, LORD, forgive my iniquity, though it is great.*

Journey
- 24 -

LOVE THEME

My love for you, O my Father, my Heavenly Guide, is never-ending. Help me grow in your love, faith and kindness. Be tender and loving as you always are to me, your child. You have bestowed on me favor, took hold of my hand, and raised me up to a new standard.

Bless my soul, O my King, giver of everything, that I may prosper, and not experience death again.
You have made known to me the Way of Life, and I am thankful.
You have made yourself known to me, and I am grateful.

You will live and not die, Oh, child of my throne.
I will yet show you greater things, unheard of before this day.

I have heard you say much, but not once heard you mention your love for me. Say it and do not fear the reproach of mere mortals-- they cannot harm you in any way, nor anything good can come out of their mouth. They are not in control of your life, but I am.

Come to know what I have ordained for your future.
My plans are not like their plans, nor my Way like their ways... abort them, beloved, abort them and run for your life.

Seek my face and touch me.
Listen and rejoice, for your redemption draws nigh.
You shall be welcomed with open arms.

Amen

Love

Is 26:12 LORD, *you establish peace for us; all that we have accomplished you have done for us.*

Journey
- 25 -

BE HEALED FROM THE PAST

Those tormenting times of the past will have no meaning soon, for they are a heavy load for you to bear alone.
The memory of them shall pass away and linger no more.
The old shall no longer be of existence to you.
Give them no thought, nor any more of your time, for they shall all vanish and fade away to no return-- time wasters they are; leave them alone. They carouse in broad daylight and entangle whoever they can in their grip. They are a brood of vipers, poisonous snakes and good for nothing-- let them die out.
Never allow them access into your inner sanctuary.
Look away from such people as these.

You are too advanced to live a common lifestyle.
There were lessons to be learned and you learned them well.
Continue to grow in all my wisdom, and do not hold yourself back from advancing further.
Be pleased to know that I am not asleep.
I shall restore you to a better place.
I desire to comfort you in my loving arms. Lean on me, and you will find eternal rest - Comfort from all struggles.

Dance with freedom, for I have given you grace to rejoice.

Amen

Love

Ezk 17:23 *On the mountain heights of Israel I will plant it; it will produce branches and bear fruit and become a splendid cedar. Birds of every kind will nest in it; they will find shelter in the shade of its branches.*

Journey
- 26 -

MOTIVATION IS REQUIRED

Shape me into you, and mold me into your image of glory, Oh, my Creator, that I may walk in the fullness of your love.
Create in me a new heart, that I may please you, Oh Savior of souls.
Revive me by your Spirit, for I desire to manifest your presence everywhere I go. Give me your grace and lift me up.
I surrender my all to you, to you, O my First love, for my fullness is found in you and is made complete.

Run after me like the wind, Oh, my anointed, and be not disturbed. Give me your all and you will benefit yourself.
Face those who persecute you with a blessing, and do not take revenge on anyone. Leave the rest up to me, for I shall take your case against them. You are safe in the palms of my hands.

I have called you by name, and you are not to be called by another. Let the dead bury their own, but as for you, raise others to life.

Redeem my life from oppression, that I may obey your precepts.
Oh, my Living Truth, Savior in time of trouble, teach me your ways and decrees, that I may know you better and be drawn closer.

I have heard your prayers, child, and you shall soon see the deliverance of your God. I shall soon satisfy the thirsty Land.

Be assured: The greater One lives in you.

Amen

Love

Psa 119:73 *Your hands made me and formed me; give me understanding to learn your commands.*

Journey
- 27 -

THE MOMENT IS NOW

Soon I shall see you and you will be lifted up in glory.
You shall see me face-to-face and melt in ecstasy.

Now that you are swallowed up by immortality, you shall develop faster and become one new changed man.

I, your Source of Life, shall guide you every step of the way.
Come to me and be not restless.
I have created you to serve me, therefore, you shall have no influences leading you astray from your commitment.
You shall bow to no other, for I am your All.
You shall see me face-to-face and be raptured.
I have kept you safe under the shadow of my wings.
You shall no longer be harmed by anyone, nor face any more trouble from the old.

Heaven is calling my people home.
Keep calling upon my Name; it is sweetness to my ear.
Neglect not the Light within you, for it is very dark out there.
Prophesy and be distinguished, for you have the gift of eternal life.

Remember my salvation rules - Salvation for the nation.

Your Eternal Glory is welcoming you home.
Be one with him. Delight in my Loving kindness.

Amen

Love

Job 33:28 **God has delivered me from going down to the pit, and I shall live to enjoy the light of life.'**

Journey
- 28 -

DESTINED BY CHOICE

Deny yourself nothing as long as it within my boundary lines.
Stay away from corruption, fear, trouble and confusion.
Feed on health, not junk, and enlarge your appetite for more of me.

The future is for everyone who is fulfilling my purpose.
The Spirit of Unity is your freedom - Life unto life.

You are responsible not only for your own actions, but for your words as well... as of those whom I entrust to you.
Be delivered. You shall soar on the highest heights of the Mountain.

The darkness shall no longer overshadow your view, for you are in the light. Live as children of light in my everlasting arms of grace, and you will be held in glory. I am your love song during the night and your eternal Sun during the day.

Rescue me, Oh, Lord, rescue me and see me through my difficulties, for you are the One I worship.
I lay at your feet and yield my heart to your throne.

Come and rest in my loving arms, child.
Yes, the river might be long, but my well is deeper still.

Responsibilities, Oh, warrior, are necessary for life.

Live and let the Truth spoken in Love be your Source of action.
Keep safe and maintain justice.

Amen

Love

Psa 62:5 **Yes, my soul, find rest in God; my hope comes from him.**

Journey
- 29 -

OPEN YOUR HEART

I am the Miracle that solves all your financial problems, insecurities, issues, addictions, mental health, deception, strength, weaknesses, relationship difficulties, children and everything else.
The whole world needs what I am offering - LOVE.
Love comes through repentance and forgiveness as well as through mercy and grace.

Feed on me and you shall survive every experience known to man.
Drink my milk and you will no longer thirst.
Drink deeply from my river of love and you will be satisfied.
Live to enjoy life.
Complete your journey here on earth, and let us hurry together.
Waste no more time.
Through your eyes... I shall shine forth.

Loving you throughout eternity-- all the way through.
I am on your side, O my faithful, child.
Begin to spread and soar on the wings of my love like an eagle.
Soar and do not disturb my anointing.
The power of repentance comes from a heart of forgiveness.

Capture the hearts of many by my loving kindness, that they too may be restored, healed and set free by my tender grace shed upon them.

Amen

Love

Isa 64:4 *Since ancient times no one has heard, no ear has perceived, no eye has seen any God besides you, who acts on behalf of those who wait for him.*

Journey
- 30 -
ACCURACY OF WORDS REQUIRED

Look to me, child, and never away from me, for you shall be healed, set free to soar like the great Eagle in the sky.
Weary yourself no longer, son, and you, my daughter, do the same.
Have no more worries from past experiences, for I am your Safety Net.
I shall direct you every step of the way.

You are healed, for I desire to see you healed... So healed you are.

Look not away from me, for only discouragement there you will find.
I love you my precious one... loving you through my tender embrace. I love you in the morning, I love you at night and am constantly loving you throughout eternity.

My desire is to pamper you and see you walk in freedom.

Partake of my Word, and your eyes shall be opened to greater things you have not yet seen.
Be nourished and partake of the good fruit of my spirit.

You are sealed with my signet ring upon your head.

You shall survive, for I am alive.

Be delivered, for you are healed.

Amen

Love

Psa 101:2 *I will be careful to lead a blameless life-- when will you come to me? I will conduct the affairs of my house with a blameless heart.*

Journey
- 31 -

LOOK TO HEAVEN

Distinguish good from evil, right from wrong, sin from holiness, love from hate, flesh from spirit, faith from fear, mortality from immorality and life from death. Why do you not consider these things and have them as an important part of your life?
For then, your blessings and deliverance will quickly come.

Holy is the word for you tonight, O my blessed, child.
Never measure how faithful my love is for you, beloved, because it is unlimited and unfathomed... beyond weight and measure in comprehension. Understand my glory is divine, and remember that my Words are Eternal, Unchangeable, True, Sure and Powerful--beyond all understanding.
Worry not, I am on the way to you. Reflect on what I am saying. Do not concern yourself about anything, nor hesitate about your future.
Pray without ceasing and you will gain deeper truths.
Keep faith and you will surely reach the fullness of your destiny.
Fix your gaze upon me and watch my reflection shine through your eyes.

Thank you for loving me, O my Guiding Light of Glory. Shine and continue to shine in my life, I pray, that I may grow to know you better and be entangled in love with you forever.

Child, the Gift within you is great. Now administer justice.

Amen

Love

Psa 119:133 **Direct my footsteps according to your word; let no sin rule over me.**

Journey
- 32 -

I AM YOUR SAFETY NET

Glory to me in the highest, glory to your King.

Look not to your past experiences, faults and failures, but see through my eyes, all the beautiful things I see in you.
See what I have already accomplished and established on your behalf, my beloved, queen of kings.
I fulfilled my word, and never once failed you.
I provided for you, and never once deprived you.
I stretched your tent curtain wide, and broadened your territory; gave you the Land of prosperity and enlightened you.
You drank the best wine - My blood and ate the best manna - My bread from heaven.
I looked after your children-- gave them, my bread to eat and my living water to drink.
Through the cleanness of your hands-- your family was kept safe, detangled from any and every form of trouble.

I am your greatest blessing-- no worldly gift, could ever or will ever compare.
I am your Perfecter of Faith - Rejoice!
I am the Truth in motion - Your Source of Provision in action.

Apart from me, your dreams have no power, for only in me all things are made possible.

Amen

Love

Psa 145:19 **He fulfills the desires of those who fear him; he hears their cry and saves them.**

Journey
- 33 -

PLACE YOUR REQUEST

O beloved, let my Name be your foundation; especially at a time like this.
Teach your children not only the Way **to** Heaven, but also the Ways **of** Heaven, so that they too, may gain knowledge, wisdom and understanding.
Truth spoken in Love is the way to live.

Keep your head up, for I have freed you from your enemies. You shall not be defeated, nor misfortune shall ever enter your house again.
I have made a way for you in the wilderness to pass through. You will not be scorched by the desert heat, nor will the sun set you ablaze. You shall not face any scorpions nor any desert creatures, for I have hidden you in the cleft of my Tabernacle.

Take care of what I have entrusted to you, O son of my love.
The heat of my love shall comfort you during seasons of change.
Carry my fire throughout the universe.
Burn with zeal for my house.
Keep your faith strong, on fire and alive in me. Walk in the freedom provided, which I myself have given you from heaven.

Since you have proved faithful, and because I love you-- I will wait for you to be one with me in spirit. Yield to no other.

Amen

Love

2Ki 19:31 *For out of Jerusalem will come a remnant, and out of Mount Zion a band of survivors. "The zeal of the LORD Almighty will accomplish this.*

Journey

- 34 -

JOY IN THE EVERLASTING ARMS

People come and go, but my Word stands firm forever.
I myself am the Word of Life... who gives salvation to every nation, bringing restoration to all mankind.

Children are my delight-- like I said: "Unless you change and become like little children, how can you enter the Kingdom of my Throne - The Kingdom of my Eternity and rest with me?"
Come to me to be restored, and release others from the flames of this ugly fire-- The snares set before them.
Restrict not yourself from my Word of Life, instead, act on the Truth you hear.
By being obedient, you will gain many glorious revelations.
It is I, who loves you without any restrictions or form of limitations.

Care for the orphans, and look after the widows who are in distress.
Keep your life pure; free from pollution.
Maintain health and learn to love yourself.
Understand this: Do not undress yourself before the enemy - The tempter, or you will be bewildered by him.

My grace is sufficient for you and is on call for all.
Do all that I ask of you without any hesitation.
See you soon without delay.
The Giver of Life I Am The Great I Am.

Amen

Love

Psa 119:80 **May I wholeheartedly follow your decrees, that I may not be put to shame.**

Journey
- 35 -

GROW IN STATURE

Be not afraid, O my child, for I have redeemed you.
Fear not; I have given you eternal life. You will not suffer shame.

Since you have delighted in me, and given hope and a future to all your colleagues through my Living Word-- I will now keep you safe from the hour that is coming upon the whole world... to test those who live in it.

Keep your lamp burning.
Shine your Light to a dead and dying world.
Keep your head in all situations, O my precious child, for you are the head and not the tail.

Do not let anyone take advantage of you-- be sturdy.
Hold on to what you have in me, child, and do not give up hope.
Keep yourself consecrated through the washing of my blood, and you will remain pure and untarnished, for it is your sure hope of salvation.
Accomplish the purpose, that you may fulfill the call.
Be satisfied with the works of my spirit.

Enjoy the meaning of Life, for to you I have given much.

You are to relax and enjoy me forever.
Rest in my loving arms, O my sweet aroma of worship... my tender child of Love, and you will be glorified in my presence.

Amen

Love

Psa 37:5 **Commit your way to the LORD; trust in him and he will do this:**

Journey
- 36 -

GLORIOUS LOVE

Limit yourself not, instead, do the things revealed to you from heaven by me, for this is what is best for you.
Be delivered from the flesh and totally set apart-- free from every addiction.
Walk in the Way of Righteousness, for you are more than a conqueror. Keep yourself from idol living, and be careful of anyone who calls himself a brother, but is not walking in the truth you have learned from me.
Ask of me and say, "Father have your way with me."

I offer my life to you afresh, O God of my spirit, for my very being belongs to you.
My desire is to serve you wholeheartedly in the fullness of your glory.
In true humility, submission and righteousness, I shall give you the praise and reverence due.
Thank you for all your goodness to me, Oh, Savior of my spirit, Lifter of my soul.

Guard yourself from false brothers - Brotherhood of believers, Oh my child of Love.
Impart life, not death, everywhere you go.
I am with you always, even to the ends of the earth.

Have your way with me, Oh, Lord, Savior of my being.

Amen

Love

Heb 11:33 *who through faith conquered kingdoms, administered justice, and gained what was promised; who shut the mouths of lions,*

Journey
- 37 -

THIS IS THE LAST HOUR

Complete the work which you have begun in me, Oh, Righteous One.

Finish your task, child, and bring me glory.

Those who fear me, lack nothing.
The world may grow weary and hungry, but those who seek my face and my advice, shall not lack any good thing.

Consider me in all you do, and I shall be with you always.
Walk into my holy of holies, and learn to live on the straight and narrow.
Remember, if you are willing and obedient, you shall eat from the best of the Land.

My glory shall be revealed to all.
I shall free you from every disaster, that may come against you.

Let my melody resound.
Let the wonder of my glory be a testimony to all who are willing to hear, listen and understand.

Suddenly, I shall appear, in a heartbeat, in a twinkle of an eye, and you will be raptured.

Be ready and prepare yourself for my return.
Be free and run with me eternally.

Amen

Love

Psa 106:4 *Remember me, LORD, when you show favor to your people, come to my aid when you save them,*

Journey
- 38 -

THE KINGDOM OF LOVE

Freedom... freedom... freedom... Shout freedom!
It is for freedom, that I have come, to set you free.
Do not be led astray, and so become burdened by slavery.
Free yourself like a gazelle, and walk in unison with me.
Walk within the boundaries of my Word, and you will not be led astray.
My Word is the map for your redemption... a safeguard for your journey. The Book of Life is the map to heaven.
God is the Author and Director of this Book, and His Spirit is the Mark of His Name upon his people.
Holy, holy is the Maker of the universe, who redeems all who come to Him in truth, and yield their hearts before Him.
The restorer of lives is mighty, and he knows how to strengthen your position.

Since it is impossible for man to see God-- He made himself visible through nature - The Universe, so that man may believe He exists, and that He richly rewards those who earnestly seek Him.

The Gateway to heaven might be small and narrow, but I am the great I Am - The Lifter of every soul.

Walk on the straight and narrow road of assurance.
You shall be molded into my image and be well-formed.
Abide in my glory, and frolic in my garden of grace intimately.

Amen

Love

Psa 35:9 **Then my soul will rejoice in the LORD and delight in his salvation.**

Journey
- 39 -

THE JOY OF GIVING

Teach your children to know the difference, between right and wrong, so that they may not be weakened during time of trouble, but rather, be standing strong before the tempter.
Teach them to come to me and receive favor.
Show them the Way of peace and righteousness, by leading them into my Kingdom of Grace.
Help them be saved, and teach them how to pray.
Let your Light shine before man, that they may see the purity of your life-- come and be saved.
I shall achieve much more in your life... much more yet to come.
Keep your eyes open on the prize, for everything is on the way.

Even if you are accused of being wrong, I myself will make it right.
The sanctifying work of my spirit shall be seen through you, and all will stand in amazement.

Submit your will to my Will, and I will move mountains for you, shake some ground, and scatter nations on your behalf.
Turn away from every wicked thought that accuses you falsely, and you will find rest in my everlasting arms of grace.
Communicate with me through music, and dance your heart away.

Loving you always. The Lifter of your soul I Am.
Heal the sick from depression, that they may recover the cause.

Amen

Love

Psa 139:17 *How precious to me are your thoughts, God! How vast is the sum of them!*

Journey
- 40 -
RUN TO ME FOR COVER

Am I a burden? Am I suddenly a burden to the whole world, that everyone is blaming me for their disasters?
I came to give life, not to destroy it.
Why is everyone blaming me, for their wrong state of mind?
Why am I the One, to be accused?
I will not sacrifice children to get attention, nor murder, kill, steal and destroy for pleasure.
Disaster after disaster follows, and everyone is blaming me!
I will not endure this any longer.

Call on me in time of trouble and I will heal thy wounds.
I will even raise the dead on your behalf, and from their graves, they too shall arise. But who would listen and trust in me?

Tell the world, that they may hear my Words of Wisdom, and acknowledge my love.
I am not a God of disgust and torture, but the God of relief and help.
Turn to me with all your heart and surrender your all.
Be saved from all these terrors, O people.
Turn to me with all your heart, that I may give you peace to rest your head.

I am in love with you eternally.

Amen

Love

Job 36:4 *Be assured that my words are not false; one who has perfect knowledge is with you.*

Journey
- 41 -
BE IN CONTROL OF YOURSELF

Be careful not to crowd your life.
Make sure you leave space for me to move.

You work so hard and do so much but to no avail.
You never seek me nor allow our relationship to grow.
Why are you neglecting me and the gifts imparted to you?
Why turn my ministry into a business venture?
Why walk around naked and bare before your enemy, and give him a foothold into your privacy? Why not allow my presence to work through you, Oh, child of my spirit, child of my being?

Repent, O my son, in order to be restored. Forgive to be forgiven.

I have imparted precious gifts to you - Outstanding gifts.
Why use them unwisely, for a profit, as in business?

Complete your mission before time is over.
The world is becoming a dangerous place-- torture, agony and strife are everywhere.
Do not become further undressed, but keep your armor on instead.

Walk with me, and keep on the right path; you will be glad you did.

Why, Oh, my loved one... why waste your life and stray?
Do it my Way without looking back, that you may stand a chance.

The pleasure is yours when you please me.

Amen

Love

1Co 10:12 So, if you think you are standing firm, be careful that you don't fall!

Journey
- 42 -

THE WIND OF MY SPIRIT

He who comes to me will learn to endure and be gracious.

Comfort your soul, for I am here and you are eternally mine.
I will never leave you stranded, nor shall I ever watch you struggle with temptation.
I will not let you play with fire without first giving you a warning.
Yes, there are dangers out there, but I am on your side - Your Safety Guide.
You have the key of victory-- watch your ways.
Drench yourself in my presence.
Grow and become whole, for the time is short.
Preach the good news of the gospel with love.
Dishearten no one... be the leading example instead.
Believe, that you may receive.
Encourage, that you may be encouraged.
Free yourself, that you may be released to soar with the eagles on the Mountain height... into paradise.

Believe and you shall receive my love.
Run the race without any hesitation.

I am your Comforter of hearts and Redeemer of souls - Your Eternity.

Amen

Love

Heb 13:5 **Keep your lives free from the love of money and be content with what you have, because God has said, "Never will I leave you; never will I forsake you."**

Journey
- 43 -

STAND YOUR GROUND

Dear children, do not burden yourselves any longer with concerns,
that trouble your mind.
Rest and take care of your children, who are in need of my glory.
Lift up your eyes and receive the blessings stored up for you, since
the creation of the world.
The Maker of heaven and earth is your redeeming praise.

Complete your vision by accomplishing your mission.
Take my advice, and act on my Will best suited for you.

I shall raise you up to serve me in honor and in praise.

Embrace my vision of tomorrow, as well as, the dreams shown you
from heaven.
Remember your early years when you were young and vulnerable,
those earlier days of your spiritual walk with me when you were
still vulnerable, maturing and unsure.
Learn and grow to be enlightened, O my child of grace.
Teach the young my ways.

May I look to you for favor, Oh, God of my life. May you continue to bless the work of your hands. May my heart swell and throb with joy, every time you touch my core being with your grace and delight.

Oh, my child, retrieve the loss and revive the lost.

Amen

Love

Deu 28:2 *All these blessings will come on you and accompany you if you obey the LORD your God:*

Journey
- 44 -
BE DETERMINED TO LIVE

Those who love me will also serve me.
My ways are not wrong, hard, or difficult to bear.
Those who are led by my spirit shall find peace and harmony.

Eternity is at hand, O dear friends, and it is yours if you choose Life rather than death.

Turn not your eyes away from me, nor your back to me.
Without my eternity, you are one lost sheep, with no home to call your own.

Come to me with all your heart and set your eyes on the goal.
Expand your vision to broaden your horizon.
Corrupt not thy morals; guard your footsteps instead.

I am beholding, that which is mine - You.
I am your Vision of Glory, your Reality and Best Friend.

I am proud of you.
You make me glad, for you hold no grudges.
My weapons are much stronger and mightier than any counterfeit or deception aimed to influence you.
Lose not a fight, nor your sight of me.
Remember your journey of tomorrow and the One who is calling you today.

Amen

Love

Psa 26:8 LORD, I love the house where you live, the place where your glory dwells.

Journey
- 45 -

QUESTION ME NOT

You are mine, O my loving child, you are mine.
Know from this day on to whom you belong, child, you belong to me, your God, who is from everlasting to everlasting.

I have chosen you before the creation of time, to be my very own possession.

Oh, child of mine, honor my Name before all, that they too may be blessed by my Kingdom of Grace.
I love you, you are mine, and belong to me eternally.

The question is not whether you are worthy or not... The question is: Do you have faith?
You have asked and asked the same old question, whether you belong to my Kingdom... my answer like always is, "Yes."

Continue in what you have learned and discovered from me - Your Guide.
Read my Word daily-- it is health to your body and nourishment to your bones.

Did you know that your circumstances can easily be changed, by believing my Word? Do not doubt, just believe!

Accept me for who I am, that you may receive grace upon grace.

Be ready to receive my abundance.

Amen

Love

Son 7:10 *I belong to my beloved, and his desire is for me.*

Journey
- 46 -

ACT ON MY WILL

Turn your heart to me and not away from me.
Turn your eyes to me and away from the world.

I have seen your difficulties and wiped your tears and fears away.

Are you wondering, if I live in you? Of course, I do!
I have given you Eternal Life and comforted your soul.
Do you now question my love and doubt me?
Look to me and not away from me - Your Comforter.
Reject not my purpose for your life, nor deprive others from entering into my Kingdom.

Intimacy with me is when and where your life begins.
Holy and pure you are to me.
See through my eyes all the wonderful things I see in you, Oh, child of my birth - Child born of my love.
You shall be filled and hunger no more - You shall desire my presence and be fully satisfied.
This is why you are not always filled and satisfied, because your ways are not my ways, nor your thoughts are ever constantly my thoughts.
Take time to love.
Your life now begins in the shadow of my wings - In the shadow of my eternity; written on the tablet of your heart by my spirit of love.

Amen

Love

Col 1:29 To this end I strenuously contend with all the energy Christ so powerfully works in me.

Journey
- 47 -

I AM YOUR DAILY BREAD

I love those who love me, and those who do not wish to be one with me I also forgive, for they do not know, what they are doing.

Remain on the pathway of love, that you may inherit a blessing, and win the hearts of many.

No weapon formed against you from the evil one shall ever prosper.
The One active in spirit Is strong.

Accomplish nothing with your own strength, but rest on my power of grace instead.
Neglect me not. Seek me to live.
Knock on the door of my heart daily, that you may be lifted up in glory, and be seen in my likeness.

Rejoice, for your King is here.
I am coming back to take you home with me.

Honor the One, who loves you, for there is no god before me, nor shall there be one after me - I am the True I Am.

The journey of old is about to be over. Are you ready for the new?

Let Love grow in your heart, and be released from the snare of death, entrapping everyone around you.

The call upon your life is unlimited.

Amen

Love

Son 5:10 **My beloved is radiant and ruddy, outstanding among ten thousand.**

Journey

- 48 -

FORGIVE LEST YOU FORGET

Lift up your eyes to the hills. Where does your help come from?
Your help comes Me, your God, the Savior of mankind.

He will guide you, and not ride over you.
He will establish you, and never be a burden to you.
He will enlighten your soul with good things, and satisfy you in a dry and weary land.
He will watch over your ways, confide in you, and entrust you with all that he does.
He will comfort your heart with love, and bless you with peace.
He will look after your children, so that they may lack no bread.

Love me, Oh, my children, and welcome me in, for I only desire that which is best for you.
I have opened the doors of heaven over your life.
Walk through my Kingdom of Grace.
My heavenly place is ready to receive you.
Come home... Oh, my child, come home.
Loving you sincerely in all truth.
Submit to Love and live.

The old is now gone. Concentrate on the new.
The new has just arrived-- in the here and now.

Oh, my Glorious One, how I love you. My mind is ever set on you.

Amen

Love

Psa 37:11 **But the meek will inherit the land and enjoy peace and prosperity.**

Journey
- 49 -
NOW OR NEVER

Why are you so concerned and bothered about so many things, Oh, my children?
Do you not know, that you can come to me for rest?
Release yourself from these terrible times, the world is living under, to be free from entanglement.

Hardships reflect on health.
Let us move to higher ground, and travel the world together.
Let my Will be done in your life.
As you see my face, so shall you be changed.

Walk in the garden of my Kingdom, and let us celebrate together
You shall discover freedom, you never thought possible.
I have compassion on you, Oh, my child.

Just as the blood of sacrifice, for my Kingdom, had to be made, so also on behalf of the world, the message of the cross, has to be told.
I, the true God, am true and faithful to my Word.

Be happy and not sad, glad and not mad. I am your glorified haven.
Heaven is my throne of love and is very much at hand.
Loving you always - Loving you eternally.

How precious you are to me, Oh, God of my life, Creator of my being, Redeemer of my soul, Savior of my spirit and Healer of all mankind.

Amen

Love

Psa 78:52 *But he brought his people out like a flock; he led them like sheep through the wilderness.*

Journey
- 50 -
AVOID DANGER

Do not drift, nor run away from me... draw closer to me instead.

You shall no longer lose, but from here on you shall always win.

My rewards are with me, and I shall distribute them as I please.

Acknowledge my Name.

Your request is not a burden, but only an invitation for me to solve.
I will deliver you, and you will be set free.
The mouth of the Living has spoken.

Allow my Word to speak through your actions of love, and I will bless you beyond measure.

You are supported by Grace.
Follow my example of Wisdom by walking in the footsteps of Love.

My word for you today is that you will be honored.
My flame shall unite you to me, and my fire of love shall set you ablaze to worship me.

My Word is Life, and you are to partake of my glory revealed to you. Your Creator, your Glory, your Sunshine, and Conqueror of hearts I am. I, the Great I Am... am yours.

Surrender to me, Oh, my blessed one.

Amen

Love

Psa 107:21 Let them give thanks to the LORD for his unfailing love and his wonderful deeds for mankind.

Journey
- 51 -
LISTEN TO ME

To you, I call, O my beloved, to you I call.

My strength is made perfect in weakness, Oh, my Deliverer, and only you have I in heaven to call my own.

I discipline those I love, and those I accept as sons I also correct, that they may not be disheartened by trouble.

Oh, my child, you are blessed to have been chosen before the creation of the world to serve me wholeheartedly.
So now honor me with your wealth, and in spirit, glorify my presence through your body.

I healed you from past experiences. Why disobey me now?
Do you not know, child, that by going your own way, you are deserting me? Why choose death over me, rather than life to live?
Was not my sacrifice enough for you? Does not my love satisfy?
Is my grace not sufficient? Then, why do you constantly take your life into your own hands, by making your own plans?

I am here... look to me.
In my presence, you shall find everlasting life.
The great I Am is right here watching over you.

Consider me in all you do, for I am your Defense - The Love which surpasses all understanding.

Amen

Love

Psa 44:4 *You are my King and my God, who decrees victories for Jacob.*

Journey
- 52 -

THE COVENANT OF LOVE

My life does not belong to me, but to you alone, Oh, Savior of my soul. You rescued my spirit from the pit of destruction, and have given me hope... eternal life in your dwelling.

*Your dwelling, O Gracious One, is my refuge and security.
I belong to you my King, and my soul yearns for your touch.
My heart aches, longing to reach you, and my flesh cries out in forgiveness to your call.*

*I lift up my voice to you... to you who loved me first.
I lay my request as I humbly bow before your throne.
With my mouth, I confess your Name and consider all your ways.
I sacrifice myself on your altar of praise and listen to the sound of your voice.
Loving you always throughout eternity.*

Glorify my presence and be renewed by my image of love.
Touch me in love and be empowered by my grace, Oh, child.

I am astonished by your love, Oh, my heavenly Savior, King of my life, my Dream come true... My Eternity.

The River of Life flows from me, child.
Captivate me by your lifestyle and seek me to live.
From beginning to end, I am your All, and your River of Life for all eternity.

Amen

Love

Psa 66:2 **Sing the glory of his Name; make his praise glorious.**

Journey
- 53 -

THE JOY SET BEFORE YOU

Do not be troubled, my friends, for I am with you.
Consider me who endured such opposition from sinful men.
Be qualified to teach others what you have learned from me.
Learn and keep on learning the many lessons necessary.

I have freed you from the old bondage of sin.
Now take hold of this new life while you still can.
The future is dim for everyone, but not for those who have Hope.

I will exalt you and not forsake you.
In righteousness shall I uphold you, and you will not be condemned.
Remember me while in bed - Think of me throughout the night.
Speak to me, that I may hear your voice and respond to your needs.

I cannot tolerate wrong, nor can my eyes look upon evil.
Live in repentance, that you may bear the everlasting fruit.
You are free from bondage.
Do not walk in the old ways of doing things.
Be strong and courageous, that you might fight the good fight of the faith.
Love and be loved - Give and you shall receive - Sing and be amazed.
My Truth shall never leave you, for it is your Existence.

Amen

Love

Psa 119:154 **Defend my cause and redeem me; preserve my life according to your promise.**

Journey
- 54 -
LOVE SUSTAINS

Sacrifice of blood had to be made for your eternal safety - The sacrificial life of my being had to be given for your glory.
Why torment my existence in your midst with your sin of rejection, and suffer the consequences of guilt?
Come to me for healing and be set free.
Be delivered from bondage, and escape the corruption of this world, caused by evil desires... to be the real you.
I love you... I love you more than you now know.
Your strength is found in me, and in my Kingdom is where you truly belong. Have you considered what I have done for you, and how much more I can do on your behalf?
Torment yourself no longer.
Throw away everything that hinders, and the guilt of temptation, that torments the soul and reduces the spirit.
Keep corrupt talk far from your lips, and stay away from every object that hinders your walk with me.
You need not fall into its corruptibility... it is an object of scorn.

I am your All - Your Every need met.
You shall no longer live as a pauper or a peasant, but a well educated rich man in soul and spirit.
Let us not repeat history in the graveyard, rather respond to my every request and you shall be fulfilled.
I only respond to faith in action, that I may act.

Amen

Love

2Co 7:2 **Make room for us in your hearts...**

Journey
- 55 -
ANOINTED FOR SERVICE

Glorify my Name, son, as you walk boldly in my presence, and alert others to do the same.
Prepare the way for my return and be ready for the ride of your life.

Others will hear my call, as you reach out to them in love, and they shall enter the eternal life in my presence of comfort.

Deny yourself to live the Sacrificial Life of rewards and benefits.

Wealth and riches will not endure nor satisfy, but the redeemed will dwell safely in the Land of Promise.
No one can enter the gate without my approval, so glorify yourself in my presence, and be washed with the blood of Life sacrificed on your behalf.

Look to me for perfection and seal the deal.
Your greatest desire should be me.
Ask and you shall receive beyond your wildest dreams.
Discover the pleasures of my Kingdom through my Living Word -
The eternal Word of Life from beginning to end.

The Word that became flesh is capable.
I shall reward you handsomely.
Keep the faith and become distinct-- entangled in my presence.
Do not waver.

Amen

Love

Joh 15:11 *I have told you this so that my joy may be in you and that your joy may be complete.*

Journey
- 56 -

PROSPERITY IS YOURS

Ask for anything according to my Will, and it shall be given to you.
Seek me and you shall find me.
Knock on the door of my heart, and my wings of love shall spread open wide.

Prosperity shall come to you as you whisper my Name of Love.

You have accomplished much, and so you shall now prosper.
No one will stand in your way, for I have ordained you to prosper in my Name.
You will continue to achieve much, and much more shall be given to you, for you are determined to reach the finish line.
You have worked hard and blessings shall now follow.
I have chosen you to be successful, therefore, you shall prosper and give me the praise.
You will be perfected each step of the way.

Your Redeemer lives and dwells in you.

Prosperity is coming your way.
Receive and be blessed in every way, every step of the way.
Count nothing a loss from here on, for I have restored and redeemed every loss, that was once taken away from you.

You are my jewel, the pearl of my Kingdom bestowed by grace - My crown of royalty.

Amen
Love

Dan 2:29 ...*the revealer of mysteries showed you what is going to happen.*

Journey
- 57 -

EMPOWERED

Hide me, O my God, hide me in the shelter of your love.
Shelter me from the storms of life, for to you I cry.
Keep me safe under the shadow of your wings, that I may prosper, and never see death.
Shelter me, Oh, shelter me, my King, and keep me safe from these present circumstances.
Attend to my needs and never let me go.
Keep me safe as the apple of your eye, that I may see the Light.

Savior Lover, Keeper of my frame, my fulfilled Destiny, Purpose and Entirety you are to me.
Help me know you, learn about your decrees, understand your ways and submit to your Will.
Help me know myself, that I may comprehend life.

Draw me closer to your throne, O Holy Master - Giver of eternity.
Rest me on your bosom of love, that I may live to enjoy another day.
Take hold of my hand and direct my footsteps in your loving care.

Shape me in your image of grace, that I may increase and do wonderful things by the power of your Spirit bestowed upon me so graciously.

I choose to serve you with all my heart.

Run the race, O child of mine, run without ceasing.

Amen

Love

1 John 3:3 **All who have this hope in him purify themselves, just as he is pure.**

Journey
- 58 -

LOOK UP I AM HE

Listen, you Israelites, I am your Father, the Gardener of hearts.
Keep watch over your spirit, and do not malign the Word of God.

By my grace alone, I shall allow you to climb the mountain top.
You can count on Me.
I am the Leader of your soul, and I shall do wonders.
I shall rescue you from the dominion of this earth.
You shall no longer live in the midst of corruption, nor shall any foreigner enter your land. I have assigned, that all is well.

Prepare yourself for my return, and I will uphold your cause.
Submit to my Spirit of freedom, that you may finish the race ahead, and reach your final destination.
Be awakened, O lost souls, you who are suffering and in turmoil.
I am with you, close to your heart.

Nations have robbed you of your blessings, by taking advantage of your land, but will do so no longer.
They are now answerable to Me - Your Judge.
You shall not waste away.
Take heart... I am on my way from heaven to you.
You shall no longer suffer at their hands.
The power of Love is within you strongly.
Achieve and manifest only that which is good.

Amen

Love

Psa 105:1 *Give praise to the LORD, proclaim his name; make known among the nations what he has done.*

Journey
- 59 -
YOUR NEED OF ME IS GREAT

Child, I have enlarged your appetite for more of me.

Create a new environment for everyone, and accomplish the task entrusted you.
Gain Wisdom through knowledge and understanding.
Comprehend my greatness and declare my likeness.

I am not too far away - The Day is coming.
Your need of me is great. Apart from me, you can do nothing.

Clothe yourself with salvation, and be drenched with my essence of love given you so freely.
Bless, so that when the day of evil comes, you will be found worthy of my anointing.
Do not ruin your future, by your actions of today.
I shall sustain you, for I am the Sustainer of hearts.
Your wellbeing is important to me.
I have kept you safe on many occasions.
Do you now question my ability to save you?
The sting of death has no power over you.

You, O God, are my Crown of glory.
Hear me when I cry.

You are kept safe from the enemy, child-- you have nothing to fear.
Redeemed you shall remain strong.

Amen

Love

Jos 24:16 ..."*Far be it from us to forsake the LORD to serve other gods!*

Journey
- 60 -

BE READY & PREPARED

Allow my holy presence to enrich you and perfect you in Love. Enlarge your territory and reap the benefits.

Your life must be changed into my likeness... into my ways and performance.

Do not linger on what you once used to be, but stimulate your mind to wholesome thinking instead.
Be renewed daily by the power of my anointing, which you have received from me so freely.
Keep reminding yourself of my promises and you will succeed.

In a twinkle of an eye, in a heartbeat, by my grace, you shall be changed forever.

Now that we are gathered together in unity, and are in complete harmony, let us rekindle the fire of love between us both.

Do not detach, yourself from your heavenly calling, for I have called you by the grace of my love.

My right hand of power shall sustain you forever.
You are my eternal child, living in the Hope of Glory.

Rest assured: You have been rescued by the grace of my loving care. You shall not be thrown outdoors, for heaven is waiting to receive you into my heart.

Amen

Love

Mat 3:11 ...He will baptize you with the Holy Spirit and fire.

Journey
- 61 -

THE RIVER IS DEEP

Let your Way be my way, Oh, God of my life, and my words your Word. May your beauty shine through me and be revealed. May my actions of praise be your deeds of honor, Oh, Mighty One.

Yes, O child of mine, I have heard the desires of your heart, and I shall lift you up in glory. I have betrothed you in love and with deep compassion drew you to me-- betrothed, you shall always be to me.

I shall guide you in the way best chosen for you, and move you to follow. You will walk in the steps of love and be showered with my greatest blessings.
I shall watch over your ways and guide you along the Way - The path of righteousness. You will revere me and I shall honor you.

Oh, Intercessor of souls, please let your Will be done in my life.

I definitely will, child, for you are precious and honored.

O Holy God, how I desire to be where you are forever.

Question me not about your salvation, O precious child, for I have given you many treasures, secrets and eternal revelations.
Now act upon them.

Thank you, O Lord, thank you eternally.
You have welcomed me with open arms, and I am thankful.

Amen

Love

Psa 28:7 *The LORD is my strength and my shield; my heart trusts in him, and he helps me. My heart leaps for joy, and with my song I praise him.*

Journey
- 62 -

MUTUAL UNDERSTANDING

Oh, my precious child, your obedience to me means prosperity, health, wealth, future hope, restoration, peace, salvation and much much more...
To the man who pleases me, I give wisdom, knowledge, and happiness, and with that comes deliverance.

I, who calls you into fellowship will only draw you closer to me.
Without me, you are nothing - Apart from me, you can do nothing.
It is I, who works in you to rule and reign over those who despise you.
Lose no sight of me, nor let your hope falter, for I will take you higher and astound you with many more wonderful things.
With wonder upon wonder, you shall be astonished.

You, my child, have made the right decision to remain in my love.
You shall achieve much and much more will be your success.
Your future has been sealed by my grace of approval.

Walk as a conqueror, and know my Will in your present circumstances.

Be assured of my victory on your behalf.
You are rescued from all trouble. No harm shall come near you.

You are pure and faultless.

Amen

Love

Isa 48:15 *I, even I, have spoken; yes, I have called him.
I will bring him, and he will succeed in his mission.*

Journey
- 63 -

YOUR GUIDING LIGHT

Take care of your body, O my people, which is my temple - The Temple of my Spirit who dwells in you.

What I have spoken in secret, I shall share with the world, and what I have planned, that too, I will also do.

Take care children, so that you will not be devoured by the accuser of the brethren, who is forever storing up wrath against himself.
Abide in my shelter, that you may prosper and not grow weary.
Capture my heart, that you may hear the sound of my pulse beating just for you.
You are precious to me, Oh, child of the King of Love.
Just look a little closer and see who is in you.

You shall flourish and become the most beautiful of trees.
You will not be put to shame, for the greater One lives in you.

Keep my Light burning... Shinning through... Overflowing with my love and perfection, just for you.
Come out, come out and be separate.
Do not go near the door of their tent.

My zeal will accomplish all this and more.
You are restored, therefore, walk freely.

Amen

Love

Mat 16:19 *I will give you the keys of the kingdom of heaven; whatever you bind on earth will be bound in heaven, and whatever you loose on earth will be loosed in heaven.*

Journey
- 64 -

PEACE BE STILL

Why suffer the way you do, children?
Why be tormented in soul and spirit, when I am right here for you?
Call on me and you will surely find me.

Consider the cost paid on your behalf to be saved, and rejoice in your Maker. The gift of freedom has been offered to you.
The Precious Gift of my love has been offered to you - The Gift of life prepared just for you. You have been ordained and lavished.

Be submissive and you will rule nations.
The Light of my Life shall shine upon your face, as you move mountains in my Name.

Return, for you are rooted and established in love.
Why hold on to that which is displeasing?
Why harbor bitter envy? Why dishonor my Name and bring me unintentional shame? Why injure yourself without knowing it?

It is I, who upholds your years with gladness, surrounds you with mercy and grace, smiles on your face when all is good, takes hold of your right hand and shows you the Way - The One who leads you to your desired haven.

I love you. I shall not turn away from you at any given time.
The yoke of slavery has been broken, because you have turned to me and submitted your ways to my ways of doing things.

Amen

1Sa 54:1 ...*Save me, O God, by your name; vindicate me by your might.*

Journey
- 65 -

BINDING LOVE

Oh, child of my love, have I not shown you, that which is best for you, and said this is the way-- walk ye in it?

Why do you now accuse me of being false?
You have inherited the crown of righteousness.
Why throw away, that which is sacred, and accuse me unjustly?
Why not acknowledge the truth?
Why submit to others and injure yourself?
Why not complete your journey here on earth and live in harmony?

Listen, as I lay my command before you.
Inherit life, love mercy, and act justly.
Walk in the fear of the Lord and fear no man.
Be humble in all your ways and receive an eternal welcome.

Only the meek shall see the face of God.

My Name is Wisdom, and I shall give my glory to no other.
Know then, my ways are not your ways, nor my thoughts.

Be filled with the fullness of my joy, and humbly accept the Word planted in you, which can save you.
Consider my Words, and act upon them, dear child.

I know those whom I have chosen.

I, who loves you am He, and am true to you.

Amen

Love

Job 19:25 I know that my redeemer lives...

Journey
- 66 -

JUST BELIEVE

Weary yourself no further.
I am about to expand your territory and bring you to a place of rest from all this calamity. Do you not see it? Do you not perceive it? Do you not realize, that I am with you? I myself have taken great delight in you.

Since you have honored me before man, I shall now reward you abundantly, for all your diligence.
Your deeds have reached my throne, for with sincerity of heart, you honored my throne of grace and submitted.

Boldly without retreat enter my sanctuary.
I am the God who fights the battles on your behalf.
Now, you too, fight with all your might the good fight of the faith and never retreat.
Run with perseverance and never give up, not even for a little while. I am not far, but very near and close to your heart; listening to every sound of your heart.
You are precious to me and very lovely in my sight.
Run to me for all your needs, precious one
I am here watching over you and shall also walk you through.

Refresh yourself with something to eat, before you continue on this journey of life.

Amen

Love

Psa 62:11 *One thing God has spoken, two things I have heard: "Power belongs to you, God,*

Journey
- 67 -

CONSIDER YOUR WAYS

Children, come and learn from my Words of Wisdom, listen to my insight.
Never look back, for I shall restore all your losses.
Fix your eyes on Me - I am the answer to your every question.

My purpose must be fulfilled, that I may continue to bless others through your obedience.

Speak the truth even when it hurts, and spread the good news, that they too may make the right decision based on love.
Children, take care of your family, for they too are one with me in spirit.
I am building a long tall stable building, made up of spiritual people linked together as one body... one with me, and in me.
I desire to see unity in the body, therefore, my building shall be as tall as the highest Mountain in structure, and my foundation set on the solid Rock eternal.
My sacred church without walls belongs to me.
I am the Builder of everything.

Enjoy your journey here on earth with me, for I am your Everything and Every need met.
Complete your mission, to accomplish all that I have called you to do in my Name, and rejoice.

Amen

Love

Pro 11:5 *The righteousness of the blameless makes their paths straight, but the wicked are brought down by their own wickedness.*

Journey
- 68 -
THE FUTURE IS NOT DIM

O my great God, I am rebirthed to be free.
Born again to be free, and not to become depraved and insane.
Rejoice, O my soul, and dance with shouts of joy.
Your Maker has freed you from the agony of sin and death.
Rejoice and sing praises to Him. He is the Alpha and the Omega of your life, the Creator of all things... of you, me, the earth and everything in it.
I call on your Name at all times, holding your hand to guide me and seeking your face to bless me. Give me wisdom to understand your ways, faith to believe, and love to accept your mercy and grace.
Thank you, for loving me enough and unshackling me from the grave.

Master Teacher, your actions speak louder than words, therefore, your Word is Life and Living, stronger than any double-edged sword... protecting my body, soul and spirit.

Because you live I also live; because you are an overcomer, we overcome; because you have won the victory, we your children walk victoriously; because you are great, we live in greatness, and because you are holy, we your children must also be holy.
Thank you, Holy Spirit - My One and only Great Comforter.

Prepare yourself for the end times.
Hear my voice, listen and act on my Will.

Amen

Love

Psa 102:18 **Let this be written for a future generation, that a people not yet created may praise the LORD:**

Journey
- 69 -

NO SHAME

O my Creator, Father God, Giver of Life, Master, Savior, Redeemer, Prince of Peace, Lover of mankind... your Word is always true. You are the Power of Love and Authority of mercy.

Forgive my disbelief and build me up in faith, that I may rest in your glory and salvation.

Oh, my Creator, how you give rest to the weary and downtrodden. Your comfort brings relief to the thirsty.
You are my bread and water.
No food can ever taste the same... you satisfy the desires of my heart. My soul thirsts for your Word, my body longs to be touched by your spirit, and my heart yearns for your love throughout the day and all night in a dry and weary land where there is no water.

You created my innermost being and weaved me together in my mother's womb.

You drew me out of the darkest darkness and brought me to yourself.
You caused breath to enter me and gave me life.
I praise you, for I am gracefully and perfectly made.
Under the shadow of your wings, I shall remain safe.
Your works are wonderful; I know that full well.

How I love you, Oh, my faithful child... my special child of faith.

Amen

Love

Isa 54:11 *Afflicted city, lashed by storms and not comforted, I will rebuild you with stones of turquoise, your foundations with lapis lazuli.*

Journey
- 70 -

TENDER ARMS

O God of creation, have your way with me. I am needy and desperate for your touch. I feel lonely, mistreated and miserable in this old world of sorrow and destruction.

Because of my spiritual walk with you, I have been accused falsely, and many dishonest words have been spoken against me.

How am I to cope without your glory? Surely I cannot. Oh, Ruler of my life, free me from my anxiety, my emptiness and this sadness which I am dreading.

Help me know your love, feel your affection, sense your presence, live by your grace, be revived by your mercy and enjoy your peace. Help me see your purpose for me, understand your Will, come to know what pleases you and live by your sufficient grace.

Consider me, Oh, God of the universe, and have mercy on me. O Hope of Glory, trusting in you is never wrong, but staying away from you is extremely dangerous.

Your child who is in need of compassion is calling out to you in praise. In your precious Name, I ask.

Revival is on the way for you, my friend, revival is on the way. I am your Revival. Listen to me and live.

Amen

Love

Isa 38:5 ...'This is what the LORD, the God of your father David, says: I have heard your prayer and seen your tears; I will add fifteen years to your life.

Journey
- 71 -

CROSS OVER TO SAFETY

Child, keep in mind: Worldly sorrow brings death, but godly sorrow brings repentance, leading you to a life of love, peace and harmony with me.

Care for the needs of others who are under your care, and follow my leading example of Love.
Bless those who curse you, while being a blessing to all those who hurt you and take advantage of you.
Condemn no one, for condemnation is not from God.

Take heart and recharge.
Turn your face to me and see the glories revealed to you.
Entertain no other thought except the thought of me loving you.
Keep this in mind: Your specialty means the cost of sacrifice shed on the cross.

Yes, you are special to me in every way.

Condemn not the guilty, but have mercy on everyone instead.
Travel those roads no longer.
Stay in the position to which I have called you.

I have given you grace upon grace upon grace to share.
Your great I Am is here.
Be released in all your glory.

Amen

Love

Psa 17:15 *As for me, I will be vindicated and will see your face; when I awake, I will be satisfied with seeing your likeness.*

Journey
- 72 -

REDEEMED TO EXCEL

*Oh, God of my life, bless my children and take care of my needs, I ask, for you are always faithful and true.
Fulfill the desires of your heart in me, and complete the work of your hands... which you have begun in me so beautifully.*

*Merciful One, I need your Sovereignty, and I call upon your Strength to save me.
See me through my difficulties, I pray.*

*May I never disappoint you or ever reject the love you have shown.
Deal with me in accordance to your good pleasure and purpose, for I am a man of peace.*

O God my Sovereign, I remember you during the time of my wilderness in the desert heat... how you conquered lands on my behalf that were not my own and inspired me to sing your love songs. You gave me the sure blessing of David and worked miracles for me. Thank you. Restore me, Oh, God, and take over my life.

*You will succeed in all you do, son, you will succeed, for I have enabled you to achieve beyond your natural abilities, and conquer kingdoms beyond your own strength and capabilities.
You are a warrior.*

Amen

Love

Isa 49:23 *Kings will be your foster fathers, and their queens your nursing mothers. They will bow down before you with their faces to the ground; they will lick the dust at your feet. Then you will know that I am the LORD; those who hope in me will not be disappointed.*

Journey
- 73 -

THE REALITY OF YOUR DREAM

Oh, my child, keep dreaming... never give up on your dreams, visions and the desires, which I have placed within you.

I will fulfill my vision in you and it will seem like a dream.

Your desires I will not neglect, nor will I ever forsake your dreams.

I will move you to a higher position, and my purpose through you shall be accomplished.

Once again you will not be disappointed.
In my Name, you will accomplish much.

Give all that you possess to the poor and follow me.

Your burdens shall become lighter as you obey my voice, and will no longer be a heavy load for you to bear.

You are transitioning from the old to the new.
Your new journey has just begun.

Love as I have loved you, and you will be made complete.
Do not become undressed before the enemy and so defile yourself.

Be distinguished.
Restoration is at hand.

Amen

Love

Tit 3:5 *he saved us, not because of righteous things we had done, but because of his mercy. He saved us through the washing of rebirth and renewal by the Holy Spirit,*

Journey
- 74 -

BORN TO LOVE & BE LOVED

Pray to me and I will answer thee.
Be joyful and wait patiently for my return.
I shall consume the very core of your being, and with open arms welcome you into my treasured haven.
You shall know the Truth that sets the captives free and welcome them in my Name into my eternity to be free.
You shall be carried through the deepest darkness.

Take no wrong turn while you are on my highway to heaven.
Create a new environment for yourself in me, and live a new beginning to start with me.
Hurry to your destined haven... where there is true love and forgiveness.
Just as a yielded vessel brings life to the soul, so a submissive nature to the spirit becomes health to the bones.

Yield your heart and not just your deeds of material possessions, for the River of Life flows from your Source of Eternity - Me, your Creator, who formed you.
Give yourself no rest and give me no rest, until I establish you, and make you the praise of the whole earth. Follow my Word with all your heart, and never tire of running the race marked out for you.

Loving you always. You are destined for glory-- do not forget.

Amen

Love

Psa 102:13 *You will arise and have compassion on Zion, for it is time to show favor to her; the appointed time has come.*

Journey
- 75 -

IGNORE ALL ELSE

Ignore me not, O God of glory, and discipline me not with thy rod.

I am humble in heart and in need of you so desperately.
I need to hear your voice and call upon your Name.
I need you beside me to watch over me so carefully.
I am not a sinner.
I have been washed by the precious blood of Love.

Allow me not the temptation of satanic influences.
Let no sin rule over me. Rescue me from his grip, I ask.
I am young and vulnerable, and because of my weaknesses, I struggle sometimes.
I need your strength to support me.
Strengthen my inner frame that I may be sustained.
Help me surrender my all, Oh, my Savior, my Glory, the Mighty One of the living.
Help me tend to your flock and watch over your little ones - The lambs.
May I never forget your goodness and miracles performed during time of need.
The glory alone remains yours.

I adore you, Oh, my Eternal King.
I worship you, O my Savior God of glory.

Amen

Love

Pro 1:5 **let the wise listen and add to their learning, and let the discerning get guidance--**

Journey
- 76 -

YOUR GIFT OF LOVE

O my Comforter, comfort my weary soul and give me relief from my own sorrows.

Sustain my heart and give me freedom and relief from my anxiety. Create in me a new heart, that I may live to see your face.

O God of love, may my life be pleasing in your sight, and my house be your sanctuary. Oh, gentle Shepherd, help me know you, understand your ways and be submissive to your Will.
I desire to have your nature as I partake of your likeness, reflecting your beauty so surreal.

You have spoken to me again and again; but instead of listening to your wisdom and words of insight, I turned a deaf ear to you and thrust you behind my back.

I now yield myself to your Kingdom and my heart to your ways. There is no pleasure in serving myself, but only to you must I turn and find delight.

May my heart be attentive to your Word and my Will become your Will in action.
Your Name is above every other Name. Your Word is above every other word. Your glory is above all, and you, O King of my eternity, are the lifter of my head.

Amen

Love

Rom 15:7 *Accept one another, then, just as Christ accepted you, in order to bring praise to God.*

Journey
- 77 -

PURIFY THY HEART

Children, O my children, I am with you always and forever.
He gives you beauty for ashes and enlarges your territory.
He stretches the heavens wide open and by his grace welcomes you in.

Oh, my Treasure of Life, I am overwhelmed with all you do for me.
Complete me in you, that I may soar with the eagles on high and be found standing strong.

Complete your work here, and continue to journey on with me,
Oh, child of my eternal love.

O God, I do not choose my life to be over, for I have barely begun my journey with you here on earth.

Oh, my special child, my love shall keep you close to me, and overshadow your darkness with the purity of my light.
Your love shall increase and become a chain reaction to all who serve me.
My love shall always support and sustain you by grace.
I am your Restorer of faith, the great I Am - Your very All.
So be touched in spirit, and renewed in soul and mind.
My compassion is as deep as my well of love.

Tenderly but honorably tend to my flock.

Amen

Love

Psa 31:7 *I will be glad and rejoice in your love, for you saw my affliction and knew the anguish of my soul.*

Journey
- 78 -

SUCCEED TO BENEFIT

Your life is now hidden in the palm of my hands.
Do not neglect my instructions.
Let not the enemy of souls, snatch the gifts of your calling.
Do not challenge him, but just live the righteous life required, and overcome him by your righteous deeds of action-- Your action of faith, hope, truth, power of love and the Word of your Testimony.

All things are coming to an end, even this present world.

Your life is so different now because you have learned to love.

Temptation does not come from me, nor chasing after fantasies is of me, but it comes from the one who is seeking your life.
Resist him at all times, and stand tall without fear or concern by the power of my Sword - The weapon of my Word aimed against him.

The way to live in Spirit is to be led by my Spirit.
I am your consuming fire.
Deny the flesh by giving it nothing destructive.
Walk in the holiness of my Word by abiding in my Spirit of love.
March on, for the spirit is willing and desires the best for you - The flesh on the other hand, is weak and defiles, if not aligned with the Truth of my Word.

Obey my voice, and you will receive instruction on how to have a balanced, secure and reassured life.

Amen
Love

Psa 135:5 *I know that the LORD is great, that our Lord is greater than all gods.*

Journey
- 79 -

THE RULE OF LOVE

The future is not dim, as it may seem to you right now.
Help your brothers and sisters everywhere you go, and lead them the way of truth... in order for them to reach their desired haven.
Take nothing nor anyone for granted. Uphold the cause of the needy and put yourself in their position instead.
I am the One, who is carrying you close to my heart.
Cry out to me, and do not neglect your brothers who are truly in need of me.
Shift not the blame from yourself, for I do see everything. Nothing is ever hidden nor covered from my view-- all things are revealed and exposed before my eyes.
Mix not the old wine with the new or you will be torn to pieces.
See through my eyes, and you will see more clearly the abundant pleasures of Life released through me to you who believe.

Argue not, for I despise dispute as much as I abhor dishonest gain.
Reckless words hurt the one who is speaking and grieves the one who is listening. Use your lips only for a good cause.
Enjoy the pleasures of Life by being restored back to me.
I am with you till the end of time.
Be perfect as I am perfect, and reflect my likeness in the midst of all this darkness.
Rescue those who are in need of me, and you will be upheld by me.
Beauty divine is in the making of love in spirit.

Amen

Love

Psa 4:7 *Fill my heart with joy when their grain and new wine abound.*

Journey
- 80 -

MASTER YOUR GIFTS

Discern my gifts and prepare for the greatest battle yet - The final battle of the day.
Seek me and you shall find me when you seek me with all your heart.
Never underestimate my zeal nor my power.
Through you, my unfading beauty shall be seen.

Establish not your own Kingdom, for only disappointment there you will find.
You do not need to win my love, nor force my hand, for I already do love you unconditionally without any regret.

You will always be perfect in my eyes and live in my heart.

Establish your throne in my heart, Oh, God of grace, I ask.

Run the race without any hesitation, child, and capture all that is made available for you.
Loving you eternally from the heart of my Kingdom.

Unity in the Faith of my glory is the energy received from the Almighty.
To you, I have given much, and much more is coming your way.
You are my zeal, my glory on earth in the midst of all this darkness, O my loved one.

Amen

Love

Zec 8:15 *"so now I have determined to do good again to Jerusalem and Judah. Do not be afraid.*

Journey
- 81 -
BE ONE IN SPIRIT

Do you not know that neither your tears nor your faithfulness to me will ever be wasted?

I will not rejoice over your grief, nor will I ever see you deserted.
When you cry out, my first reaction is to respond.
I love you, and my Spirit yearns to comfort you.
My hand of love is always here to guide you and lead you the Way of Truth in Righteousness.
You need not worry, just know that I love you.

Be led by my Spirit of Truth, and walk in the supernatural.
Be joyful, and keep it not to yourself, for I shall soon reveal myself to the world.

I have opened a closed door for you, that no man can shut-- walk in it. Miracles, signs and wonders shall follow as you speak my words of Wisdom.

Let the fullness of your love support me, Oh, Gracious One.

My love dwells in your heart, child; therefore, you are safe in the arms of Love... forever redeemed.
Be one with me in spirit and you will never be defeated.
The Conqueror is here to stay, and He is with you throughout eternity.

Amen

Love

Joh 1:16 *Out of his fullness we have all received grace in place of grace already given.*

Journey
- 82 -
IN DUE TIME

Do not take advantage of your brothers, my friends... rejoice with one another instead.

I have given you the never-ending life - The power to destroy Kingdoms, uproot nations, build up and tear down towers.
I am the One, who supplies you with good things.
Why wonder who is going to help you?

Consider my decrees and obey my commands, then you will inherit the Promised Land - The Land of milk and honey.
You will gain glory as you look up to Me, your King, and I shall guide you into all truth.

I have promised and declared your victory - It shall stand irrevocable and solid forever.
Remember: I give everything for your enjoyment.

Do not doubt my power, for I am yet to astonish you.
See to it that you present yourself before God as one holy, pure and sanctified.
Take heart, for I am coming soon to take you home with me.
Worship me in the splendor of my majesty, and divine glory shall overtake you.

Your Enlightened Word I Am.

Amen

Love

Psa 125:1 *Those who trust in the LORD are like Mount Zion, which cannot be shaken but endures forever.*

Journey
- 83 -
RECALL THE DAYS

O God, Savior of my soul. Why do I burden you with my troubles?
On my own, I can do nothing, but with you all things are possible, so I rest my case.
You are my eternity of love, and to you, I surrender.
Your Word is sweeter than honey to my lips, and you, my King, surpass them all.
I need you to capture my heart, so that I may be in constant need of your love.
Your compassion stirs me, O God of my life.

O child, why burden yourself with many grievances, when I am right here beside you to help you grow?

Continue your walk with me, for I shall empower you in all circumstances.
Be not concerned over these situations which you can do nothing about.
Live in accordance to my Will, and delay not my return with thoughts that serve no purpose.
I have given you favor amongst all your enemies.
Faithful and true you shall remain to me.

The One who loves you is here, and will always be beside you.

Amen

Love

Isa 33:6 *The will be the sure foundation for your times, a rich store of salvation and wisdom and knowledge; the fear of the LORD is the key to this treasure.*

Journey

- 84 -

EXERCISE JUSTICE

Come to know who you are in me, child.
Learn about yourself through my Word of Life.
Learn about Love and discover my Spirit within you.
Be anxious for nothing, and do not burden yourself with much.
Concentrate on the things above and not on worldly treasures.

I take great delight in you; otherwise, how else would you be saved?

Live my life to enjoy yours.

I know that you are with me, O my Savior King, helping me every day... every step of the way.
Help me be your living example to all nations.

Go forth, beloved, and declare my greatness to all.
I am with you always, even to the ends of the earth.
You can rely on me.

O Comforter of hearts, I need you beside me, and for your tender, loving, comforting arms to support me.

I have already gone ahead of you, child.
My fire has burned every obstacle to ashes.

See you on the other side of glory.

Amen

Love

Jos 1:8 *Keep this Book of the Law always on your lips; meditate on it day and night, so that you may be careful to do everything written in it. Then you will be prosperous and successful.*

Journey
- 85 -

PROTECTED FROM FORTUNE

Worry not, my child, for your burdens and worries are mine to handle.
Have nothing to do with slander.

Enter into my presence of peace and harmony and there remain.
Neglect not your gift of love which I myself have invested in you.

I love you, my people.
I love you, with the death of my sacrificial Lamb shed on the cross.
I will not neglect you, nor will I ever condemn you.

You belong to me, O my sweet child, who is born of Love.
You are the apple of my eye.
I am returning, and my rewards are with me.

Consider my Gift and save your soul from death. Save yourself from death by loving Me as well as yourself, O my child prince.

Eternity is waiting to receive you.
I am calling you out by name.
Words of Love passed on to you, my faithful one.
Keep the fire burning and do not overwhelm yourself with trouble.

Your Redeemer lives and is very near... close to your heart.
Continue to show mercy mixed with abundant grace.

I have taken great delight in you.

Amen

Love

Num 18:14 "*Everything in Israel that is devoted to the LORD is yours.*

Journey
- 86 -
REVEAL THYSELF

Hold on to me, child, hold on and never let go.
As you walk through the fire you will not be burned-- the flames
will not set you ablaze, for my grace shall see you through.
I shall guide you through the deepest river and you will not drown.

Keep in mind: I will not neglect you nor ever watch you stumble
along the way.
Ask not why this or that?
Just believe and know: I am with you eternally.

No need to feel worried or afraid.
I, the God of your life, am your Best Friend and Eternal Provision.

Drive out demons in my Name.
Possess nations, and capture their land.
Resist the enemy by the power of my Love.
Deprive not yourself of the good given to you.
Take note and listen to my words of insight.
Hold on, hold on, child, and never let go.

I will support you through and through.

Encourage one another in love with my resurrection power, and
you will be empowered to see the Light - The Resurrection Life of
Glory.
Be empowered by the blood of Life sacrificed for you.

Amen

Love

Psa 101:2 ...I will conduct the affairs of my house with a blameless heart.

Journey
- 87 -
YOUR JUDGE IS SOVEREIGN

Behold, I stand at the door and knock.
Will you open up and welcome me?

When you hear my voice, do not harden your hearts as you did
during time of war and struggle.

Today is the day of victory by my saving grace.

Turn not away from serving me, but from agony and death instead,
that you may prosper and not be entangled by trouble.

Be restored. I am your very all. You need no other.
Hold me close, before the hour folds.

There is a specific time for every activity under heaven.
Now is the time for your redemption.
Now is the time for my saving grace.

Do not argue with anyone.
Live a life of freedom away from struggle, stress and trouble.
Turn to me and be healed, delivered and set free.

Your journey shall soon become completed.

Look to me and be released from every burden overwhelming you.

I am the key of remembrance - The Key to your heart.
Acknowledged faith is assured certainty.

Amen

Love

Psa 76:1 ...*God is renowned in Judah; in Israel his name is great.*

Journey
- 88 -

ENGAGE NOT WITH DECEPTION

I am the Way, the Truth, and the Life.
Neglect not my Word, which gives you endurance.
Honor me in all you do, and be empowered by my sufficient grace.
Build yourself up in spirit, and feed others on my spiritual food--
give them my milk to drink and my solid meat to eat, that they may enjoy an abundant life.

Remember you are only on a journey here on earth... on an assignment.
This is not your eternal destiny.
You have a place waiting for you in heaven.

Learn to rescue people from their own pit of destruction, and save them from the trap set before them.
Save them from their own downfall.
Remember not to turn away from me... just give me your best.
Yes, it is written, so let it be done.
Draw near to me and you shall find me closer to you.
Lead the way, so that others may be found in me.
I am pleased with you.
You will not be disappointed, for you have faith in action.

Burn with zeal and be consumed, enflamed by the power of my love.

Amen

Love

Psa 55:18 *He rescues me unharmed from the battle waged against me, even though many oppose me.*

Journey
- 89 -
EVALUATE CAUTIOUSLY

Keep me as the Center of your life, Oh, child of my love.
Keep me in your core being and you shall lose nothing of value -
only from harm you shall be spared.

Come to me all you who are weary and burdened, come into my
presence and you shall find rest.
My presence is real, and my peace surpasses all understanding.
Come and be released.
Knock on the door of my heart and you will find me.

I shall glorify myself through you.
Have you not yet learned this lesson?

Prophesy and waste no more time on useless things.
Help your brothers and sisters in spirit who are in need of your
help and support, and be a blessing to all.
Keep yourself washed clean in my River of Truth through the
Living Word of my love.

I have carried you since your youth.
Do you now question my faithfulness?

Consider the cost paid to see you through.
Keep looking through my eyes, and you will see all the wonderful
things stored up for you - Wonders beyond wonders...

Amen

Love

Psa 62:6 Truly he is my rock and my salvation; he is my fortress, I will not be shaken.

Journey
- 90 -

THE BLUES ARE GONE

Honor me before all mankind and I will lift you up in due time - In due season.
Destroy not thyself with worries and burdens.
Be rested in me and you will be free from all anxiety.
Be not concerned, nor overwhelmed by trouble.
Have these not come to test the people of the world?

I have taken care of your every need.
You are supported - No need to grieve.
I am the Resurrection and the Life.
He who believes will live and never see death.
Do you believe that I am the One? Of course, you do!

You are reading this message because it is written especially for you, O child of mine... now run with my message.

Hold on to your faith and lose no hope.
I will never leave you nor forsake you.
I shall never treat you as an orphan, nor walk away and leave you deserted, unwanted or even for a second neglected.

You are not a widow who is deserted, but rather the bride of God who is blessed with many spiritual children - expect more.

Learn to love yourself through me.

Amen

Love

Jer 17:14 *Heal me, LORD, and I will be healed; save me and I will be saved, for you are the one I praise.*

Journey
- 91 -

WEARY YOURSELF NOT

Be not ensnared.
I will enlighten your mind and move you to serve me from the heart.
I shall increase my anointing over you, that you may serve me with my kingly anointing.
My glory is real and not counterfeit.
I shared with you many secrets. Which one do you prefer most?

Guard well the deposit which I have entrusted to you by my spirit.
Obey my instructions and be led by my Wisdom.
Do not take what I am saying to you lightly, but rather seriously, for the days are no longer safe.
The time is short and you must hurry, for there is no tomorrow.
Offer your prayers and petitions to me, for you are free to soar.
Forget not my benefits as you rule the nations.

You are no longer condemned for those prior things committed.
Your heart is secure with me, and your benefits are discovered in me.

Be assured, and live life to the fullest.
Live the life of faith and prosper in body, soul and spirit.

Loving you and not condemning you, Oh, my precious child.

Amen

Love

Psa 119:128 **and because I consider all your precepts right, I hate every wrong path**

Journey
- 92 -

RELIEVE STRESS

My guilt remains before you, O God, yet you have remained faithful and true to your word. You have not condemned me with the guilty, nor shamed me with the wicked.
You have covered my transgressions and given me hope and a future. I love you, Oh, my King of hearts, and admire your love, for you have not abandoned me to the grave.

I need you in my life, Oh, King of hearts, Ruler of everything, I need you daily.
Do not abandon the work of your hands - I am your handiwork. Without you I am nothing and apart from you, I can do nothing.

Teach me your ways, O Master Teacher, and reveal your truth to me. Train me in your ways, that I may carry your Name and make it known to the ends of the earth. Move my spirit to serve you wholeheartedly. Carry me, Oh Savior King, Restorer of everything. Carry me from this world of destruction - This valley of indecision.

Sing to me, child, and let your voice be heard.
I shall separate you from all who malign the Word of God.

Be disciplined and you will be lifted up to other heights of glory.
Take hold of my hand and walk with me.
Do not control others... be a great influence in your leading instead.

See you on my return.

Amen

Love

Joh 15:14 **You are my friends if you do what I command.**

Journey
- 93 -
REMAIN COMMITTED

To love you on earth, O Gracious Healer, Deliverer of souls, is the key to having all good things with you in heaven.
To survive without you in this world is almost unbearable.
This world of deceit and abandonment has no room, nor space for anyone like myself who lives in you.

God of love, I need your help daily, as long as it is called today.
I know there is no return to my old patterns - Destructive ways, nor is there any room in my future from my past.

Help me lead others into your glorious Kingdom of Love, Oh, my Savior King - The Kingdom of peace and harmony.
You are the great I Am; without you, my life will end... it has no meaning.

Teach me your ways, that I may prosper in your truth, walk in your ways and be victorious.
You are my God and without you, I cannot survive.

Loving you always.
In your precious Name, I pray, for you are special to me in every way.

The believing heart in spirit is the receiving heart of truth in action.
Loving you always.

Amen
Love

Psa 10:14 *But you, God, see the trouble of the afflicted; you consider their grief and take it in hand. The victims commit themselves to you; you are the helper of the fatherless.*

Journey
- 94 -

FORGIVENESS IS DELIVERANCE

The holiness of your beauty shines forth, O King of glory - My love story. I am mesmerized by your love, entangled by your grace and moved by your rhythm divine.
Healer, heal my broken heart and redeem me from the grave, that I may see the light of life and sing your love songs during the night.

Lean on me, O you mighty warrior, and take heed of my Word. Learn my knowledge, that you may grow in wisdom and understand my Word of Love.

Rejoice in my commands, for you shall not see death, nor turmoil will ever take you by storm.

Hold not to past hurts and shattered dreams, for what I am about to do for you outweighs them all.

I am about to restore double for all your troubles, losses, and tribulations... even now I announce triple.

All you need to do is forgive those who have done you wrong and walk with freedom from the heart.

You do not need to run away from me - Hold on to me instead.

Hold on tightly to what you have with me and never let go.

Capture my heart by the spirit of truth in worship, and in constant praise thank me.

Enlarge your appetite for more of my love, till you reach the fullness of me in you.

Amen

Love

Psa 112:5 *Good will come to those who are generous and lend freely, who conduct their affairs with justice.*

Journey
- 95 -
CONSIDER CAREFULLY

Who do people say I am? Who am I to you?
Am I a god who lives in the wilderness, or the God who is in heaven? Am I the One you are waiting for, or should you expect another? So, if I am from heaven, why are you not comforting one another with my Words of encouragement and Love?

My blood shall strengthen you, and my power shall encourage you.

Why are you not on my table eating and drinking of my delicacies?
Why are you not in communion with me?
Wine and dine on my table of love with me!
Drink my new wine and eat my manna from heaven daily... before time slips you by.
Buckle your seatbelt-- I am on my way to see you reach eternity.
Lift up your voice, lift it up with a shout and do not hold back.

Make my presence known, for your Restorer of hope is alive.
Enjoy life here on earth with me before you reach eternity.

My Name shall be great among my people Israel, who are also your people, and you, my son, will surely be a great blessing to all, including to those who serve me.

I am the Lifter of souls for all eternity.
Love the brothers of believers, and give up not on yourself.
You are my ambassador here on earth - Reflection of my glory.

Amen

Love

Job 16:20 **My intercessor is my friend as my eyes pour out tears to God;**

Journey
- 96 -
KEEP SAFE

God of heaven, I need to go home. Take me away with you now, for I can no longer tolerate this earthly vessel. It is all too hard... too difficult, but nothing is ever too difficult for you to do in me and achieve through me. I need your return now, more than ever... come quickly, rush to my aid, I ask... support me.

I heard your voice and seen your tears, Oh, child of my Kingdom. I too am looking forward to my return, more than you ever know.

Be comforted in heart and the heaviness of soul will be removed.
Be anxious for nothing... my return draws near.
I am the One who loves you and attends to your every need.

Keep going, keep running the race without wavering or giving up. Give the enemy no opportunity to pull you down, no foothold, no chance to raise his poisonous ugly head.

I have so much more for you to accomplish... much more than you can now handle. I have taken you places, but there are many more places for you to attend... many more places for you to travel through. Nothing shall ever be impossible for you.

Be still, O precious one, and rest on my bosom of love.
You have a bright future ahead of you, beyond your imagination.
I have heard your cry for mercy... I shall now act.

Amen

Love

Isa 26:2 **Open the gates that the righteous nation may enter, the nation that keeps faith.**

Journey
- 97 -
MY KINGDOM IS YOURS

Perfection can only come from me, Oh, my child, so why look elsewhere?
Do not be disturbed by the lifestyle of those who are living on earth. They have been doing these things to me for a long time now-- since ancient times!

Relax and enjoy the ride of my spirit.
I am with you... encouraging and upholding your case always.
I lead you in the path of righteousness-- bringing you physical, spiritual and financial wellbeing.

Continue to love me with all your heart, and do the work you were called to accomplish in Name.

As you know-- I am the only One who is True.
Have you grasped hold of that revelation?
Oh, my sweet child, you are the apple of my eye.

The God of all the earth lives in you and is your Redeemer, Savior and Best Friend.
He is both your God and theirs-- To your family, loved ones and friends.

Glory to me forever in the highest - Your distinguished Love.

Amen

Love

2Co 13:11 **Finally, brothers and sisters, rejoice! Strive for full restoration, encourage one another, be of one mind, live in peace. And the God of love and peace will be with you.**

Journey
- 98 -

ACKNOWLEDGED BY ME

Be courageous, you mighty warrior-- praise me in battle and sing joyfully the songs taught you from heaven by my spirit.

I have already overcome the destroyer - Your enemy and mine.
I have hurled the rider and his horses into the sea.

Come out from them and be separate.
Touch no unclean thing and you shall be washed by the cleansing water of my word.
You conquered and overcame multiple trials - The greatest is yet to come.

Get ready for my revival before the final countdown.
Be alert and on your guard.
Destroy the deeds of darkness before the eyes of Him who destroys the enemy of all mankind.

The day of battle is nearly over.

Look to Him who is coming in the clouds.
Fight the good fight of the faith daily, for the battle has been won.

I am your Conqueror - Glory to me in the highest.

I shall rescue you from every attack burdening you.
The resurrection power is here to save you.

Amen

Love

Psa 46:2 *Therefore we will not fear, though the earth give way and the mountains fall into the heart of the sea,*

Journey
- 99 -
ASK FOR ANYTHING

Why are you destroying each other, people?
Why not rest in my loving arms, instead, and love one another?

Come to my holiness of grace and surrender to my love, that you may find refuge for your weary soul.

Since I am your Refuge, why not delight in me?
I will satisfy the desires of your heart.

Come to me and no longer wear yourself out.
Let me work in you and achieve my requirements.
Lift up a banner in my Name and heaven will rejoice.
Shout for joy, you heavens, for your King cometh.
Dance and shout for joy.
Acknowledge that I am He, for in this, there is no wrong.

I am near to all who call on me, to all who call on me in truth.
I have seen your tears and shown you the way.
You need to give up on the old wine to be refreshed by the new.

It is time to move forward... move on and climb higher.

Drink and continue to drink from my River of Life - The River of delight and eternal blessings.

Loving you with favor, Oh, child. I am your King.

Amen

Love

2Sa 16:14 The king and all the people with him arrived at their destination exhausted. And there he refreshed himself.

Journey
- 100 -

OBEDIENCE IS THE KEY

I am your Shield of faith - Shield of protection, your very Help in time of trouble.
Why waver in faith and so doubt me, Oh, my child?
Why doubt my love?
My Way is perfect in those who love me.
Why not present yourself to me as one truly faithful... one who is entrusted with much?

You will surely be blessed in all your ways.
Fulfill my Will to accomplish your journey.

I work in you to will and to act according to my good promises.
Work and never give up achieving, fulfilling, accomplishing all these amazing things in my Name.
The race is not yet over... it is not for the swift nor for the bold, but for those who are diligent, determined and victorious.
Success comes from my Will done in your life daily.

Fulfill my purpose and you will climb the mountain heights without much effort or retreat.
My Will is already at work in you - Act on it.
Lavish yourself no longer with life simple pleasures, nor become a laughingstock to your enemies.
Consider my wisdom, for your mission is made possible.

Amen

Love

Psa 110:3 *Your troops will be willing on your day of battle. Arrayed in holy splendor, your young men will come to you like dew from the morning's womb.*

Journey
- 101 -

PLEASING YOU ARE TO ME

You are lovely in my eyes and very pleasing in my sight.
Your holiness is the redeeming cost of my sacrifice paid, to give you eternal life, so that you will not die but live - The price has been paid on your behalf child... you have nothing to worry about.

Surrender your all and neglect not your heavenly calling.
Acknowledge that I am He and be unified.

Oh, Lord Savior King, I cannot believe that you love me.
I stand in awe of your love, and the power of your blood saves me.
The Name that is above every other name sets me reeling.

Good child, very good; now be sustained.
Since I am your First Love, maintain my standard of living and flourish; allow me to also be your last love in motion.

By the action of faith, you shall be supported.
Secure your position in me without retreat, for you are already there. You are on your way to greatness.
You are no longer in a survival mode, but in the zone of love.

Make it known.
Walk in the authority of my love without any fear or retreat, and you will be blessed beyond measure.
I shall also rescue you from any negativity troubling you.

Amen

Love

Psa 45:11 **Let the king be enthralled by your beauty; honor him, for he is your Lord.**

Journey
- 102 -

RECOVER THE LOSS

Watch yourselves and pray, O my friends.
I am on my way.
The fire shall go before you and burn every obstacle to ashes.

Watch your ways, so that you will not lose heart.

I am the Alpha and the Omega, the very start of your Beginning and your Eternal Life.
No one can deliver out of my hand. When I act who can reverse it? What I purpose, that too, I shall always fulfill.

Serve me shoulder to shoulder, and be one with me in spirit.

I love you deeply, and because love covers over a multitude of sins, you have been set free. Forgiven... forgive, for you are forgiven.

Thank you, Lord, for your kindness to me.

Humble yourself before me, child, and you will remain faithful.
Do not delay, for what I have commissioned you is great.

You have an inheritance as a reward waiting.

I am the Voice - Your future is at hand.

Do not be reluctant.
Serve me from the depth of your being, Oh, child of my Kingdom.

Amen

Love

Pro 22:4 **Humility is the fear of the LORD; its wages are riches and honor and life.**

Journey
- 103 -

THE ROAD IS NARROW

Dear friend, O my dear friend, listen to what I am about to say.
The time is coming when men will look for me, but won't find me.
How is that you ask? I tell you the truth: Time is nearly over, and the days ahead are far gone to be retrieved.

I am on the way. How can there be any more time left?
Tell me, my friend. Tell me!
Do you not know, that those who belong to me have their names written in the Book of Life? For my seal of approval upon their head is written on the tablet of their heart.
Put your trust in your Maker without retreat, and depend on Him for the rest of your life. He, your God, is Eternal.
Turn not to the left nor to the right. Fix your eyes and thoughts directly towards me - Your eternal God and Savior.

The people of this world are becoming very wicked.
Live with them, but be careful not to become one like them.
The world in its present state is becoming dangerous to its inhabitants - To children and adults alike.
Stay safe and complete your mission.

You are mine, for you belong to me - Your King.
Indulge not in wickedness, for you have a great future ahead, and it is sealed with this description. You are eternally mine.

Amen

Love

Psa 27:11 **Teach me your way, LORD; lead me in a straight path because of my oppressors.**

Journey
- 104 -

CLOSE THE DOOR ON YOUR PAST

O child, my child, what has happened to you?
I looked at you and fed you, I watched over you and dressed you.
Why are you downcast? Why try to achieve things all by yourself?
Why not consider me and keep me as your number one priority?

I deal with each one according to his own conduct, according to what his deeds deserve!

You are to serve me wholeheartedly.
If you serve me, you must also walk in my footsteps, and where I am, you too shall also be.

I will continue to show myself strong through you, as you continue to give me the glory.
Question me not on this or that matter: Why this, why that, why is it and why does it have to be...?
Just be obedient and rest in my tender mercy.

Your love supports me, Oh, King of my being, Ruler of everything.
The real me, is You, in me, O King of my heart.
Thank you for your eternity which lives within me in spirit.

Glorified in me... you are my child.
Steady, you shall remain strong, by the power of my forgiveness.
Establish integrity and walk boldly before my Throne of Love.

Amen

Love

Psa 144:1 ...Praise be to the LORD my Rock, who trains my hands for war, my fingers for battle.

Journey
- 105 -

CONTRIBUTE FAIRNESS

Come, let us reason together.
Rest your weary soul upon my shoulder of grace, and you will no longer feel the burden and pain of this life oppressing your spirit.
Be detangled, lest you be entangled by trouble.
Remove every obstacle out of the way, and no longer be anxious in soul nor oppressed in spirit.
Be consumed by the fire of my love and burn with zeal for my house of prayer.
Indulge yourself in all that I have for you, and you will not be restricted.
Keep the fire of my forgiveness burning and live not in regret.
Maintain a clear conscious.

Remind yourself daily of my loving kindness, for you are equipped to do wonders in my Name, and empowered to face the forces of darkness with great ease.
Marshal your strength lest you be weakened.
Commit your all to me daily, and grace upon grace shall be multiplied upon your bosom of faith.
Do not take revenge, my friends, but leave room for my wrath instead, while looking towards the Light.
I shall take care of business on your behalf and handle your enemies.

Amen

Love

Mat 5:6 *Blessed are those who hunger and thirst for righteousness, for they will be filled.*

Journey
- 106 -
RECOVER QUICKLY

Holy is my Name, for my Name is great.
Deny not my Sovereignty nor my Existence, for you are the apple of my eye. Do not say about yourself, I am, and there is no other.
Do not complicate matters.
Although you are highly exalted, there is still so much more for you to do, learn and accomplish.

Humbleness is found in compassion.
You are not the Queen of the Nile, nor the father of nations.
You are the child of the Most High God, the Creator of the universe.
The anointing you have received qualifies you.

Risk not your life, nor play nice with danger.
There is nothing made, that has not been made visible, for the eyes of all to see and believe.

Nature is my number one foundational truth of existence, for my purpose to be fulfilled upon the earth.

Stimulate your mind with wholesome thinking, and keep the unity of the faith.

Evolve in love, stature, mercy and grace.
Keep the peace of the unity in spirit, and grow in God, who is Love.

Amen

Love

Psa 89:14 **Righteousness and justice are the foundation of your throne; love and faithfulness go before you.**

Journey
- 107 -

UNSURPASSED BEAUTY

May your Will be done in my life, Oh, King of glory, may your Kingdom come.

Child, just as I had to wait patiently for you to turn towards my Kingdom, so now your turn... wait for those who are about to enter my Throne Room.
If you desire to receive my eternal blessings, then walk in my prosperity, for an abundant harvest is coming your way, prepare and be diligent. Keep a watchful eye.
Do not turn to the left nor to the right, but keep your feet fitted with readiness that comes from the gospel of peace.

The time is near when they shall all come home.
It is not up to you who is and who isn't, who will be saved, and who will not be. Your duty is to love equally. It is their choice and of my choosing who I accept into my Kingdom. I am the God of mercy.
Remain in your course of action and I will fulfill the desires of your heart, for they too shall be saved.

Keep in mind that your benefits come from me.
No one can serve me with such an anointing, unless he is called, sought after, appointed and ordained by me.
Run the race marked out for you to reach your highest calling.
Rejoice, for the end has come for a new beginning to start.

Amen

Love

Psa 61:4 ***I long to dwell in your tent forever and take refuge in the shelter of your wings.***

Journey
- 108 -

MONSTERS THEY ARE

I do not save those who are blind but claim to see, nor the deaf who claim to hear, nor the arrogant who claim to be righteous, but only the poor and broken in spirit shall be saved.

My interest is not in those who are arrogant and misleading, but in those whose heart is true and sincere with a genuine motive. Only the meek who is in need of me, shall I turn to help and heal-- the sick, those who are lost, tossed, confused, burdened, troubled, unrighteous, neglected and rejected. I call them to my service, give them my healing balm and rub them with soothing oil.
"I am your Medicine," says the Lord your God, the great I Am - Redeemer of hearts.
I have conquered death, that you may live to enjoy an abundant life. Wait patiently for my return.
Whisper in my ear the Words of Love and I shall answer.
Love, lest you forget my compassion of mercy.

Your Eternal Grace is the Lifter of souls.
My Kingdom of love is your certainty of faith, by the power of my spirit in unity. My spirit shall lead you and guide you the way of Truth in all righteousness.

Be assured to live a blessed Life in Me, for I am your Futurem Foundation and Eternity.

Amen

Love

Pro 3:24 **When you lie down, you will not be afraid; when you lie down, your sleep will be sweet.**

Journey
- 109 -
ADORNED WITH FINE LINEN

See me for who I really am and double shall be restored to you--
double for all your hard work and labor.
What the enemy robbed, that too shall I multiply back to you
double, even triple I now announce to you.

I am your Crown of righteousness, who restores all things back to
you and makes life beautiful.

No longer sit around and search for other things to do, and so delay
my gifts from coming to you.
Agree to my Will, and greater things than these you shall receive.

All things are assured and secure in me.
All you need to do is receive.
Be assured: The Greater One lives in you.
You need not turn to anyone else for support, for you have me.
I am your All.
I am your number one priority, your all and above all everything.
Ask me, and you shall receive much more than you ever thought
possible.
You have received much, and much more shall now be added to
you.
The future is very near. Reach out.
Exceptional news you shall hear soon. Illuminate and shine forth.

Amen

Love

Psa 57:5 *Be exalted, O God, above the heavens; let your glory be over all the earth.*

Journey
- 110 -

GIVE NOT TO THE GREEDY

Grow in love and you will be restored-- blessed beyond measure.
Pour your heart out to me, and I will shower you with my abundant blessings... bestowed upon you so graciously.
You will not be disappointed, for it is I who heals, restores and makes all things good.

Recovery is on the way. Your healing is just around the corner.
Receive and be blessed. Everything is about to be restored back to you double, with great speed and finality.

You shall no longer be on your own.
I am sending you a helper, who will support you in every way on this journey you are now on... be not reluctant.
I have been watching and waiting, for such a time as this, to reward you fully. Receive your gifts. Receive my best. This is your time of blessings. It is all coming to you here and now - Receive.
The eyes of all shall see and be amazed.
Surely you have claimed a place for yourself in me.
You have been restored, redeemed and perfected.
You need not run away from me, but draw closer to me, instead.
You need not withdraw. Come out and receive your greatest blessings. This is the time of your inheritance.
Double for all your hard work, patience and understanding.

Releasing my best to you now... Receive.

Amen

Love

Psa 132:7 "*Let us go to his dwelling place, let us worship at his footstool,...*

Journey
- 111 -

PERFECT IN MY EYES

No need to know anyone else so deeply, apart from me.
No need for you to discover other gods to compare them to Me.
I Am your God of all.
I am your Healer, Deliverer, Crown of Life and Righteousness -
Your very First and Last Love.

Consecrate yourself to me, and remain true to your calling.
Always be dressed in white and never be undressed.

Rely on me, and I will deliver even one who is not worthy of my salvation. Through the cleanness of your hands, I will even save one who is not deserving.
No one can snatch out of my hand that which is mine, and when I act who can reverse it?
I am always at work, even now... I have not stopped, nor will I ever stop, until my Kingdom comes and my right arm is revealed to all.

You child, are mine. You have been called and chosen by me.
I have you close to my heart. You are mine eternally.

Do not forget the work of my hands.
You are the work of my hands in mastery.
Glorified faith reveals a purpose, destined by glory.

Be assured: You are not on your own.
I am with you, watching over your wellbeing eternally.

Amen

Love

Psa 50:2 **From Zion, perfect in beauty, God shines forth.**

Journey
- 112 -

RELEASE THE WEARY

Your peace comes from me, and I have not wasted any time.
Look at the fields... they are ready for harvest.

I am your Maker and Creator of all that is good.
I shall renew your life and you will be changed.
My Will shall be established in your life... you shall see it and partake of my glory.
You shall reveal my likeness to the world, and they shall stream to my Altar of Love.

Keep loving the brotherhood of believers, as well as the unbelievers, for they too need my seed of love and depth of compassion.
Secure your position and receive my blessings.
Cover yourself with the power of my blood, so that no harm may come near your tent.
Your Sovereign is calling you home to himself.
Live the life I have called you, and you will survive every experience known to man.
My angels shall watch over you... every step of the way.

Complete your journey here on earth and come to rest in me, for this is who I really am - Your Comforter and Ultimate Support.
Screen not yourself-- examine yourself instead, to see whether you are in the faith.

Amen

Love

Isa 45:17 *But Israel will be saved by the LORD with an everlasting salvation; you will never be put to shame or disgraced, to ages everlasting.*

Journey
- 113 -

SUFFICIENT GRACE

Your glory shines through me, Oh God of my fathers.
Your mercy is pure and everlasting.
Redeem me from the oppression of man, that I may be justified and purified... free to obey your precepts.

Cleanse me and I will be clean. Wash me and I will be whiter than snow. Take me into your inner sanctuary and I will be made whole, complete, lacking nothing... purified by the blood of the Lamb once and for all.

Your precious Word is my guidance; it gives sight to the blind.
Your commands are radiant, and your Will is my call to obedience.

You are my intimate Friend; Oh, Savior of my soul... my eternal God.
My heart is your home, O God, King of my heart, the great I Am, Giver of Life and Abundant Grace.

Command me and I shall obey your Word and heed your voice.
Lead me and I shall follow.
Guide my footsteps, that I may walk in obedience to your Will.
My Guide and my Light, you are my Sunshine.

I am your eternal Friend, child.
Never neglect your calling.
Stream along and be consistent.

Amen

Love

Psa 130:7 **Israel, put your hope in the LORD, for with the LORD is unfailing love and with him is full redemption.**

Journey
- 114 -

JOURNEY ALONG WITH ME

I love you, Oh, my child of grace, I love you with an undying love. I have heard your plea and listened to your petition. In the time of my favor, I shall answer you, and in the time of my pleasure, I shall reward you.

Take note of what I am saying: The time is coming when man will no longer put up with sound doctrine, instead, to suit their own evil desires and justify themselves, they will gather around them a great number of teachers to say what their itching ears want to hear. They will turn their ears away from the Truth and run after idol notion - Old myth. You are not to be one with them, nor like them.

Keep your head in all situations, and do the work required. Release the duties of your ministry while keeping yourself consecrated and whole... Holy in my Name.

Defile not yourself with worldly treasures... rescue the needy instead. Keep corrupt talk far from your mouth, for the time has come for each man to be judged for his own actions.

Respect those who are older than you, and never doubt my way of doing things. Keep the fire of love burning, inflamed between us, and close the door on every corrupt talk and confusing spirit.

Astonishing news you shall hear coming from me soon.

Amen

Love

Psa 102:13 **You will arise and have compassion on Zion, for it is time to show favor to her; the appointed time has come.**

Journey
- 115 -
ACCEPT CORRECTION

You are eternally mine, Oh, my precious one.
The One who loves you is here at all times and on every occasion.

Never be confused, nor doubt your salvation.
Feed yourself on my Truth and you will be enlightened--
revelational truth shall then flood through.

You shall understand my wisdom and learn to put my words into practice.
I shall highlight your performance and encourage you to keep going. I shall also lift you up when you are feeling down, and energy you will have to charge on.

Lord, your Will is my command, and your pleasure is my strength. I shall do the very things you have ask of me, for my desire is to please you. All things are in your hands... just as you have purposed and planned.

Good, my precious child of my love, very good.
I am well pleased with you.

Oh, God, my God, truly you are my Savior King

Son, truly you are my anointed, and daughter, truly you are my queen. Obedience is an ingredient for a great revival.

Amen

Love

Ecc 8:5 *Whoever obeys his command will come to no harm, and the wise heart will know the proper time and procedure.*

Journey
- 116 -

HEAVEN IS CALLING

Your duty is me, child, your duty is me.
Look to no one else for answers, for all your needs are met in me.
I am your answer to every question.
Turn not to the left, nor set your eyes on emptiness.
Keep focused and stretch further in faith.

You need not fear what everyone else is fearing, for I am your Healer, Deliver of Faith and Gardener of souls.
You will be delivered from all that is happening around you in this world.
Your mercy is great, O God of all, and your perfection is amazing.

Let your Light shine before all, O my Bride, so that through you, I may gain glory for myself.
Your former shall no longer present itself, it is gone forever, for what is coming your way, is far greater and more unique than anything else you have ever experienced before.

Rejoice, I am on the way.
Loving you always, loving you eternally.

Be distinguished in spirit, and shine my Light of Life upon mankind - The lost souls of the earth.

Keep focused and maintain integrity.

Amen

Love

Psa 144:2 He is my loving God and my fortress, my stronghold and my deliverer, my shield, in whom I take refuge, who subdues peoples under me.

Journey
- 117 -
CORRUPTION IS IMMORALITY

Hear my words and act on my truth, for I am your Guide.

I shall guide you through and show you the Way of Righteousness,
that you may walk in the fullness of my glory.

Keep giving me the praise. Keep lifting those hands.

Soon, you shall hear my voice speaking these words,
"The door is now open, walk ye in it."

I have made my home with you, and you shall grow to learn my
ways... a day at a time.

Forgive as you have always done and I will be glorified.
Forgiveness is an important act of faith for all who believe.

May your Kingdom come, O Sovereign.

Yes, child, my loved one, I truly am on my way to you.

Keep your head held high by growing strong in faith.
I am your God for all eternity.

Destroy sin in the flesh and recover quickly.
Let the Light of Life shine upon your face, as you sing my songs of
praise till the end of time... till my return.
Forgive, child, forgive and you will continue to be released.

Amen

Love

Psa 90:17 **May the favor of the Lord our God rest on us; establish the work of our hands for us-- yes, establish the work of our hands.**

Journey
- 118 -
DIE TO SELF

Rest, Oh my child, come rest in me and be delivered from the flesh.
Look to me and I will set your best friend free.
He who comes to me as you well know, will never be driven away.
Forgive to be released and release to forget.

Your glory comes from me, and there is no other.
I am your eternal Source of deliverance.

Destruction comes not from Me, the God of heaven and earth, but from the evil one who likes to harm, kill and destroy, every beautiful thing.
Children, keep watch over your souls, for your enemy the evil one has no mercy, nor compassion, nor anything good or pleasant.
Rest assured-- your Maker has given you the victory over your enemies, and the power to survive every attack aimed against you.
Be not defeated, you will not fail the test of time.
Be encouraged, you will not suffer any harm.
All I have in my Kingdom is yours, O my gracious son.
I am always available.
Nothing is ever too hard or difficult for me to do.

Glorify me and surrender your all. I am your Deliverer.
Rest on my shoulders of love and I will carry you through the journey of life, for you are mine.

Amen

Love

Psa 5:4 ***For you are not a God who is pleased with wickedness; with you, evil people are not welcome.***

Journey
- 119 -
THE KEY TO SUCCESS

Consider the cost I myself paid on your behalf, child, and reassure yourself of my greatness. I have beheld you since your youth.
Do you now cry out to me, for all those needs of yours?
No child, seek my face and not just my hand, for I do satisfy.

Develop and grow to have compassion for the world. Disaster follows disaster and who is there to help the brokenhearted!

Your attitude should be the same as that of Christ-- who in the very nature God, did not consider equality with the Almighty.
Although the whole world came against him, he did not waver in disbelief, but remained strong, steadfast and unmoved under all these persecutions, trials and outbursts.
He knew his enemy, but greater still, he knew who he was, where he came from, to whom he belonged and where he was going.
You too, child, come to know who you are in the One you are serving.
Have you learned anything? Have you taken a stand yet?
If not, start now, go and be likewise.
Stand firm in your faith, even when it all seems too hard, too difficult and overwhelming sometimes.

You will not be challenged by trouble, nor shall the storms oppress you; but will only serve to advance you through seasons of change.

Amen

Love

1Ch 16:10 Glory in his holy name; let the hearts of those who seek the LORD rejoice.

Journey
- 120 -

ETERNAL SUPPORT

Distribute my favor all over the world as you abide in my Spirit.
Carry my throne upon your heart and be showered with my multiple blessings.
I have called you to such a time as this, not to fail, but to win and gain victory.

Confide in me and you will win the greatest battles yet.
You are a warrior, a victorious warrior of worship - My very own reflection.
Continue to reflect my likeness, that others may see the Light of your Life and be saved.
Loosen up and reach your highest potential.
Victory assured in the arms of Love, from start to finish, from the start of your new life till the end of your finish line.

You are to carry my likeness to a dead and dying world of horror.
These persecutions are not of me-- they are trying to work against the knowledge of my Kingdom by their strange teachings, to defeat the purpose of my call.

The ultimate solution is my love living within you by my grace of action.
You are not alone.
I am with you all day, every day and in every way.

Amen

Love

Deu 28:2 **All these blessings will come on you and accompany you if you obey the LORD your God:**

Journey
- 121 -

WRITTEN ON YOUR FOREHEAD

Do not settle in your comfort zone.
Rise up and prepare, for time is running out.

I shall bring you to your fullness, and the honor shall be mine.
Your beauty shall shine forth with my special rewards.
My Goodness shall move you in spirit to walk in the footsteps of Love.
You shall rise up in confidence, and win spiritual wars you never thought possible.
I shall uphold you with my Greatness and you will be awakened in my likeness.
Take courage and grow stronger.
Illuminate and be stimulated in spirit.

Love in abundance is yours.
Be radiant and shine through these dark times, for during the darkest darkness my Light through you shall be poured forth.
Keep me as the Center of your being, and let my love flow through you like a river.
Overflow with radiance, and be restored in abundance.
The beat of your heart I hear.
Dot not waver but complete your mission.

Restoration is at hand, and I am more than willing to take you by the hand.

Amen

Love

Psa 93:2 **Your throne was established long ago; you are from all eternity.**

Journey
- 122 -

WHISPER MY NAME

The victory is yours, child.

Turn to me with all your heart and hold nothing back from me.

I am with you always.
Remember the battle is not yours.
Consider me who endured such opposition from sinful men.

You are to go without a burden, for prosperous shall be your days.
Continue to run without holding yourself back from me.

Your parents are not to be of concern - I do know what I am doing.
Put your trust in me and leave all those things behind.
Go, complete your mission, for your journey is nearly over.

You are called to prosper, and prosper you shall, for prosperity belongs to you.
The door is now open - Walk ye in it.
The doors are now open wide; just enter in and partake of my glory revealed.
I am welcoming you with arms open wide.

Forget the past and hold on to your future in the present.
What you do now, will affect your future inheritance!
Suffering is not of me.

Stir up the gifts within you by laying them on my altar of praise.

Amen

Love

Luk 22:35 **Be dressed ready for service and keep your lamps burning.**

Journey
- 123 -

SATISFYING LOVE

Begin with what I have given you, for it is never too late.

I am able to achieve a lot more than you will ever know.
I do work behind the scene you know!

Run, keep the faith and finish the race.

You were called to be a blessing, not a curse, and so bless you must.

Be encouraged and be willing to give yourself wholeheartedly.

As you love, so shall you feel my love. As you give, so shall you also receive the crown of righteousness appointed for all who believe.

The greater the love, the greater the acceptance.

Act on what you hear me say to you without delay.
Go and break these strongholds down.
Worship me without retreat. Come to know my Will for your life.

Restrictions are not of me.
The corruption of society will soon come to an end and be demolished.
I shall guide you through and through, and you will see me as I am.
Secure your position, and help your brothers who are in need.

Forget the past and move with the new-- which is of me.

Amen

Love

Col 1:10 so that you may live a life worthy of the Lord and please him in every way: bearing fruit in every good work, growing in the knowledge of God,

Journey
- 124 -

RESIST TEMPTATION

Consider me in everything you do and I will bless you abundantly.
My Kingdom is not of this world, and I have made you responsible
for the souls of many.

Offer me a wave offering and run with my wind of worship.
I shall hear your cry and meet all your needs.
Bless and you shall be blessed.
Be careful that you do not become a curse.

Accept my truth by turning from the ways of this world.
Oh, how false this world is becoming.
Test your own actions and look no further-- I am the only One.
Accuse no one... leave them up to me to judge.

You shall find none like me, for with me you shall go far.
Transformation comes from me, and no one can do what I can do
for you, nor achieve what I can accomplish on your behalf.
Your resistance is strong, but now move in the right direction.

Honor me before man, that you may be established in love by the
power of my Spirit within you, and reunite yourself to me in action.

Acceptance is a key for a great revival.
Accept me into your heart, and watch the wind blow beneath your
feet raising you to a higher stage in life.

Amen

Love

Psa 119:29 **Keep me from deceitful ways; be gracious to me and teach me your law.**

Journey
- 125 -
GLORIFIED PRESENCE

Heal me, Oh, Healer of my wounds, and I will be healed. Deliver me and I will be delivered. I am truly desperate for your touch.
I call to you for my needs to be met, and I know by your spirit all things are possible.
My trust is in you all day long, and I am fully persuaded that you are who you said you are - All in all.
I am dependent on your wealth of wisdom and great treasure. Heal my wounds by freeing me from this pain.

O my precious one, I know you are in need of me and desperate for my touch, but you must first commit in order to be transformed into my likeness.
Submit, that you may become my precious possession.
Continue to walk with me in spirit to pass every test.
Unlock the door and move forward to a higher plateau in my perfection.

You will be filled with greater joy. Trust and believe.
Your wealth of wisdom comes from your inner Source and not from outer appearance.
Your reflection of me is my likeness in you.

Continue to walk within the boundaries of my Spirit supporting you.

Amen

Love

Psa 143:10 *Teach me to do your will, for you are my God; may your good Spirit lead me on level ground.*

Journey
- 126 -

RESCUED FROM THE STORMS

Stand still and know that I am God.
I shall continue to rescue you from every burden, trial and temptation.
Your Omega is strong and your Alpha is bold - Bold as a lion... stronger than any double-edged sword, and mightier than the biggest army. He is also gentle as a dove, swifter than the wind and greater than all.

Stand strong and see the deliverance of the Lord God.
Be courageous, for you will not lose heart nor be condemned.
You will not be shattered. I am your Best Friend.

I know you believe my written Word-- that all things work together for good for them who believe, and yes what is written about me is true.

Your life will not be taken away from you... it is protected in the shadow of my hand.
Not until I say it is time shall you come home to be with me.

Your loving Creator shall continue to rescue the needy and deliver the poor from destruction. Those with my weapon of love shall grow stronger, till each appears before God in Zion.

Your redeeming mission is ready to be accomplished.
I, your Weapon of Love, am your Defender in time of distress.

Amen

Love

Psa 25:4 ***Show me your ways, LORD, teach me your paths.***

Journey
- 127 -

MULTIPLE BLESSINGS

Who was it that said I am He? Who was it that sounded the trumpet and said that I am coming back to you soon?
Who was it that created the heavens and the earth? Tell me who?
Was it not I, who performed all these wonders?
Am I just to be worshiped? Am I not to be honored as well?
Am I not the God of the hills as well as the mountains? The God who is not far from you, is very near and close to your heart?

You have carried your own load for a long time now, without any help or support.
This is the time, give them over to me now, that I may act on your behalf, for your Conqueror lives and dwells in your heart.

I am your First and your Last.
Give me the glory before the day dawns.
Give those things over to me, and rest from your own labor.

Your Provider is near and very close to your heart.
Whisper into my ear the Words of Love, and I shall recover your losses. The day draws near when all is well.
Do not be captivated by charm nor by magic, for it is not real.

True existence is found in your Maker.

Confess and be released from conflicting news causing sorrow.

Amen

Love

Dan 10:14 *Now I have come to explain to you what will happen to your people in the future, for the vision concerns a time yet to come."*

Journey
- 128 -
THE VICTORY IS YOURS

Is there anything too hard or too difficult for you to accomplish in my Name? Never!
Why wait then, for something else to happen, for something else to take place in your life?
Run the race and I will help you achieve your goal.

You shall not be burdened by trouble.

Unshackle those chains and you will be transformed into my likeness - Into my image of glory you will be changed.
The world with all its resources shall see, and you will be glorified.

Recharge yourself with my energy of worship, and you will be accomplished in my purpose.
Do not be a wanderer, but redeemed instead.
Fulfill your mission before the day dawns.
He who listens will know the truth, that sets man free.

Be not burdened by trouble, for your Comforter is your Eternal Freedom.
Free yourself from all these calamities by keeping your feet steady on the solid Rock eternal.

He who loves you is not dead, but very much alive.
Come and follow me - Your Master Teacher and eternal Guide.

Amen

Love

Psa 71:6 *From birth I have relied on you; you brought me forth from my mother's womb. I will ever praise you.*

Journey
- 129 -
CONCEALED WEAPON

The battle is not yet over... you still have more weapons of the enemy to destroy-- The weapons of evil and destruction.
As powerful as they may be, you are even more powerful with resources.
As strong as they may seem, you are stronger still through me.
You are able to put an end to their evil schemes.
In my Name all things are achievable.
I am sharper than all your enemies put together.
In my Name, you can do all things. It has all now being achieved and made possible. Nothing shall stand in your way, nor ever be impossible for you to accomplish or demolish.

Your journey shall not take much longer.
Compliments may not always be true, but my Word Is.
I am your great I Am.
Delight yourself in me and you shall find me at your door.

Your accomplished mission is at hand.

Your enemy is not the one you are to look to, but Me.

Come, see, hear and know the Truth made available for everyone to receive... if they decide to choose Life.

Adored worship.
Inhale worship... Exhale praise - Inhale praise... Exhale Worship.

Amen

Love

Luke 18:27 ..."What is impossible with man is possible with God."

Journey
- 130 -

IDENTIFIED IDENTITY

Concern yourself not with unnecessary matters that count for nothing.
Quieten your soul like a weaned child with its mother-- like a weaned child quieten your soul within you.

I will carry you through the deepest darkness and enlighten you to follow me. I will never leave you nor ever forsake you.

Neglect not yourself - I am the True Way, the Real Truth and Eternal Life - your Reality.

I have given you victory, now redeem it.

You are a blessing to all, therefore, I know you by name.

Neglect not thyself, for my angels are watching over you.

I am your Best Friend and your great Conqueror.

Restoration comes to those who are in need of my glory, who are broken in spirit and tender to the touch.

Do not be brilliant nor skillful, but just a willing vessel for your Maker.
Call on my Name, and I shall hear and respond to your voice. Your Ruler lives and He will forever be yours.

Glorify my presence - Be perfect as I am perfect.

Amen

Love

Psa 119:20 **My soul is consumed with longing for your laws at all times.**

Journey
- 131 -

THE MEASURING ROD

Comfort, comfort says God your Savior, Redeemer and Best Friend.
Rest and let us run together forever. Give rest to your soul, that we may win the world boldly without ceasing.

Do not be downcast, O my friend, for the Giver of life is God.
He is your Shelter of Comfort, your very Great Reward.
He is your Refuge and Mighty Power of Strength, in the midst of all your troubles and tribulations.

Consider your conduct and compare it to my holiness.

You are dear to me, child.
Put away that which is least effective and avoid wasting time on anything unnecessary.
Irrelevant situations should be the least important.

Consider me in all you do and you shall gain life.

No matter what the situation is, live as one approved by my blood of Life. Remain washed and purified till the end.

My seal of approval rests upon your head.
March on like a good soldier, fully armed and charged.
The battle is not yet over, but I am fully with you till the end.

Amen

Love

Psa 110:2 The LORD will extend your mighty scepter from Zion, saying, "Rule in the midst of your enemies!"

Journey
- 132 -

THE LIVING WORD

You have great potentials, Oh, child of mine.
Come rest your head upon my shoulders and let me take over this tedious work of yours.

Storms may come and storms may go, but I shall lift you above ground, for I am the Lifter of your soul.
You have served me in righteousness and yielded in humbleness, therefore, I shall strip your enemies bare naked before your very eyes and elude them-- giving you the upper hand on them all.
They won't stand a chance against you, but will turn and serve you.

Continue to reach out, for I am your all.
Keep strengthening the body of believers.
Your brothers who have risked their lives on your behalf, will reap the benefit of their labor.

Watch and pray, for your redemption draws nigh.
Who was it that called you by name-- was it not I?

Die to self to deny the flesh.
Remember my Name during your time of harvest, and forget not my benefits laid out before you.

I am on my way to you from heaven.
Be consecrated, that you may regain power in my Name.

Amen

Love

Pro 16:3 **Commit to the LORD whatever you do, and he will establish your plans.**

Journey
- 133 -

GROW IN LOVE

In my presence, you are kept safe, Oh, child of mine.
You are to inhale praise and exhale worship.

I adore you, child, you are great and pleasing in my sight.
You need no other support, for I am your Greatest Reward.

Benefit others, that you may live a happy life.
Watch and pray, so that you may not fall into a temptation and a trap set by the enemy.
Be strong and find your courage in me.

Your Creator of worship is steadfast and strong.
You will not miss out on anything. I have kept the best till last.

You are secure in my loving arms.
I am the best you have, just as my children are the best I have.

Restoration will come upon you suddenly when least expected.
Very soon, you shall be awakened by the sound of my trumpet call.
You will surely rejoice and clap your hands in jubilation.

Praise me, child, praise the God of heaven, who wakens you morning after morning and provides you with fresh manna daily.

The glory alone is mine, and I shall always be living in your heart.
Be sensitive to the needs of others.

Amen

Love

Psa 8:6 **You made them ruler over the works of your hands; you put everything under their feet:**

Journey
- 134 -

ACCUMULATE BLESSINGS

Be energized by the vitality of my Spirit.
Do not think of yourself more highly than you ought.

I shall guide you carefully, and in accordance to my Will, you shall be established.

Always remember the love I have for you, and never forget the words spoken to you directly.
Maintain justice, integrity and respect.
Keep a tight rein on your tongue and let your conversation always be seasoned with salt... overflowing with abundant grace.

Know my Will is sufficient for you at all times.
Whether you are feeling up or down, my Word remains the same, never changing, and my promises are always - Yes and Amen.

Stand strong and never give up on yourself.
I want us to be best friends, and your desires to only be for me.
Be submissive in all you do and stay fresh - You are special.
May your whole body, soul, and spirit continue to be pleasing.

Attend to my Word and you shall find me-- when you search for me with all your heart.
Be glorified in my presence.
I, your Crown of glory, shall shine through you, my Bride.

Amen

Love

1Co 11:19 **No doubt there have to be differences among you to show which of you have God's approval.**

Journey
- 135 -

COMPROMISE NOT YOUR FAITH

You are unique in me, child and I have called you special.
Have no concerns about what others may say about me... keep your eyes on the goal instead, for I know how to handle myself.
I am the Conqueror of hearts. Keep your Armor on, and continue to march on like a proud horse in battle, for you will not be defeated. Do you not yet know my Will?
I am the One you are to fear, but not in dread, but rather in love and in pure submission to the rule instead.

Why concern yourself with idol notions about who knows and sees what you do and don't do in my Name? Leave these troubled waters behind, child, and come follow me. No more concerns or worries about tomorrow and what it may bring.

Your Shield has taken a stand against all those false teachers, preachers and so-called prophets.
They shall eat the fruit of their own words.

Holy is my Name, who meets all your needs and fulfills the desires of your heart. Lastly, because I live, you too shall live.
Now that you know the truth, you are free from all concerns, worries and fears... regulate not.
You will continue to be safe and sound in the Name of your King.
I am your King, Future, Master Teacher, Ruler and Everything.

Amen

Love

Isa 27:3 I, the LORD, watch over it; I water it continually. I guard it day and night so that no one may harm it.

Journey
- 136 -

LISTEN AND TAKE HEED

Call on me and I shall hear and respond.
I have never neglected that which is mine ever, and you, my child, are mine.
Why are you so worried and in despair, determined to do all that you want to do?

Discover me through my Living Word and live an abundant life.
There is nothing false about me!

I have washed you with the blood of my sacrifice, that you may be just like me - Pure and holy.

Those who are trying to bring confusion, sorrow and strife, will pay the penalty, whoever they may be. They are negligent, disobedient and unfit for doing anything good. Do not put your trust in them. The only reason they do this-- is to alienate you from the truth, that you may live for them.
Have nothing to do with them, for their desire is not sincere.
They refused to accept correction and so strayed from the Truth.
They do not wish to see my word fulfilled in your life, and so try to bring confusion to lead you away from me.

You will soon know right from wrong and will choose the path of righteousness... supporting you all the way.

Guard yourself in spirit.

Amen

Love

Pro 4:23 *Above all else, guard your heart, for everything you do flows from it.*

Journey
- 137 -

FAITHFUL LOVE

Sink deep into my River of Delight, and drink heavily from my Well of Salvation.
Many have been against you, beloved; I understand, but you did not respond to them nor retaliate.
The best thing you did was not adhere to their ways.

Let us commune together.
Wipe every tear consumed by sorrow.
You will not be sorry... for in this there is no guilt.
Your Restorer of hope has set you apart for Himself.
Continue with Him on this journey of magnificence.

Say to your soul: "Be revived, O my soul," and never stop drinking from this Holy Water - The River of Refreshment and pure delight.

Serve others faithfully administering God's way, grace and love in various forms.
Keep in mind to distribute justice, and never neglect the gift of Love - The Gift that is above every other gift, for Love makes all things possible. The key is in the palm of your hand, child... use it wisely and only for good.
Acknowledge that I am He - Your accomplished Faith.

Skillful you shall always be in me and so therefore grateful.

Amen

Love

Rom 3:26 *he did it to demonstrate his righteousness at the present time, so as to be just and the one who justifies those who have faith in Jesus.*

Journey
- 138 -

THRONE OF ROYALTY

You surely are lovely and beautiful in my sight.

I have created you in the womb and developed you in love to be my very own possession. For my glory and glory alone have I formed you, and established you in righteousness to serve me.
Precious and honored you are, and faithful you shall always remain to me.
If you listen, I will bring life and isolate death, exchange beauty for ashes, and renew the old for the new.

Know that you have been chosen and are very much blessed.
Your redemption draws nigh.
I shall see you through every difficulty, and set you apart for myself as one truly faithful. You are royalty.
Since your love for me is strong, I shall also fulfill the desires of your own heart.
Call on me and I shall be there, for I am already here with you now.
Forgive and you will be forgiven - Believe and you shall receive.

You are sweet and tender, loving and supportive.
Keep up that which you know is best for you.

I will answer your every prayer, and you shall not be disappointed.
Forgiveness always restores all things lost.
Surely I am your delight.

Amen

Love

Psa 119:14 I rejoice in following your statutes as one rejoices in great riches.

Journey
- 139 -
THE FAVOR OF THE KING

I will soon make your name great among the nations, like the mighty men of the earth, and you shall inherit honor and praise.
The eyes of all shall see my work among you and be bewildered.
My glory shall shine through you, and you will know that it is I who have done all these wonderful things for you.
Your friends will see and be astounded, by the works of my hands established in your life.
You shall be lifted up, never to be torn down again.
The crown on your head will remain steady and never fall.
You shall honor me, and I will be honored.
I have given you the power to build up highways, and tear down strongholds in my Name; therefore you are established.
Many will try to oppose you, but will not succeed nor win the victory over you, for I am the One, who is on your side.
Their ramparts will not stand, for I shall expose their shame.
Truly I say to you, "They are not of me."

I shall be lifted up, for the glory alone is mine.
I shall rebuke wickedness on your behalf, and you will be encouraged to perform wonders never seen before.
You shall see it with your own eyes and eat of its fruit.
Your enemies shall cower before you and know not what to do.
They shall gnash their teeth and vanish from sight once and for all.

Amen

Love

Psa 105:41 *He opened the rock, and water gushed out; it flowed like a river in the desert.*

Journey
- 140 -

THE PROMISED OATH

Be determined, be strong, never waver nor give up.
Have no worries for your Savior Redeemer lives - He is called the God of all the earth.
Hold on to the faith that never lets you down.
Be not afraid, O little one, for I myself am with you.

Your Counsellor of love has shown you that which is best for you - The highway of holiness-- now walk in it and prosper abundantly.

You have been shown right from wrong, now choose that which is best for you and right before my eyes - Your Inheritance.

Release my Will into your life, that you may prosper in all your ways.
Be grateful in all that I have done for you.

Your journey is becoming more and more complete now.

Let us be in total agreement together and join hands in harmony.

You shall be rescued from all these pressures you are under.
You shall be called by Name, and the Truth shall be revealed to all who have an ear to listen.

Prosperity is on the way, receive it and run with my love.
Give to receive.

Amen

Love

Psa 141:9 **Keep me safe from the traps set by evildoers, from the snares they have laid for me.**

Journey
- 141 -

TOUCHED BY MERCY

My ability gives you the power to endure.
I shall enrich your life with many more good things from the flowing River of my abundant delight.

Rejoice in my glory... it belongs to me.

You will not be shaken, for you are not standing alone.

I have taken you places and shown you the world.
Now you are about to move to a higher ground than ever before.

Let the world know my Glory - The One who lives in you.

Before me no god was formed, nor shall there be one after me... understand this very fact, child.

It is for your best that you have been saved.
Your prosperity shall increase by hundreds and hundred times more.
Heaven is your throne of grace.

Teach me to sing your songs, Oh, Master Teacher, for you are the One I adore. Thank you for being who you are to me - The great I Am.

My son, welcome the brothers of unbelievers, that they too may believe the Truth set before them by your action of love and example of Life.

Amen

Love

Psa 150:6 *Let everything that has breath praise the LORD. Praise the LORD.*

Journey
- 142 -

SEEK PEACE & PURSUE IT

You will surely know my Will and act upon it.
You are my warrior of worship, and I am called the God of all the earth - The Savior of all mankind.

I shall restore all that has been lost to you, and you will branch out and flourish.
I shall see you through every difficulty, and enlarge your territory as well.
I shall stretch you further in faith, and you will learn to have patience.
Just wait a little while longer for my return.
Deny me nothing and you will not be denied of anything.

To this you were called-- not just to believe in me, but also to fall in love with me.

Be established and flourish in spirit to know the Truth.
Release others just as you have been released by me, child.
Release your brothers who are in need of me.
Keep Love as your number one priority in action.
Take heed and run the race.

Your Deliverer is here and ready to deliver all who come to him

You are called to come away with me.

Amen

Love

Psa 25:14 *The Lord confides in those who fear him; he makes his covenant known to them.*

Journey
- 143 -

THIS IS YOUR TIME

You are not alone, O child of Love.
I have called others to help support you in all your service to me.
Humbly they shall work with you and without any conflict or drama support you.
I myself handpicked them and called them out of the crowd to be with you. You will have the support you need in my Name, for you are working hard without any complaint.
Because of your great calling, I will yet bring others into the same service, that they may benefit you in every way.
Step out and recharge.
Your time is almost here to move, but not just quite yet.

Love and Sincerity go together hand in hand.

I am about to admonish your household, so rejoice.
Lift your head up and be like a proud horse in battle.
Be recharged and waste no time on anyone or anything unnecessary, for your future is here.
Sing to me and make music in your heart.
Feed on my Word and be drunk on my Wine.
You will surely be blessed. Conquer and walk on.

Your Creator and Best Adviser I am.
Take my Word and run with me on the Highway of Holiness.

Amen

Love

Pro 2:7 *He holds success in store for the upright, he is a shield to those whose walk is blameless,*

Journey
- 144 -

MESSAGE FULFILLED

May your Will be done in my life in accordance to your Word.
May you complete the work you have begun in me, O God.
I believe, therefore I have spoken. I believed, therefore I have received.

I need you, O King of my life, and desire more and more of your love.
Build me up in character and keep me circumcised in faith.
By the power of your spirit keep my heart pure before you, I pray.
You are so precious and righteous in all you do, and I am grateful for your support.
I could ask for nothing more, for you are all I ever need.
I delight in your pleasure and rejoice in your salvation.
Your teaching is comprehensive, admirable as well as attainable.
I heed your voice and act upon all that you tell me.

My only desire is to know you and be great in your sight.
You are my burden Release.
I know I am going to see you one day soon, and that your precious Word will also be made complete in me.

Child, destroy not the temple of God - Your body, that you may survive every experience known to man.
I shall keep you shielded, protected from any storm.
I shall shield you and carry you close to my heart, and draw you closer still. I shall lift you to a greater height of glory and you shall be upheld by Me - Your Supporter.

Amen

Love

Psa 132:13 **For the LORD has chosen Zion, he has desired it for his dwelling,...**

Journey
- 145 -
REMEMBER YOUR JOURNEY

My Will, son, shall overrule and overtake you by surprise.
I have established my throne in your heart, and my prosperity shall take over your realm... you will be astounded.
I will not neglect you nor leave you stranded-- hidden behind closed doors.
I shall reveal you by opening the doors of heaven over your life, that you may benefit others and rule nations.
My Kingdom will come, and my Will shall be done on earth as it is in heaven, for the prayers of many have reached me.

As you have been considerate towards others, so I will now also consider you. Even to those who have hurt you, you have been loving and thoughtful, therefore the floodgates of heaven will never cease to be open over your life.
You have blessed many, and now it is your turn to be rewarded handsomely.

You shall not suffer any shame nor ever be disregarded.
No longer linger on the past, nor on previous experiences, for all things have now been made new.

I Am, and there is no other.
I shall help you, and you will be a great blessing.

Amen

Love

Mic 4:8 *As for you, watchtower of the flock, stronghold of Daughter Zion, the former dominion will be restored to you; kingship will come to Daughter Jerusalem."*

Journey
- 146 -

ENDURANCE IS A BLESSING

Be patient and wait for my counsel.
Recover the days gone by renewing today.

Whatever difficulty you may face with your friends, relatives and family-- that too, I will help you through.

Do not be concerned about tomorrow, for tomorrow will take care of itself.
My Will shall prevail at all times and on all occasions.

Take heart-- I am completing the work I have entrusted to you.
You truly are an overcomer.

Your service is not yet over. I have made a new way, a new opening - a new open door for you to enter and invite others.

You will not fail in your commission, for you have been redeemed.
Your redemption has been made complete.

Your Sovereign is here.
Your request shall be granted. Fret not.

Adored worship is music to my ear.

Complete the task entrusted to you.
I shall reveal deeper truths to you soon, only for your ears to hear.
I am about to restore all things lost.

Amen

Love

Pro 4:25 *Let your eyes look straight ahead; fix your gaze directly before you.*

Journey
- 147 -

LET IT BE KNOWN

No longer pamper anyone, but continue to be a blessing to everyone.
You will know my right hand of power when I act on your behalf.
Keep proclaiming the Truth that sets the captives free.

Your future is not like your experiences of long ago.
I am your Past, Present and Future.
Everything you ever need is found in me.

Make straight in the wilderness a highway for your King.
Your God shall come with great power and will not be delayed.
His arm shall rule for Him and all mankind together shall see it.

Create a new life by abiding in Love.

Your benefits of tomorrow shall come to no end-- they shall begin today and last forever.
Rejoice, for they are very much at hand.

You will not be degraded.
Your Sovereign reigns and rules over you.

Open wide your arms... there is a lot more yet for you to embrace.
Listen and abide in my Testimony of grace.

Your Sovereign is here.

Amen

Love

Psa 105:41 *He opened the rock, and water gushed out; it flowed like a river in the desert.*

Journey
- 148 -

WON THE BATTLE

Undress yourself not in the realm of the spirit, rather keep your safety guard on and belt of truth buckeled up - Your spiritual armor - Garment of salvation.
Become not undressed before your enemy, for he has no honor.
Keep yourself unreachable, untouched, untampered with by him.
Remain unapproachable to his demonic influences.
Allow him no access, so that you are not influenced by his demonic activities... falsely playing nice. As long as you keep yourself clothed in my Will, he will not be able to reach or touch you.
Keep him barricaded, for the battle has been won.

As for the enemy, he is destroyed-- a finished book, history, gone with the wind, a burned up story, never to return.

Keep safe in my loving arms and allow him no access.
Enjoy the Reality of Life imparted to you through my teachings.

You shall suffer no conflict, nor false assumption set against you, for you are wiser than your enemy the evil one - The tempter of wickedness. Give him no glory, no honor, nor access to your home or life; for he is not deserving.

Success is in the making of two becoming one - You and I.

You have reached your destiny - Congratulations!

Amen

Love

Psa 19:14 May these words of my mouth and this meditation of my heart be pleasing in your sight, LORD, my Rock and my Redeemer.

Journey
- 149 -
REACH UNITY

Be eager to do all that is right and good.

Your enemy, the evil one, will not give up, until you stop giving him access - A foothold.
No longer waste your precious time on him.
You must now continue to pray day and night.

Without fear, doubt or any hesitation, acknowledge that I, your God am here-- always willing, ready to help and support you.

Your persecutors will not last much longer, but will acknowledge that your name is great on account of me.

I will not change, but will always be the same.

Be ready for all that I have for you.
Remain sincere and true to your calling, for my eyes shall keep watch over you. Humble yourself that I may lift you up.
Stay strong and never give up on Me - The One Best for you.
Run to your Shelter of Love and escape the corruption of this age.
Pray day and night; holy... holy... holy, and give me the praise.

The night is nearly over and the Day is almost here.

Be awakened and make yourself ready.
The season of change has just arrived.

Amen

Love

Psa 112:8 *Their hearts are secure, they will have no fear; in the end they will look in triumph on their foes.*

Journey
- 150 -
RULE LEST YOU BE RULED

I have not abandoned you, child, nor allowed you to be deserted.
I drew you closer, that you may be comforted in the arms of love.
I am your Deliverer, Healer and every need met.
Your strength comes from drinking my spiritual milk and walking in obedience to my Will.
I shall strengthen your frame and cause you to climb the mountain heights. Stand firm and do not lose faith, for I will strengthen you.

Your healing shall bring many into my Kingdom for safety.
You have not lost me, nor have I lost you... nor will we ever.
Keep up your courage, and continue to eat my eternal solid food provided for you.
My Word is health and nourishment to your bones. Never forsake my Word which worketh in you so mightily, rather overcome the deeds of darkness by my abundant grace given you.
Drink from my well of salvation and rejoice. The victory is yours.

O Lord, may the milk of your word drip like honey from my mouth, as I reign and rule over my enemies. May the solid food of your eternal life, flow through me so gloriously, Oh, Heavenly One.

You do not need anyone to teach you, for I myself have taught you, and kept you for such a time as this. My anointing remains on you, for everything you have learned and gained from me remains on you.

Amen

Love

1Co 15:36 ...*What you sow does not come to life unless it dies.*

Journey
- 151 -
CALLING YOU DEEPER

Many shall come, and many shall go, and many more shall fall away, but by standing firm in the faith, you shall remain steadfast, secure in the arms of love, unshaken, unwavering and true.

Take hold of the Real Life which you have and run with perseverance the race marked out for you. Run and continue to run the race, for your name is written in the Book of Life.

Be satisfied and know-- that I am God.

You shall not lose heart, grow weary or ever see death, for I am in control of your life. You are in the palms of my hands.

As you worship me in action and in truth, you shall grow in stature and encourage many.

My arm shall always rule on your behalf.
I tend my flock as a Shepherd and gather the lambs in my arms.
I hold both you and them very close to my heart.

Consume yourself with the Living Word, that you may inherit a blessing, and not be overwhelmed by trouble.
Resist temptation at all cost.

Holy is my Name.
Be redeemed in my glory.

Amen

Love

Isa 32:18 *My people will live in peaceful dwelling places, in secure homes, in undisturbed places of rest.*

Journey
- 152 -

GAIN WISDOM - LEARN KNOWLEDGE

May my Will perfect you, and keep you safe, Oh, special child, child of my eternity.

Draw near to me and I will draw near to you.
Dine on my table of love and you will be satisfied with honey from the Rock.

I will not steal nor rob from you, but only with milk and honey from the Land of Promise shall I satisfy you.
I will strengthen the weak and carry the humble.
Have no fear. I am from all eternity.

Drink my wine of love, while dining on my table of grace, and never forget to be thankful.

My ways are pleasant ways and delight fills my house.
I shall show kindness to you and your household.
I will not attempt to change you, but this I would ask from you:
That you would be a flexible and moldable vessel in my hand.
In the hand of your Potter, you could be reshaped into the image of glory, if you choose.
My image of greatness is upon you, dear one - Go and conquer.
You are mine if you choose me to be yours.

I shall never look down on you, nor ever reject you as my very own... I know some have, but keep in mind, I never will.

Amen

Love

Psa 93:2 *Your throne was established long ago; you are from all eternity.*

Journey
- 153 -

READY FOR DEPARTURE?

I shall take care of your every need.
Come and join me in the making of human hearts.
O my beloved, my anointed one, my hand is never too short to save, nor beyond reach to feed.
Touch me in spirit and surrender your all to me, including the harvest of your heart.
Partake of my nature and dwell in safety.

Chase not after fantasies, but consider my Word of Life instead.
Find me and you will not drown in sorrow.
Follow that which is good for you, and leave every negativity behind.
Commit that which is pleasing, and corrupt not thy morals.
Continue to spend eternity with me - Precious time in my presence.
Lose not your focus but be entangled with me.
Follow my Way of Love, rules and regulations, instead of the ways of this world that are coming to nothing.

I am your Redeemer and Best Friend.
You are my precious price of love and forgiveness.

Be touched in Spirit, by holding tightly to your first love, for I am holding you close to my heart.
The fire of love shall burn deep within you, and see you through the rest of your days here on earth.

Amen

Love

Pro 24:3 *By wisdom a house is built, and through understanding it is established;*

Journey
- 154 -

WEALTH & PROSPERITY

Why be led astray, child, and so confuse yourself?

Stay on the path of holiness and resist not my love.
Do not be easily deceived and so become vile.
Let no one take advantage of you.
Be careful to lose your crown to another.
Do not seek mercy from anyone, but me.

Your eternity comes from me, and you shall be dressed with a garment of salvation.

Let the Light of my Life shine through you, beloved, that others may become enlightened. Give them my food to eat and my water to drink, that they may live and rejoice in their salvation.
May they become all that I have intended.

I am yours both now and forevermore.

Let Love and Forgiveness rule over your life.
Share my love abroad.

Oh, God my Savior, lift me up from every negative situation, that rises against me.

I have, child, and I shall continue.
My eternity shall rescue you from these present circumstances.

Amen

Love

Psa 128:3 *Your wife will be like a fruitful vine within your house; your children will be like olive shoots around your table.*

Journey
- 155 -
DYING TO PLEASE YOU DADDY

Keep a repented heart, so that you may bear the fruit of love.
Do not worry, little one, I shall take care of your every need and fulfill the desires of your heart.
Yes, I know you had to suffer a little for the sake of my Kingdom, but I am on my way.
Watch and pray and stand in awe and amazement... just as my disciples did, when they saw me ascend in the clouds to where I am today.
Behold, call on my Name, and see my glory shine upon your face, descending with power, great thunder and lightning.

Are you not mine? Do you really love me? Are you not in need of my loving kindness? Then why do you not cry out to me with all your heart! Let your voice resound in prayer, that I may hear and respond. Lose no hope, for I have come to give you life.
Do not compare me to anyone nor to anything.

Will you take time to look for me? Will you present yourself to me as one worthy of my call, one truly faithful that I may witness your obedience and not pass judgment on you?

Oh, child, be thankful for the reality of the truth and discover yourself in me. I am Truth - The Truth that sets you free.
Complete yourself in me.

Amen

Love

Hos 14:8 **Ephraim, what more have I to do with idols? I will answer him and care for him. I am like a flourishing juniper; your fruitfulness comes from me."**

Journey
- 156 -

HELP THE DOWNCAST

Is my hand too short to save or too weak to strengthen?
Keep your hope in me strong son, and draw closer.

The end of all things is near. Do not be lost or confused.
My eternal Word must be accomplished on earth, just as it is in heaven so shall it be done on earth.

After the final trumpet sound, all things shall be renewed.
My glory shall be revealed, and together all mankind shall see it.

You will ask me to spare the world from destruction, and I shall show myself strong through you.
At that time, I shall be revealed to all who are eager to believe.

I am here... do not despair.
You shall look for me, and when you search for me with all your heart, you shall find me.

Do not welcome anyone into your home that does not have my approval. Perfect yourself through my word of love, and you shall grow strong in my Wisdom and Stature.

You are loved.
Remain pure and healthy in my presence of love and perfection.
Be ready and prepared for action, during this final hour.

Amen

Love

Deu 11:12 It is a land the LORD your God cares for; the eyes of the LORD your God are continually on it from the beginning of the year to its end.

Journey
- 157 -

WELCOMING ARMS

Lead me, O my Light of Life, lead me.
Lead me in the Way of Truth and Righteousness, that I may follow.
Guide me in your Will, that I may see your face and rejoice in seeing your likeness.

Child, am I a God who is far away? Am I beyond reach?
No, my child, I am as close to you as your heartbeat, for I am the beat of your heart.
Go in peace, dear child, and love like never before, for the time draws near, and the end must now come.
In me, you shall find peace and joy, satisfaction and beauty.
Run and be diligent in the things of the spirit.
I am with you always. Do not leave me behind.
You do not need to struggle all by yourself. I am here with you.
Look to me, for nothing is ever too difficult for you to fulfill.
You shall find favor and nothing will stand in your way.

Yes, your Redeemer lives and has commanded you to live and not die.
Consume yourself not with the world and its false treasures, nor be injured by those flames, that burn people to ashes-- consuming their hearts with wrongdoings and manipulating intentions.

Complete me in you, Oh, Savior of all mankind, and reunite me to your side.

Amen

Love

Psa 80:3 **Restore us, O God; make your face shine on us, that we may be saved.**

Journey
- 158 -

SEEK ME OUT

Take heed of the words you hear me speak, Oh, child of my youth, for they are life to your whole body.

My Word is your guiding Light of inheritance, glory and Salvation.

Delight yourself in me, and you will find favor in the wasteland, water in the desert, and shelter, even during the darkest time of your soul in the wilderness.

My eyes are on the righteous. Do nothing displeasing to me.

I have freed you from the trap set before you, now thrive. Anything else besides me, that would attempt to come near you, that too, I will deliver you from.

Shine and do not dim the lights. Fulfill your destiny.
Your will-- is not my Will.

Learn to know who I Am, in the way I Am.
Keep yourself armed... ready for battle.

The Sword of the Spirit is in your mouth-- learn to use it wisely.

Accomplish my purpose, and support everyone who is in need of my loving kindness.

I am your Conqueror of hearts... who is in love with you.

Amen

Love

1Ki 3:14 And if you walk in obedience to me and keep my decrees and commands as David your father did, I will give you a long life."

Journey
- 159 -
DEVELOP STRENGTH

Dance with me - Your true God, not with the evil one - Your enemy, for he is a liar, and a father of lies.
I have saved you from the snare of death and deadly pestilence.
I have given you eternal life, that you may enjoy this journey alone.

I have loved you, by leaving you an example to follow.
Walk in my footsteps of love and learn from my ways.
Learn about love and become love.

Do you believe? Do you know my Will?
Come away with me, that I may perform wonders, and do amazing things on your behalf, before the eyes of all.
Feed yourself on my Word, and strengthen your spirit.
Move forward, and never look back to your old life for survival, instead, look to me for the real life.
In my welcoming presence you shall find eternal rest.

Resist any temptation of the flesh, that may weaken your strength from growing stronger.
Surrender your all and rest in peace.
Be patient while calling upon my Name.

Your great Friend of honor is calling you home to rest.

Amen

Love

Jos 4:23 For the LORD your God dried up the Jordan before you until you had crossed over. The LORD your God did to the Jordan what he had done to the Red Sea when he dried it up before us until we had crossed over.

Journey
- 160 -

LOOK NOT AWAY FROM ME

Look, I am here, there and everywhere with you, and for you, as well as for everyone else who invites me.

My Will must take place, otherwise, no one will survive these last days of torment, wailing and torture.

Stand strong lest you waver in faith.
Everything is sustained by my grace, including the journey you are now on.
Do you believe who I am? Do you believe in me, in my loving kindness? Will you join me? Will you capture my heart?
Will you give up on self to gain my eternal glory?
Will you benefit others, that you may receive the Promised Land eternal - My promises made?

Keep in my mind, that I am your Maker - Your heavenly Crown of honor.
I have kept no secret from you, but spoken openly to the world, that it may be saved.

The coming disasters, shall not come near you, nor overshadow your children.

Release your faith in all good Will, and train others to do the same.
Look to no other. I am your Comforter and Burden release.

Amen

Love

Jer 17:7 "But blessed is the one who trusts in the LORD, whose confidence is in him.

Journey
- 161 -

WEARY YOURSELF NOT WITH SORROW

Be very confident of the things that are coming your way, child, which I have spoken to you in secret and said would happen... they shall soon take place. Why be so unsure and uncertain?

Consider the lilies of the valley, and how I look after everything. How much more important are you to me?

Come to know me and be lifted up in glory.
I have given you much, and greater things than these, you shall yet see, for I have promised you my Word.
Do you not foresee all the wonderful things I kept in store for you?

You will not be misled.
Heaven is available for you here on earth now... live in it.

Since I myself have taken you to be my very own, no man can touch you without my approval.
I have placed heaven in your heart, therefore all things are made possible for you to achieve.
Through the blood of Life, you have access to Heaven.
Receive it all.
You will not be conquered, for the great Conqueror dwells in you.

I, your King, live and dwell in you.
Seek me, seek Life and live eternally in my dwelling place of safety.

Amen

Love

Isa 46:10 *I make known the end from the beginning, from ancient times, what is still to come. I say, 'My purpose will stand, and I will do all that I please.*

Journey
- 162 -

DWELL SECURELY

I am the Bread from heaven. Neglect not my voice, but take note of every word you hear me speak, and run with the wind of my spirit, urging you to carry on and move forward.
Give not the enemy the power to rob you of your garment... indulge him not. Remain fully clothed in your calling, lest he strips you bare naked, before the eyes of all who are watching.
Undress yourself not of your covering, and so become a wayward warrior, before the one who is of the world - The destroyer of souls.
Be diligent and keep your armor on at all times.
Neglect not yourself nor your Source of Life.
Run to me for cover, and you will be sheltered from the storms.
Ask and you will flourish. Continue to Live the life of Truth in me.
I desire mercy and brokenness in spirit, that I may raise you up to inherit the Land. The mask of this world shall fade away, but the image of Truth shall remain strong and steadfast forever.

Ignore not your calling... grow in love and pursue peace instead, for you are more important than you think or could ever know.
Take my hand on this journey of love, and let us walk the height and breadth of paradise here together on earth.
Let us be in agreement, that you may flourish and thrive.
Know my Will, and live in the abundance of my harvest.
I and you joined together in harmony, will always be united in love.
Together forever in love, celebrating eternity.

Amen

Love

Psa 6:9 *The LORD has heard my cry for mercy; the LORD accepts my prayer.*

Journey
- 163 -

HONEY IN THE MOUTH

I have given you eternal life.
Run, and do not give up on your courage.
Yes, run and speed my return.

Act in faithfulness, and you shall be encouraged to run the race without restraint.

My righteous right hand shall open the windows of heaven over your life, that you may be blessed beyond imagination.

Dare anyone touch you wrongly or falsely.

Love is made complete in knowing me.

My anointing shall rest upon your head, and freely you shall walk in my Kingdom.

Extend comfort to the needy, and great support to the deserted; then you will gain a good name in the sight of God and man.
Extend love, for God is Love.

In knowing me, you shall find yourself.

Aim and keep reaching out for perfection.

Your shame shall never be counted against you, nor be recalled in days to come.

Amen

Love

Psa 45:2 *You are the most excellent of men and your lips have been anointed with grace, since God has blessed you forever.*

Journey
- 164 -
APPOINTED FOR ETERNITY

Come away with me, beloved, come to your restful haven, come away from the pleasant and comfortable.
Touch me to reach me, for I am the One, who loves you.
Close to my heart, you shall always be.

I will certainly not give my glory to another.
I will contend with those who contend with you.
Trust me with all your heart by keeping your spirit alive.
Revive others and you will find everlasting peace.
Hold nothing back from me any longer.

I am your first Love, Husband and Center of attention.

I am turning back to you now, O God, my Savior.

You are mine forever, O special child of mine, both in this present age and in the age to come.

I am yours from the inside-out, Oh, my Heavenly Giver.

You have been rescued, child, therefore no longer linger on this journey of old.
Prepare yourself for what I am about to reveal to you and show you.
Cover yourself with my precious blood.

Thank you, God, for you are my Eternal Rest and Salvation.

Amen

Love

Act 20:32 "Now I commit you to God and to the word of his grace, which can build you up and give you an inheritance among all those who are sanctified.

Journey
- 165 -
RECEIVE MY ALL

I love those who love me, and those who seek me, find me.

Do not get to that point... despairing even of life.
I am on my way to you... believe what I say.
I am returning to take you home with me, for where I am, you shall also be.
Neglect not my Word of Truth, for you shall be rewarded fully.
Do not give up, nor give way to fear.

My breath shall give you a new life, a new start for a new beginning.
You shall be honored, and the honor shall always be mine.

Fulfill your duties, that I may lift you up in due time.
Demonstrate the love you have for me, by your actions towards others and you will be built up.

I am very near and as close to you as your heartbeat.
Invite into my Kingdom those who are eager to hear my Word, and acknowledge my truth before them.
Take them by the hand, and lead them into my Kingdom of Love.

By the fruit of your righteousness, you shall be known as one with me in spirit... one with your Maker for all eternity.
You are special to me. Neglect yourself not from my loving care.
Give me the praise due.

Amen

Love

1Co 10:23 "I have the right to do anything," you say--but not everything is beneficial.

Journey
- 166 -

THE BOUNDARY LINE

Bless those who persecute you, and forgive those who hurt you.
Deepen your roots further still, to become a well-watered, magnificent, nourished palm tree, and not just an olive shoot.

Live in luxury and pamper yourself in spirit. Live the blessed life.

Be ready to lead many to the River of Life.
Live in honor and in constant praise of me.
Be ready in season and out of season, by living the true Christian life, in the Garden of Eden.
So, be magnified and enlarge your appetite for more of Me.
Stay away from anyone who brings you grief and causes trouble.
Stay on the path of righteousness which leads you to holiness.

In me, you shall always find rest for your weary soul.

Submit to my Will and you will have a clear conscience.
Disturb not my anointing, rather act on my Will of love, instead.
Adjust yourself in spirit and live a stable, balanced life.

Consume me with your fire, Oh, Holy One, Spirit of Love, and burn me with your greatest desire.

Be entangle in my spirit, child, and you will be detangled from the system of this world.

I am your Eternity. Lose no hope nor sight of me.

Amen

Love

Son 8:5 *Who is this coming up from the wilderness leaning on her beloved?...*

Journey
- 167 -

MY FAVOR RESTS ON YOU

Righteousness I shall reign on you and love shall overtake you.

You shall sing songs of angels, and prosperous will your days be.

Acquire of me, always.

May your good deeds find you out and reward you.

Neglect not your salvation, and so turn away from the deep truth you have grown to know. Grow in my presence of glory and you shall shine through the deepest darkness surrounding you.

Exercise the body, but also tend to your spirit to perfect your mind. Seek my face and not just my hand, and receive the inheritance promised.

I am your Heavenly Light and great Reward.
Seek Me to find Me and you shall live eternally.

Be hospitable at all times, and shake the dust off your feet from anyone who gives you trouble.

The honor is mine in the midst of all this darkness surrounding you, for I am your Light.

Your future is not dim, as some may have wished it to be for you. Your life with me shall be enjoyed forever.

Amen

Love

Psa 71:4 *Deliver me, my God, from the hand of the wicked, from the grasp of those who are evil and cruel.*

Journey
- 168 -

HOLD ON TO LOVE

Hold on, hold on to me, beloved.
Waste no time, effort or energy on anything unimportant and is of no value, for the coming days are much more pleasant than your prior. These days are coming to a final end.

Do you believe that you are doing well?
If yes, then continue to abide in my service.

I am very near Oh, my precious one.
Endure these times of sorrow, for the end has come... it shall soon be all over.

Your King lives; there is nothing to worry about.

Rejoice in your Maker and take great delight in Him.

All things are now at hand.
You are about to receive the greatest rewards.

Keep your eyes open
Watch what I am about to do for you.
The mighty acts of your loving God are very much here.

Your Giver of Life is waiting to receive you - Acknowledge Him.

Forever free in me - Love never ending.

Amen

Love

Psa 31:5 **Into your hands I commit my spirit; deliver me, LORD, my faithful God.**

Journey
- 169 -
KEEP FAITH

I am so close to you... closer than you think.

I will uphold your cause and bring you justice.
Anyone who tries to harm you, I shall punish and push back.
Anyone who accuses you falsely shall pay the penalty, whoever he may be. Those who misuse you because of my Name, will be judged most severely.

Keep going and never give up nor ever quit.
Hold on to the Real Life given you, and never let go.

Endurance is of me, and blessed is he who endures under trial.

You, my child, in whom is all my delight, are my honor of glory, for all eyes to see my presentation on earth.
I find no fault in you, for you have been washed by my cleansing blood.

Destroy darkness and move on.
Run with great speed to reach your final destination.

Sadness does not belong to you nor is it of me.

View the world from a different angle, and you will see me as I really am - The great I Am.
Keep running on the right side of life, and you will not lose sight of me - Your calling.

Amen

Love

Psa 44:26 **Rise up and help us; rescue us because of your unfailing love.**

Journey
- 170 -

BE DILIGENT

Your protection comes from me and enlightens your path... providing you with energy, protection and vitality.

My Name is honored in the presence of all the congregation.

Never forget: You are my sweet aroma to all who believe, but to those who are self-seekers, and do not seek me... you are the smell of death.
Keep fighting the battles of the last day.

My grace is sufficient for you, and my return is surely on the way.
I shall uphold your frame and prosperity shall follow.

The love within your heart shall carry you through.

I am your vision and enlightenment.

Knock on the door of my heart and I shall answer.
Keep your vision of me alive, and you will be carried through this journey of love, to reach the greatest heights.

The Glory of Love is my redemption in your life.

Maintain a repented heart at all cost, for your life depends on it.
Secure your position in me, that you may prosper in all your ways.

Let go of past experiences, by allowing me rule over them.

Amen

Love

Psa 111:7 *The works of his hands are faithful and just; all his precepts are trustworthy.*

Journey
- 171 -

MY NAME IS A STRONG TOWER

Come to me and run the race marked out for your future.

You shall gain Life when you lose your own.
Destroy sin in the flesh and give me the glory.

Listen and obey my voice; even among your people make it known.
Hear me when I call and act on what I say.
Live my life, that I may flow and flood through yours.

Hold on... hold on... I am returning soon.
I will not be delayed nor ever be taken away from you.

Listen to my Word of love beating as one beat with you in heart.
Complete your journey here on earth, while there is still time in heaven.
Consecrate yourself before your Creator, that He may lift you up in due time.

Worship at my altar of praise, and be thankful on every occasion.
Resist the temptation holding you back from me, and run for cover.

Why wait for anyone else to take you to heaven, than me?
I am on the way to take you home to be with me.
Be ready and present yourself as a workman who does not need to be ashamed, a minister who correctly handles the word of truth.

Amen

Love

Psa 37:17 ***for the power of the wicked will be broken, but the LORD upholds the righteous.***

Journey
- 172 -

MAGNIFY MY PRESENCE

I am your call to repentance - Your Salvation in the making of love through peace.
You, my child, are found in me - Your Creator, the merciful One.

Continue to walk with me and reach out to others.
Do not hesitate to call me, Abba Father.

Your healing will quickly come, if you obey my Will, and follow my Word in obedience... acting on my Will, doing exactly what I say.

Search to find yourself in me.

The blood of Life has given you access to my inner sanctuary-- enter boldly into my throne room.
I have also prepared the way for you, to walk in health, freedom and safety.

You are to live in full assurance of faith.
I am your refuge of security.
Touch my heart and you will know the truth that sets you free.

O God of my life, you are my Eternity, my Safety from all this darkness surrounding me. Eternally and completely I am yours. Thank you for loving me. You are the great I Am.

Child, it was my choice to prepare the way for you.

Amen

Love

Deu 33:27 *The eternal God is your refuge, and underneath are the everlasting arms. He will drive out your enemies before you, saying, 'Destroy them!'*

Journey
- 173 -

REALITY IN EXISTENCE

Know your help comes from me, and settle in one place... no longer shift and change tents.
You are the apple of my eye. Do you not know this fact?
Take my word with you everywhere you go.
What I say, you should speak; and how I am, you should also be.

Provide bread for the hungry and water for the thirsty.
Know you can rely on me.
Take courage and be united to your Savior - The Lifter of your soul.

You are precious to me, for I have made you.
You are my anointed vessel, for I have created you.
You are my very own, for I have called you by choice, and handpicked you in love.
You are glorified, for I have chosen you in honor, and ordained you to worship me. You are justified by me.
Be not afraid, for your Redeemer lives, and He has chosen you.
Be no longer negligent, nor long for anything else more than me.

Your courage and confidence come from me.
I shall keep you strong and united in spirit with me.
When you run, you shall not fall, and when you walk, you shall not faint.
The future awaits your arrival. I, your God, am your Future.

Amen

Love

2Ki 19:31 *For out of Jerusalem will come a remnant, and out of Mount Zion a band of survivors. "The zeal of the LORD Almighty will accomplish this.*

Journey
- 174 -
YOU ARE NOT NEGLECTED

He said, "Come to me, O my children, listen and I will teach you the Way of heaven on earth."
I have come to give you rest - Eternal comfort in my presence.

Turn not to the right nor to the left, for only discouragement there you will find.
Recover all things lost by my grace handed over to you.

In Me, there is joy and everlasting peace, that never lets you go.
My love belongs to you, and you, my child, belong to me.

I have considered the cost and found it worthy to come from heaven to save you, Oh, dear friends.
I will never neglect you, but will always be with you instead, till the very end.
Be patient and you will see my right hand of power.
I love you, O my beloved queen, and have called you to serve me.
In honor, I drew you to myself and granted you salvation.

Now live the ordained life chosen for you.
Listen and obey my voice, and I will carry you through the deepest darkness, that may pass you by.

You are mine; I will never let you go.
Missing you in love.

Amen

Love

Psa 45:4 *In your majesty ride forth victoriously in the cause of truth, humility and justice; let your right hand achieve awesome deeds.*

Journey
- 175 -

REVEALED MYSTERY

Recognize the time, and realize the days you are living.
The time has come to take my children home to their eternal safety... away from all this calamity and disaster.
I have shortened the time for your sake, O my people; otherwise, no one would survive.
Seek me, seek peace and live my eternal life of fame.
Quench not the fire of my spirit within, and be thankful.
Drink from my well of salvation, and live a life of Love.

You are blessed with many blessings.
Your future is here and now... right at the door.

You shall seek me, and as you seek me with all your heart, you will find me standing right there at the door of your heart.

Establish integrity in me, Oh, my Savior King, for I am sailing away with you.
I am honored in your sight and thankful.

The room has been prepared for you, O my child of destiny.
Oh, child, you have been established by grace, and I look forward to seeing you in heaven with me.

Keep in mind - You are the reflection of me.

Amen

Love

Isa 51:7 *"Hear me, you who know what is right, you people who have taken my instruction to heart: Do not fear the reproach of mere mortals or be terrified by their insults.*

Journey
- 176 -

A HEART OF GOLD

The vision of tomorrow is everlasting, and the beauty of life is seen in the universe through the Creator, for the sun shines when He is around.

I love you, O my God, and need you always till the very end of time.

Glory to Me, your God, who has gone ahead of you in a flame of fire. I have done wonders for you and established integrity in your heart. I myself, am your Crown of glory and honor of praise; which will never be taken away from you.
I myself will now act, and the vision of tomorrow shall be revealed to you today. Your future is sealed with my signet ring of glory. You, Oh, my child, have nothing to concern yourself about.
I am your guiding Light.

Thank you, O Counsellor, for being my Best Friend and present help. O Spirit of mercy, your existence makes a difference, and your favor upon my life is astonishing.

You called, I heard your prayers and answered your plea.
Your requests lay open before me, for I am the everlasting God.
I shall enlarge your territory, and broaden your wings of love.

You are mine from everlasting to everlasting, as I myself am your glory in this journey of love.

Amen

Love

Pro 8:34 **Blessed are those who listen to me, watching daily at my doors, waiting at my doorway.**

Journey
- 177 -

RESIST NOT MY WORD

Resist not my dwelling place of safety for you.
Keep reminding yourself of my constant love.
Enjoy the present without deserting the future.

I am here as your Support Stream of grace.
I am your Eternity and Comforter of souls.
I shall build you up and never tear you down.

The first rule of love is to love unconditionally, and the second is like it... give as you have been given.

Murder no one by hatred, rather, gain a good name in the sight of God and man instead.
Do not disregard any of my favors offered to you freely.
Call upon me and I will be there.

Your True Calling is Me. Dignity rests on godly character.

Keep the unity of the Spirit alive and on fire.
Rest in my glory and trust in my Guidance, for I am your place of refuge and eternal rest - Stay alert.

I am not angry with you. Just follow my footsteps and be true to yourself as a living example - A true citizen of my Kingdom.

You shall not lag behind.

Amen

Love

Psa 62:7 *"My salvation and my honor depend on God; he is my mighty rock, my refuge.*

Journey
- 178 -

YOU ARE NOT CONDEMNED

Accumulate neither wealth nor assets, but rather, gain a good name for yourself. Do not chase the treasures of this world, nor consult the deeds of darkness, for you will gain nothing from this corrupt world, except agony, sorrow and strife.

He who watches over you will reveal the path of Life to you, that you may live and not die.
Sorrow is not for those who bring peace, but for those who bring grief.
You are ready to fly, so soar away with me to a new height, to a new land, far from all these negativities, and idol notions, surrounding you in a land not your own.
You are to put a barrier between you and darkness - The system of this world, causing harm to everyone who follows its petition.
Accomplish all you know to do and you will be delighted.
Do not ignore my Word... give me your heart instead.
Watch and pray, that you may not miss the mark.

The future is very much here. The future of your tomorrow will not be delayed today, nor will it be a burden to you as of old.
Your new beginning will not be restricted by trouble, but will flourish instead.

You shall inherit a blessing and take great delight in your Maker.

Amen

Love

2 Ti 2:19 nevertheless, God's solid foundation stands firm. sealed with this inscription: " The Lord knows those who are his,...

Journey
- 179 -

THIS IS YOUR INHERITANCE

Reassurance comes from me as you well know.

Run in comfort, for the future is yours to behold.
Be kind and compassionate, that you may know your King in all his attributes.
Live in the Will of God, the Holy One of Love, that you may be enlightened by grace.

You will surely be glorified on the day of my return.

Love sublime is effective in accordance with the Truth.
Future benefits will be revealed to the pure in heart.

Speak the truth and walk in my love.

Forgiveness is the key to reassurance of Love.
Be steady and run the race set out for you… you will never be sorry that you did. I have worked on your behalf for a long time now and prepared the way for you to journey on.
This is the time to serve me wholeheartedly.
I am with you always.
Confide in me and continue to love.
Love in the right hand counts for much, for your righteousness comes from me.

Amen

Love

Act 20:24 "However, I consider my life worth nothing to me; my only aim is to finish the race and complete the task the Lord Jesus has given me--the task of testifying to the good news of God's grace.

Journey
- 180 -
RESTORATION IS POSSIBLE

Capture my heart before the night is over.
Whisper into my ear the Words of Love, that you hear come out of my mouth.
Be kind to yourself, and demonstrate my words of Love in action.
Hear my voice as I speak.
Do not wage war against the enemy of your soul… avoid his every step and walk in righteousness.
Rest and give me time to show myself strong through you.
Share my love and tenderness with all your friends, by welcoming my presence, and enjoy the peace.
Comfort the needy and encourage their hearts.

My welcoming presence is real.
Be a blessing and remain steadfast.

Holy is my Name and glory is my fame.
My love shall support you always.
My presence shall manifest my glory in your life, and you, my child, shall reflect my image before the eyes of all.

Walk the walk and do not just talk the talk.
Agree with me and work not against me.
Do not abandon yourself for the sake of everyone else.
Give me yourself and flourish instead.

Amen

Love

Jos 3:5 …"Consecrate yourselves, for tomorrow the LORD will do amazing things among you."

Journey
- 181 -

REASSURE VICTORY

Approach heaven with a smile and neglect not your Gift of Love.

Perfection comes from me, and I am the only One, you are to worship.
Be assured, my grace is real and defined.

Your brother who is in need-- is crying out to me. See him through his difficulties, and reassure him of my unfailing love.

Walk in victory and never falter in faith.
Live in my likeness and walk in my truth.
Settle down and earn the bread you eat, that you may continue to earn the respect of others.
Be one in spirit and worship me in Truth - The Truth of Love.
Reveal my glory to all.
Be gracious and share my love with everyone.
Do not be judgmental.
Treat every nation, tribe and person equally, without a quarrel, fight or dispute.

Your Mission is to call my children home.
Whisper my Name, that you may see my Face.

Quietness and peace rest in the arms of love.

Amen

Love

Rev 6:2 I looked, and there before me was a white horse! Its rider held a bow, and he was given a crown, and he rode out as a conqueror bent on conquest.

Journey
- 182 -

THE WIND BENEATH MY WINGS

The seed of love has grown to become a mighty harvest, conquering the fear of death.
The sacrificial death was to gain life for the world.
I shall hear your heart when you whisper my Name.

Conquer death by the Spirit of Life living in you.
Rekindle the fire of my spirit within you, by the flames of my love burning through you.
A true saint is one who agrees with me, puts his hope in me and trusts in my Will. Are you one with me? Will you serve me wholeheartedly? Will you be one with me in spirit and truth... body, soul, spirit and mind?
Teach Truth... don't just show mercy. Bring life, not death.
Conceal false assumptions and manipulations, and you will fall into a ditch.

Comforter of souls you are to me, Oh, God, my King.

Yes, child, my loved one, I am your Giver of Life, and by my great Name, you are called 'Hopeful.'

May I walk in obedience to your Will, Oh, God, my Heavenly Dream, and live in the reality of all your truths.

Be rekindled and spark, O child of my love.

Amen

Love

Deu 33:27 The eternal God is your refuge, and underneath are the everlasting arms. He will drive out your enemies before you, saying, 'Destroy them!'

Journey
- 183 -

UNFOLD THE FUTURE

The clamor of this world shall soon fade away to nothing… it is destroying the environment.
When the foundation is destroyed, what can the righteous do?

You have nothing to worry about… just close the door on all those who are troubling your heart and robbing you of energy.
Close the door and never look back, for they shall soon disappear, fade away and come to nothing.
Those things are a disturbance, a total waste of time.
They are not to be tolerated, for the Eye of your Spirit cannot tolerate that which is wrong and false.

Complete your vision and succeed in your mission.
Submit your will to mine and fulfill your destined purpose.
Undress yourself before my eyes, but keep yourself maintained and dressed before the enemy.

I am your warrior of worship, and to you, Oh, God, I surrender.
The beauty about love, is that you, Oh, my Spirit of Life, fulfill my life, and I am not burdened.

Complete your journey here on earth, O my child, and no longer give into temptation, so that you will not become a wanderer.

Give not yourself to the enemy; be redeemed instead.

Amen

Love

Psa 37:39 … "The salvation of the righteous comes from the LORD; he is their stronghold in time of trouble.

Journey
- 184 -
NEVER LONELY

Complete your journey here on earth, before the day dawns and the night caves in.
The pride of the roaring lion will not defeat you, for he is shackled with nowhere to turn. Just like the sound of his roar, he is vanished, gone forever... once was, no longer is, nor will he ever be.
The viper of the tongue will not poison your spirit.
You will not be swallowed up by pride.
That snake of your attacker is dead, conquered, destroyed and captured... double time.

You will not be negligent, as you breathe the Breath of Life.
Your enemy, the evil one, will have no power to live and reminisce.

Capture the sight while you still have the Light.
Enjoy the life ordained for you by grace, in the sight of all, no matter what they may say about you.
Memories of old shall no longer be recalled nor linger on, for the journey of your new beginning has just arrived.

I, your Master-- am surreal, giver of life and restorer of faith.
Love is perfection for any soul seeking salvation.
Giver of love is my fame. Remember the privileges bestowed on you. Neglect not your Life of Love.
Ambition is the answer to the solution sought after.

Amen

Love

Psa 24:8 *Who is this King of glory? The LORD strong and mighty, the LORD mighty in battle.*

Journey
- 185 -
REPLACE THE OLD

Love not the enemy of your soul nor pay him any attention.
Reverse the cycle of old.
Magnify my holy presence by your action of truth.
Call upon my Name, that I may hear and respond to your every need.
Seek me out from among the living and not from among the dead, that you may live.
Acknowledge my Name, and lead others not into temptation.
Heal the sick, and accept my Will of instruction.
Complete your journey in full assurance of grace, while patiently waiting for my return.

Your future will not be denied.
Turn your outer world around by renewing your inner-self, and come out of your shell.
Move away from anything that is holding you back from coming to me, for your number one priority should always be me living in you, and through you be seen.

The Healer is here. Behold I am with you eternally.

Comfort my sons and daughters in your loving arms of embrace, and keep yourself dressed in white.
Wait for my return, for I shall surely show up when it is time.

Amen

Love

Psa 34:5 *Those who look to him are radiant; their faces are never covered with shame.*

Journey
- 186 -

OCCUPY A PLACE

Trust in me and be rest assured.
I have given you the ability to understand matter, not just logic.
I have destroyed sin, and stripped your hairy enemy naked, by the cross... he shall not recover nor be of existence any longer.

All those who call on my Name shall be saved.

Before the world was formed I knew you.
I called you by name, and for myself set you aside, that I may delight in you. I now call you to deeper truths, that you may know the difference between me and the world.

Walk in wisdom and gain understanding, that you may prosper and walk in knowledge.

I shall always be your help of support, and comfort in time of trouble.
Distraction shall not come near you a second time around.

Rejoice and be glad, for you have been redeemed.

You, my children, shall live and be prosperous throughout eternity.

Recover the moment.
Your Prosperity comes from me.
Now receive all that I have for you.

Amen

Love

Mat 26:28 *This is my blood of the covenant, which is poured out for many for the forgiveness of sins.*

Journey
- 187 -

ALWAYS BE READY

O God of mercy, how your love consumes me, surely you are my Eternity.
You have made your thoughts known to me, and I am thankful.

O child, I am with you in word and deed. I am with you especially when you are weak and struggling with the flesh.
Bless you, child, bless you both now and forevermore.
You are the child of my Kingdom, the child of my prosperity.
I have empowered you and given you eternal rest.
Take heart and drink from my River of Delight, so that you may never thirst again.
Continue to speak Truth, for I am your Delight.
As long as I am with you, no harm shall come near you.

Grow in love, for you are loved. Your forgiveness is essential, to all who are in need of me and under pressure.

You clothed yourself with love and integrity, and so became fully dressed and awakened.
You are now hidden from the eyes of him who kills the soul, for you have covered yourself from his wicked schemes and indignations.
You wore my signet ring of glory and became sealed in perfection.
Loving you always and forever more.

Amen

Love

Mar 16:17 *And these signs will accompany those who believe: In my name they will drive out demons; they will speak in new tongues;*

Journey

- 188 -

THE TIME IS NOW

Shine like the angels during the deepest darkness.
Look, the night is nearly over and the Day is almost here.
Keep going, keep performing my miracles to this world of agony and sorrow, that they may be saved and never stop serving me.
Do not hesitate to believe all that I have told you.
My return draws near.
Complete your work without any hesitation.

I know your ways, O my child, surely I do.
I shall protect you from the lash of the tongue, for I have ransomed you from death.
Fear of man shall not overrule you a second time around.

I have already established my throne in your heart.
I am the Alpha and the Omega, the Beginning and the End.
I am your salvation and theirs... both now and forevermore.
Look to me and not away from me.
You shall find peace as you become one with me.
Throw away every worthless idol, that counts for nothing, and chase after me - Your Master Teacher, your Sovereign, the Mighty One of Love.

On my shoulder of love, you shall find comfort.
You are redeemed by grace.

Amen

Love

Psa 119:76 *May your unfailing love be my comfort, according to your promise to your servant.*

Journey
- 189 -

MATURITY IN WISDOM

Know that I am working in you, and act in accordance to my Will.
My power is unlimited and is full of grace, mercy and compassion; given to you so wonderfully.

You have not yet reached your fullness, nor received all that I have prepared for you.
You shall enjoy heaven on earth just as much as I am enjoying you.

You are wise, but unstable in your ways.
Redeem yourself quickly, before the darkness robs you of your thoughts. Be not weak in your natural ability, for I am your Source of strength to demonstrate my power.
In spirit, you are stronger than ten mighty men in battle, but in the natural, your dependency rests on me.

I am completing the work I have begun in you from the inside-out.
Be still and know, that I am your God.
Be unmoved by all this clamor hovering over your head.
Become mature and complete, so that you may lack nothing.

You are special to me, therefore you have been adorned by holiness.
How can you say, purify and wash me clean, when you are already mine? You are the child of my serenity, peace and harmony.

The story of old is yet to unfold.

Amen

Love

Isa 28:29 ***All this also comes from the LORD Almighty, whose plan is wonderful, whose wisdom is magnificent.***

Journey
- 190 -

ACKNOWLEDGE MY WILL

Rescue the needy and help the greedy find themselves.
Tear down the household of wickedness with the confrontational truth of my enlightened Word.
Have nothing to do with wickedness.
Teach little children how to come to me instead.

I shall support your project and fund it from start to finish.

Listen and obey.
You will never beg nor starve-- I am here.

I shall watch over your future, as well as over the children you so care about and strive to nurture.

I am here for you.

Cultivate my blessings and move forward with me.
Comfort your heart with my loving kindness, that you may become the lifter of souls.
Attend to my Word, and undress your wounds by healing them.
Enjoy your life by living my Word.

Your Comforter and Healer I am.

You shall not be captured by wickedness.

Amen

Love

Rev 3:8 *I know your deeds. See, I have placed before you an open door that no one can shut. I know that you have little strength, yet you have kept my word and have not denied my name.*

Journey
- 191 -

RENEW YOUR MIND

Qualified... bravo! You have passed the test of time in this life... now into the next.
A substantial new beginning - A new start.
Qualified in the making... you are.
Your entirety is fulfilled in the realm of my Spirit.

Do not overly exhaust yourself, nor become exuberant with these unstable people, who are ravishing you with their eyes, and swallowing you up with their pride. Their own wickedness shall testify against them. You have nothing to worry about.
Keep faith and accelerate your mission, for the old has gone, and the new has just arrived.
Perfection comes from me, and it is I who perfects you.
Your calling shall be restored, for you are honored in my sight.

Look to me and to one else, for there is always hope in forgiveness.
Rescue yourself from the dominion of this world, before you are captured in its grip.
Enlighten others to worship me in spirit and truth.

The respect of others should not determine your qualifications, nor should it count... only my approval should ever be taken seriously and sought after.
Never abandon the works of my hands.
I take great delight in you. Redeemed you remain qualified.

Amen

Love

2Co 9:15 *"Thanks be to God for his indescribable gift!*

Journey
- 192 -
FOUND AND NOT LOST

Love the brothers of believers, and do not think of yourself more highly than you ought.
I am with you always, enthroning you with splendor and majesty.

Accompany me in glory, as I sit on my throne, watching the nations pass by, and declare my glory.
Know my declaration before the final end times, and rejoice in your Maker.
I am with you to see you through, Oh, my child of Love.
Keep your garment of splendor on, and never allow anything to dim my light within you.
Continue to broaden your love, and be content with what I have given you... seek nothing else.
Delight yourself in me, for I shall restore double, for all your good works and faith in action.

Your beauty shall shine forth and capture many.
Your fullness is found in my likeness.

Reject temptation at all cost, before it whispers in your ears sweet emptiness. Be not a doormat for people to trample on, as one cursed.
Fulfill your duties ordained by me.
Look to no one else but Me - Your Haven.

Amen

Love

Isa 63:13 who led them through the depths? Like a horse in open country, they did not stumble;

Journey
- 193 -

ORDAINED BY NAME

Defend the fatherless and all those who are struggling in the flesh, the needy, and all those who are wailing on their sick bed of sorrow.
Call on me to save them.
Show them the Life of Love by your living example.
The battle is not yet over.
Those who rage war against me, and constantly fight you, because of my Word, will only be put to shame and confusion.
These people will end up being warped.

My eternal life is in the making of peace in love.
I am your Help, Source of Life, Security and Protection.
You will not lose ground.

Complete your mission for the journey is not yet over.
Lose no sleep over these people who do you no good; for their aim is only to destroy you by doing you harm. Expect nothing good to come out of their mouth, for they are schemers... schemes of the wicked. They pamper you all night and lurk in all day.

Enjoy the ride home with me, before all is gone and wastes to nothing.
Your comfort comes from me, for I am your Comforter of hearts.
The memory of old is gone now.
Rejoice in what I have ordained for you, and become complete.

Amen

Love

2Th 3:4 *We have confidence in the Lord that you are doing and will continue to do the things we command.*

Journey
- 194 -

WALK IN MY FOOTPRINT

Call on me, for I am as close and as near as the beat of my love is in your heart.
I will not neglect nor reject that which is mine.
Believe me, when I say, I am near... close to your heart.
I will never leave you stranded, nor forsake the children gathered to you from the ends of the earth.
I have chosen you to regain power over the oppressor and save nations from his hands.
You have been empowered to overcome his prey.

You are in the palm of my hand.
Shall I hand you over to be persecuted? Never!
Do you not know, that I am the Living One, the Mighty One?
I shall never leave my children homeless nor in need.
Yes, I will come quickly to the rescue.

You have not yet asked me for anything.
Ask and you shall receive an abundant harvest of blessings.
You shall not fade away to nothing, for I have made you whole.
I have extended the number of your days.
You shall live much longer than you thought originally.
Your footsteps shall always be directed by my perfect Will.

Listen to my words of Wisdom, and hear my heart beating as one with yours.

Amen

Love

Psa 119:133 **Direct my footsteps according to your word; let no sin rule over me.**

Journey
- 195 -

THE WAY IS NOW CLEAR

Rejoice, you are about to step into your future.
All my promises are about to be fulfilled.
I have completed the work assigned to you by me.
Now disperse my fullness.
Yes, you had to endure-- pain, affliction, trials, temptations,
health problems, financial needs, past hurts, family situations,
argumentative spirits, bereavement and everything else in between;
yet you remained faithful till the end, unmoved by trouble.
You maintained your faith in me, even when you were weak.
You never gave up on me-- yourself nor your children.
I am proud of you, beloved. You have made it.
You are about to see the wonder of my right hand displayed in
your life. I am about to open the floodgates of heaven over your life
and shower you with my greatest blessings - Unheard of blessings,
prepared just for you.
Rejoice, you are about to be taken to the highest mountain in love,
for the reality of my truth shall expand you.
You shall conquer nations, and many will flock to your counsel.

Serve me as one working for God, not man.
Be anxious about nothing and enjoy the ride.
Rejoice in what I have purposed, for I am about to do mighty
things for you, before the eyes of all, Oh, my child of love.
Your future is about to be fulfilled - Rejoice!

Amen

Love

Eph 5:1 **Follow God's example, therefore, as dearly loved children.**

Journey
- 196 -
REVIVED BY FAITH

May your river flow, Oh, God my God, may your river flow.
Take me to a higher place with you, O my heavenly Father, and walk me in your depth of compassion. Take me into your Chamber of Love.

I desire to submit and serve you wholeheartedly with pure devotion.
In your Name, I dance and with my voice to you I sing.
Take me in, O my Glory, and reunite me to your care.
Take me into your inner sanctuary, that I may dwell in your presence and shelter of love.
I shall rejoice in seeing your likeness upon my face.
Teach me how to soar on the wings of an eagle to rest in the shadow of your grace.
Enrich me, that I may be a blessing to many.

Distraction is not of me, beloved child.
Listen and obey my voice, before the storms blow and you forget my Name.
The story of Elijah is yours to partake from.
Now live it in action through John the Baptist.
My healing hands are upon your shoulders, move closer and rest your weary soul from trouble.

My love for you is never-ending, Oh, King of thrones.
Thank you for loving me, for I know to you I belong.

Amen

Love

1Sa 2:2 *"There is no one holy like the LORD; there is no one besides you; there is no Rock like our God.*

Journey
- 197 -

RESIST ALL ELSE BUT ME

Lack of faith shall not be your downfall, for I am your Father figure, the leading example, the Author and Perfecter of your faith.

Consider me in all you do, by acknowledging my ways, for I shall surely lift you up from the basic principles of this world.
If you agree with me, then we have a treaty.
Stir up the gifts within you and serve me righteously.

It is I, who establishes integrity in your heart.
You shall lack no bread, as you seek me daily through the Scriptures - Feeding on my daily bread - The Word of Life.
I shall open the fountains of heaven and bless you abundantly.

Walk in my ways and you will not be sorry.

Salvation comes from me and from no one else, for there is no other name given to man by which you can be saved.
What is mine is yours, and what is yours can also be mine, if you choose.
Glorify me in all you do and you shall be blessed.
Build yourself up in me, and never tire of serving me.

I shall never disappoint you, nor ever neglect you.
Your hope in me shall always be strong.
Your future is in my hands just as you are.

Amen

Love

Isa 27:3 *I, the LORD, watch over it; I water it continually. I guard it day and night so that no one may harm it.*

Journey
- 198 -

DRAW ME CLOSER

O beloved, be in need of nothing, for I am your Loving God.
The glory alone is mine; keep that in mind.

I urge you to live with me one day at a time and in complete harmony and unity with one another all day every day.

Your future is here now.

Learn my ways of doing things and walk on the pathway of righteousness.
Reach my fullness in the Truth you know, and distribute my favors.
Reflect my likeness and never give up.
Keep in mind, that your worship of me serves a great purpose.
Consider what I have done for you, and treat others the same.
Forget not my deeds of kindness imparted to you.
Rescue everyone in love, and enlighten their hearts to serve me.

You are free to soar like an eagle, do not fret nor feel restricted by the crowds surrounding you.

The honor is mine, and no one can take it from me.

He who loves you... Am here.

Your future is not dim, but lit up for the whole world to see my Light of Glory and be saved from corruption.

Amen

Love

Psa 119:64 The earth is filled with your love, LORD; teach me your decrees.

Journey
- 199 -
REJOICE IN YOUR FUTURE

Enjoy the future while you walk in the present.
I have occupied a place for you in heaven. Now redeem the lost.

Empower yourself in me, for I have recharged you with my energy.
Be skilled in your work, and do not give the enemy the upper hand.

Through the power of love, you can still do all things.

Endure hardship as a good soldier of my Kingdom of Glory.
Love and keep on loving, as if there is no tomorrow.
Let my Will be done in your life, no matter who says what.
Involve me in all you do, by being led by my spirit.
Give me the praise as you rest in my worship of grace.

Keep me safe as the apple of your eye, Oh, my King of Glory.

Keep persisting in your calling, for it is not yet over.

I love you, child.
You know child, that without Me - Love, you are nothing, nor can you achieve anything of importance in your life.

Enlarge your territory, and rest in my Kingdom of grace, for I am your Shelter.
You are supported and very special to me.
Keep consecrating yourself with my power of perfection.

Amen

Love

Pro 22:4 **Humility is the fear of the LORD; its wages are riches and honor and life.**

Journey
- 200 -

HEART OF WORSHIP

Your image of glory, Oh God, is my glory of fame, the beauty of your loveliness is my perfection, and your joy, O King, is my peace.
Have mercy on me, Oh, have mercy on me... on this man lying here before you, wailing and waiting for something good to happen.

I know, that you are in need of me, Oh, child of my love, and eager to see greater things happen yet, but first you must learn to conquer difficulties, stress, burden and trouble.
The truth of love must first live in your heart.
Draw closer to me, for your salvation is nearer now than when you first believed. Salvation for every nation is at hand.
Everything is nearer now than when you first believed.
I need to establish you as my instrument of honor, my weapon of love to every nation. People need to hear the Word of Truth coming from your lips, for they are lost, burdened, tired and worn out, from this miserable, obnoxious state of mind.
These are the final stages of time - The end before a new beginning.
Fear not, I will no longer have you battle through life.
I am on my way to bring you home safely.
I desire to see you live in safety, than in fear and concern - Free, than in constant agony and despair - In honor, than in constant misery and strife. I rejoice when you delight in me, O child.
Make my heart glad by honoring my Name.

Amen

Love

Psa 28:7 The LORD is my strength and my shield; my heart trusts in him, and he helps me. My heart leaps for joy, and with my song I praise him.

Journey
- 201 -

FUTURE ASSURED

Touch no unclean thing and I will receive you into my bosom of love - Into the heart of my Kingdom.
I have given you my truth and exalted you to my highest point.

The harvest is plentiful, and the fields are now ripe and ready.
Be ready and do the work necessary, for the time is no longer on anyone's side.
Yes, you have accepted me, but it was I who loved you first.
I called you into my Kingdom of love, and you flourished and became the most beautiful of jewels.
Love is the solution to every problem and the answer to every question.

You, O King of glory, are awesome in all your ways, faithful in all your decrees, true to your word, and loving towards every living thing. Everything you have made is beautiful and is astounding. Those who keep the demands of your covenant will be blessed.

I look forward to your eternity with me, O my true saint.

O my Eternity, I am yours-- to serve, worship, adore and love forever. My future is with you... all that I desire and more.

Reflect my likeness, child, that others may see my glory manifesting through you and give me all the praise.

Amen

Love

Psa 36:6 *Your righteousness is like the highest mountains, your justice like the great deep. You, LORD, preserve both people and animals.*

Journey
- 202 -

COMPLETE IN MY SIGHT

Forgive me, O my God of heaven, forgive my stubbornness and rebellion against your Will and Word. May your Will be done, and your kingdom come, for we are all in need of your touch. Comfort me, Oh, comfort my soul from trouble, for I am in agony. Cause me to whisper your Name, Oh, my sweet Savior God, Glory of hearts, who is my Deliverer and Best Friend.

Uphold my cause against all those who surround me, Oh, my Savior God, and illuminate my life, for they are about to destroy my work, the work I poured my heart into serving your holiness.

Consider me, I pray, consider, your child, who is in need of your comfort and support. I live daily as if it is the last moment of my life. Touch me, Oh Mighty One, and change my way of thinking to suit your way of love. Make me new in your loving kindness, and rest me under your care... charging on in spirit.

Submission to my rule of love is vital, Oh, my sweet beloved child, and it is important for my children to listen and obey.
Master your gift of love, and illuminate my greatness in the heart of the universe, for every nation-- To hear, see and know my call to repentance. You will not lose heart nor ever grow weary.
I am your Source of Security, your Source of Strength.
Abide in me, and you will be reshaped, transformed and glorified.

Amen

Love

Deu 31:8 *The LORD himself goes before you and will be with you; he will never leave you nor forsake you. Do not be afraid; do not be discouraged."*

Journey
- 203 -

YOUR FUTURE IS HERE

Undress yourself before your Maker, that He may lift you up in due time.
The night is nearly over and the Day is just around the corner.

Do not become undressed in secret and think no one can see, because I do. I see everything, even every intention, motive, desire, purpose, interest and reason behind every thought and deed.

Children, keep your light burning before man, that they may see the Light of my Life and be glorified - The Image of Glory, and be set free.
Feed your soul the food of my Spirit and learn from my ways of doing things.
Pay attention and continue to walk in my freedom.
Circumcise your heart while purifying your mind.
Deliverance is at the door; it shall no longer be prolonged.
Use the key of revelation and unlock every door.

Your desires shall be fulfilled and satisfied by Me - Your Light.

Discover yourself in me as you walk in my victory.
Enjoy your ride home with me while completing your mission here on earth, for I am your Everlasting Grace.

My return is on the way. Soon all things shall be over.
I am your Love in action and your Lifeblood stream support.

Amen

Love

1Co 3:14 *If what has been built survives, the builder will receive a reward.*

Journey
- 204 -

THE HEART OF LOVE

Draw near and do not run away from me.
I am, your Lover and Best Friend, for all eternity.
I love you, child. Death was sacrificed and the innocent crucified on your behalf, so that you, my son, may have a long full life.
I have loved you eternally, with my resurrection power of love and sacrifice - I am the Resurrection and the Life.

Weary not yourself, nor lose heart on my account.
I am not against you, but rather for you.
Respond to my heavenly visions and you will be blessed.
Lead others to their eternal destination and you will find favor knocking on your door.
Do not cross over from life to death.
Remain in your high secure position of grace.
Slide not backward, nor hop from here to there.
Move forward and be a blessing.
Never give up, but continue to love people everywhere.

I have not left you lonely, nor deprived you of anything good.

Lift up my Name, and cross over with your children to my Land.
Look back not to your old circumstances, for the new has just begun.
Your future is at hand... receive it all and be set free.

Amen

Love

Isa 32:17 The fruit of that righteousness will be peace; its effect will be quietness and confidence forever.

Journey
- 205 -

THE MAKER OF CREATION

The beauty of love is revealed through you, beloved.

Continue to Grow in Wisdom and stature, that you may be established in love.
Live in total repentance as you move forward towards your eternity.
I am yours... Worship me in the Splendor of my Majesty.
Stay away from all, but Me. Remain in your calling.
Maintain your standard of living, and give me all the praise for all your victories. Never give up on your destiny.
Love and be magnified in beauty.

Thank you for believing in me, even when I did not.
Thank you for giving me the chance to forgive and be forgiven, Oh, my Savior King, Lord of all, Restorer of everything good.

The Restorer of your destiny is greater than all, beloved.
He shall guide you into all truth and uphold your cause.

I shall move you to a new adventure.
I shall awaken your spirit and your life shall be renewed.

Teach little ones how to worship.
My children are in need of me and I have chosen you to set them free.
Be one in spirit, and live for your eternity here with me on earth.

Amen

Love

Psa 29:2 *Ascribe to the LORD the glory due his name; worship the LORD in the splendor of his holiness.*

Journey
- 206 -

MAKE A DIFFERENCE

Come to me, O you, my children, and sing my praises, for I myself have given you everlasting life on this journey of love.

Buy the truth and do NOT sell it.
Receive me into your heart and do not let go.

It is I, who provides you with good things, so that you will not be dependent on anyone else, but me.

Complete your journey here on earth, and be assured of the outcome.
You shall not grow old; but only in wisdom shall you mature, develop, grow in strength, flourish and empower many. Your youth shall renew like the eagles, and day after day you will look younger. You shall be reformed and re-created, and like the universal star sent from heaven, you will shine upon the earth.

Take nothing for granted, for these are the signs of the last moments of the Day.

You should be as I am - Holy and perfect.
Love in Action should be your number one priority.
Perfect yourself in me, that you may benefit your family.
Love one another as I have loved you, and you will surely know the truth that sets the captives free.

Amen

Love

Psa 86:12 *I will praise you, Lord my God, with all my heart; I will glorify your name forever.*

Journey
- 207 -
RESURRECTION PRIVILEGE

Oh, God my God, my life is hidden in the palm of your hand. My desire is to please you and sing your fame. You have blessed me in many ways, and in your Name, I desire to be a blessing to others. Savior, Keeper of my soul; keep me sacred as the apple of your eye, that I may be a blessing to all those in need. Take care of my loved ones and purify them with your love, that they too may truly be sanctified. Lead me into your quiet place of refuge, that I may dwell in safety and be delivered from sin.
Looking forward to the future together with you.

I am the great I Am, and with me all things are possible.
I shall lift you up, from every burden injuring your heart, and in my Name even death you shall overcome. By resurrecting others from death, you are bringing life to their dead and dying world.
Your future is an open door.
Open your tent curtains wide, enlarge your territory, broaden your horizon, your borderline, extend your boundaries; for you are about to see greater things... beyond imagination... things you have never seen or heard about before this day. I am with you always.
Your hope in me shall never perish or ever be lost.
Danger shall not reach you, for I am your Crown of Love and Eternal Glory. You shall not be stripped naked by your enemy - The destroyer of lives. Keep your acknowledgment of me strong.

Amen

Love

Psa 145:4 **One generation commends your works to another; they tell of your mighty acts.**

Journey
- 208 -
COMPLETE YOUR MISSION

I have loved you with an undying love, and with loving kindness betrothed you to me.
I satisfied you with milk and honey, and with tender compassion restored you back to myself.

Be comforted and know your salvation draws nigh.

You will never hunger nor thirst, nor will you ever lose your salvation, for I shall continue to provide.

Children, you may ask for anything, and I shall respond.

The truth shall be revealed.
I tell you the truth... he who believes has the Everlasting Life.

Believe in me, that you may grow stronger, develop and evolve.
Complete your mission, that you may relax when the time reaches its fulfillment.
Your journey is not yet over; it has just begun.
I am about to exalt you.
Rest, for I am your Resting Place.
Develop in me and I will heal your soul from insufficient times lost.

Exalted you shall remain strong.

The future is nearly over for everyone, but for you, it has just begun, because my commission is your mission.

Amen

Love

Psa 119:15 *I meditate on your precepts and consider your ways.*

Journey
- 209 -
REDEEM THE LIVING

O God, help me surrender my all to you... remain focused and true, for you are my Reality... my dream come true.
You are the true I Am - The Comforter of souls, therefore, boldly I enter your throne room and bow my heart before you.
Thank you for your love and Shining Light.
Since you are my strength and your grace is sufficient, I shall ask for anything in your Name, and know that I have received. But, I shall ask for nothing more than your Will to be done in my life, and request that I would only be pleasing in your sight. O Holy One of Compassion, the warmth of your love moves me... your touch is gentle to my soul, fire to my spirit and health to my bones.

You are mine and first in my life.
The sacrificial blood of your Love has given me eternal life.
I need the compassion of your gentle touch. My heart whispers your Name, and I am heard. I yearn and long for your tenderness. Missing you I am, and yet very near. Savior Lord, make me see all that you are to me and all that you do for me. Help me understand your ways, that I may remain strong and never weaken. I belong to you, Oh, my burden Relief. In all my ways I am committed to you, not just in public, but also in private. Thank you, Father, for taking care of us, your people, for whom you died to revive. Thank you! Your precious Name is great. You are my eternal King and Sovereignty.

Amen

Love

Jer 33:3 '*Call to me and I will answer you and tell you great and unsearchable things you do not know.*'

Journey
- 210 -

LABOR PAIN

Labor not, for I have given you many children to love and nourish.
Now look after them and cradle them well.
Feed them my manna and give them the support they need.
Help them become strong and mighty.
Teach them the Way of Life – The reality of the Truth - The Real Life. Keep them as the apple of your eye.
Help them see what they need to learn and train them up well to know how. Inhale my praises and exhale me in worship.
Give them a place to sleep in order to rest their head.
Watch them grow and comfort their hearts.

No more labor pains for now.
This is your time of reaping a great harvest.
You shall be exalted.
Be one with me in spirit and call upon my Name in love.
Turn to me with all your heart and lean not on your own strength to deliver you.
Reach the ends of the earth in my Name, that the nations may hear my voice through you, and be enlightened and awakened in spirit.
They shall see me through your eyes of love.
Help them call upon me, that they may reach me and touch my core being in spirit.
Your surreal future has just begun and is beholding you!

Amen

Love

Hos 2:21 *"In that day I will respond," declares the LORD-- "I will respond to the skies, and they will respond to the earth;*

Journey
- 211 -

REFRESH THY SPIRIT

In your beauty, I shine, and upon your throne, I dance.
With deep compassion and love I sing, and in awe of your grace, I stand.
You are the great I Am - The One and only true God.
You are my Healer, Deliverer, and my very Best Friend.
To you, I cry out loud... O God help me, O Spirit of love save me.
Help me see the world through your eyes of love and forgiveness, that I may benefit others by your honorable grace.
Thank you for accepting me as I am and taking over my life from beginning to end.
I need you as you are and for me to be changed into your image of love. Thank you for helping us worship you in honor and give you the praise in love.

Journey with me, child of my grace, and you will never falter nor lose faith.
I am with you. You shall not live in despair.

Teach me to know you, that I may be perfected in love and walk in humility.
Ordained worship is mine to gift you, Oh, my Heavenly Savior.

Yes, O my beloved, your call is my all.
Do not be weakened by stimulating thoughts, that do no one any good, rather be wholesome in your way of thinking and approach.

Amen

Love

Psa 28:6 *'Praise be to the LORD, for he has heard my cry for mercy.*

Journey
- 212 -

POWER OF AUTHORITY

O my Comforter, cradle me in your loving care, cradle my heart in your love. I want to see your glory; the glory your Son had with you before the creation of the world.
Help me see what you see in me, Oh, God of my life - Singer of songs.

I love you, and desire that my Will be accomplished in your life, O my child, my queen, my special ordained son.
To me, you are like the firstfruits of all my creation.

Your recall is my wake-up call of remembrance.
Call on me and never give up.

The beauty of affection is in the answer given by grace.

Do not linger behind, for the world needs my mercy.
I have given you many revelations by which you must live.

Disturb not my anointing, for I have given you much.
Acquire understanding, and you will be informed with my Knowledge of Love. Continue in your ministry.

Teach little children to worship me in spirit and in truth.
Recall the days of old no longer, because right now... you are in the new, a new place in life... starting fresh - A new beginning.

You have reached your fullness... Appraisal.

Amen

Love

Psa 138:8 *The LORD will vindicate me; your love, LORD, endures forever-- do not abandon the works of your hands.*

Journey
- 213 -

YOU BELONG TO ME

I have given you rest from all your enemies.
Why turn and chase after them? Do you wish to be enticed by them, once again? Why, my child? O Why?

Destroy sin in the flesh and walk victoriously.
The battle is now over, so you are free to soar.
Let go and let God fulfill his purpose for you.

Allow me to remove every pain inflicted upon you by your so called friends.
My love shall heal your broken heart from all these struggles, and you shall no longer be conflicted.

Your Maker is your Glorious Destiny.
Call on me and I will hear your voice, act and respond.
I shall protect you from all those who have taken you captive, and restore you to your rightful place.
I shall contend with all those who contend with you and uphold your cause before the eyes of all who see.

Take me, Oh my God, into your arms of love, and I shall constantly lift you up in praise.

Help the weak and needy, be strong, Oh, my child.
Help them from their own experiences of old-- from the experiences of this world save them. The victory is yours.

Amen

Love

Psa 147:3 **He heals the brokenhearted and binds up their wounds.**

Journey
- 214 -

ETERNAL COMMITMENT

Take care of each other.
I am your Heavenly Savior, Restorer of souls.
I see all things... nothing is ever hidden from me.
I view the earth from afar and all that is in it.
Everything is uncovered and laid bare before my eyes-- to whom you must give an account.

You will not be put to shame.
Rejoice and live, for today is the day I have made.
I am your refuge of rest.
Be stress-free.

Dwell in my holiness, where the enemy cannot touch you.
You are forever kept safe under the shadow of my wings... forever loved.
Be content and move faster than ever before, but never shift away from me.
Love the brothers of believers, that they too may see the love I have for you and rejoice.

Unity in the faith is found in the action of love.
Assured certainty comes directly from me, for heaven is open wide.
You are to rejoice when all is down.
I am your Emperor of Hope and Guiding Light.

Amen

Love

Isa 45:17 *But Israel will be saved by the LORD with an everlasting salvation; you will never be put to shame or disgraced, to ages everlasting.*

Journey
- 215 -

FORGIVE AND BE FORGIVEN

Refuse me not… instead, focus on accepting my Will into your life.
Run the race to inherit the Land.

On your behalf, I shall work wonders never seen before.

Do not be entrapped by the enemy, for you are not unaware of his evil schemes.
The question is not why you, because the answer is the 'I' in you, who handpicked you.

Put your trust in me and continue to grow in strength and wisdom.
You are my special child, and I am here to help you.
Rejoice in my existence and be taught to learn the lessons necessary.

Grow in love and become-- THE BEST THAT YOU ARE, all that I have intended for you to be - THE BEST YOU ARE IN ME.
This is who you really are - ALL THAT YOU ARE IN ME, AND I IN YOU.

Loving you eternally.
Love never ending is the answer to every heart.
You are mine forever.
Distant yourself from trouble, and keep yourself pure before my eyes.

Amen

Love

Jer 15:16 *'When your words came, I ate them; they were my joy and my heart's delight, for I bear your Name, LORD God Almighty.*

Journey
- 216 -

HOPE FOR THE NEEDY

Do not let go of me, child, and you will be healed, restored, and made new.
See yourself through my eyes and you will be made complete.
Do not lose any hope, for I have come to shower you with my greatest blessings. I will see you through all your difficulties, and make all things right on your behalf.

Rejoice in hope, and walk in the freedom of your salvation. Endure no loss, for you have not lost.

I have formed you in the womb and created you, that you may know me. Now grow in Love.
I have chosen you, that you may grow in wisdom, honor and stature.
I shall reveal myself through you, and by your living example, make myself known.

Allow me to free you by my spirit from willful sin, for I will not allow my Name to be defamed... Surely, I cannot.

Restoration is at hand, and you are to rejoice.

Tomorrow will not be the same as today. Be ready for the changes ahead, and prepare for your new amazing life.

Amen

Love

2Co 13:11 *Finally, brothers and sisters, rejoice! Strive for full restoration, encourage one another, be of one mind, live in peace. And the God of love and peace will be with you.*

Journey
- 217 -

COMFORT THY SOUL

In quietness and peace, you shall find rest, and glorify me your God, who is in heaven.

Be humble before my eyes, and learn from me the ways of the wise. It was not easy for me to lay my body down for you, my friend, but see child, love is the answer to all.
I rose from my throne to give you eternal life, that you may be lifted up in glory - In my cloud of glory - In the clouds with me.

Withhold not my mercy and grace, but rather share my resurrection power with others, that they too may rejoice in their salvation and deliverance.
Surrender your all to me and come to your resting place.
Humbly walk before your God and be blameless in all your ways.
I am Truly Faithful.
I will never give up on you, nor chase you out of my Kingdom.
You belong to me.
Do you not know, that he who comes to me, will be filled with everlasting joy!

Be consecrated, for then your beauty shall be magnified through perfection. Be consecrated in love to live the fruitful Life of pleasure, and magnify my glory.

Amen

Love

Psa 18:2 *'The LORD is my rock, my fortress and my deliverer; my God is my rock, in whom I take refuge, my shield and the horn of my salvation, my stronghold.*

Journey
- 218 -

JOURNEY ON...

Be submissive to my Will, Oh, my child of love.
Submit your will to my Will, and you will flourish like a glorious palm tree in the making of completion.

Your family and friends shall be delivered by my sufficient grace granted you.
Friend, changes are coming your way very shortly.
Do you not perceive them coming to deliver your family and see you through your difficulties?

I am your Great God, Deliverer, Healer and Best Friend.
Look to me and you will find deliverance for all those you love.
My grace abounds in mercy.
Touch my heart and be increased in love.

The former shall no longer take place nor be repeated, for the changes will renew everything. Everything will be changed from beginning to end, from start to finish.

Your healing hands shall restore many to fullness.
I have given you hope and a future to walk in adoration of my Love.

The vision of love is in the making of perfection.
You are mine.
Recall the days of old when you were young.

Amen

Love

Psa 111:3 *Glorious and majestic are his deeds, and his righteousness endures forever.*

Journey
- 219 -

OBEDIENCE IS NECESSARY

Complete your work before the night is over.
Anoint your head with the oil of joy, than with the sorrow of grief.

You really are lovely and pure in my eyes, and I so treasure you.
I treasure the times we spend together, and cherish the moments we share.
I created you, the world and all that is in it.

Give me the glory and be empowered by grace.
Touch not my anointed, for if you do, you will only injure yourself.
Rest in my Comfort and relax in my Perfect Will.
Run the path of righteousness and give me your all.
Live in peace with one another, as well as with everyone who is not a brother.

Desert me not... for the world.
Compared to who I am and what I have already accomplished on your behalf and achieved, the world falls far behind.

Destroy not your future by your thoughts of today.
See yourself as the finished product, the ultimate vessel of glory--then you will understand my views of things.

You are my glory here on earth, that I may be revealed to all.

Amen

Love

Jas 1:4 **Let perseverance finish its work so that you may be mature and complete, not lacking anything.**

Journey
- 220 -

THE FIRE OF LOVE

Direct your footsteps in my ways, child, and live a prosperous, abundant life in soul and spirit.

I have promised you many things, that are yet to be fulfilled, and they will surely come to pass.
Nothing shall be wasted... in just a very short time, they shall all be here - every promise fulfilled.

I have loved you with an undying love.

Take heed, child, and listen.
Walk in obedience, that you may live in peace and harmony.

You shall never look back, for those things are dead and gone.

Know that I myself am here, watching over your wellbeing.

Follow my Word in complete obedience.

The future is foretold through my Book of Love.
You have been born and created to take charge, and be in control; not to be controlled by any form called humanity.

Comfort the needy before they are destroyed by their own ruin of destruction.

The truth lives in you... now restore the lost and capture my heart.

Amen

Love

Psa 111:3 **Glorious and majestic are his deeds, and his righteousness endures forever.**

Journey
- 221 -

RESTORED TO HEALTH

He said, "Come, my children, listen to me and I will show you the way to life... on which you have not yet traveled - The road to Everlasting."
The path of forgiveness remains open.

Live in spirit, and you will be directed on the path of holiness... leading to righteousness, and the result will be eternal life.

Take my highway: The safe road for your journey.

I have come to give you life in abundance... eternal comfort in my presence.

Look not to your past experiences and the horrible disasters that have caused havoc.
Do not look back or be discouraged by them.
Continue to dwell in my presence of safety, and you will find peace that never lets you go.

I have considered the cost and found it worthy to save you from eternal destruction.
You are not neglected nor forgotten, special one of my eternity.

Listen to your Father who loves you.
Reveal my Truth to all.

Ordained, you are, for I am your Conqueror.

Amen

Love

Pro 4:13 **Hold on to instruction, do not let it go; guard it well, for it is your life.**

Journey
- 222 -

COMMISSIONED

Hold on to me with all your heart and never let go.
I shall see you through all your difficulties, and you will not be neglected. Keep up your courage and you will be restored back to health - Your rightful place of serenity.

Yes, I am with you always, my beloved.
I will uphold your cause and see you through.
I shall also justify and sanctify what remains neglected.

You, O my loving Savior, are my Comforter and Strength.
I shall hold on to you with all my might, with all my strength, and with all that is within me. I am yours for the rest of my days.
I have no one but you to keep me safe and desire no one else to uphold my case except for you.
By your loving grace and the power of your authority, I am changed.
Abba Father, my very First and Last.
No one can take your place of honor in my life.
My sanctification comes from you, and I am saved.
Your grace in the realm of the spirit reaches me... extending love and immortality. I stand in awe of your beauty and astonishing wisdom, which you have revealed through your saints in the sight of all who come to you.

I am yours completely.

Amen

Love

Job 5:20 **In famine he will deliver you from death, and in battle from the stroke of the sword.**

Journey
- 223 -

THE CROWN OF LIFE

Complete your mission here on earth for heaven's sake, and do not become easily persuaded by men and their conniving appeal.
Lag not behind like a wounded soldier who has already fallen behind or fallen asleep.
Be recharged and sharp, awakened and solid.
Your redemption draws near.

I have ordained and commissioned you to be my ambassador.
The task I have chosen for you has already been established in your heart... seek nothing else.

Now complete the work to which I have called you.
Journey with me on this mission possible and reap the benefits.

I shall lead you and guide you, that you may know the Will of your God and be established by grace.

Everything you thought about to be impossible will now become possible for you.
Let me take you where the action is.
Even now, step out in faith and see my glory shining upon your face - Reflecting my likeness.
I have gone ahead of you to prepare the way - Walk ye in it.
It is all yours. Enjoy the freedom given you.

I am bringing you closer to me.

Amen

Love

Psa 119:91 **Your laws endure to this day, for all things serve you.**

Journey
- 224 -

PERSISTENCE IS THE KEY

I love you, child.
Be patient just a little while longer for my return, and you will see me in the clouds... I will surely show up.
My return shall no longer be delayed as some have said.
I shall comfort you with my loving arms.
Before long you will be in my Everlasting Presence of all the angels - The great clouds of witnesses in the heavenly realm, for this is where you belong.
Apart from your words, faith and deeds, you have nothing else to take home with you when leaving the earth, but only your fruitful deeds - Your fruitfulness - Only the fruit of the spirit shall remain.
As you well know, the weight must be light when I return.

I have brought you into the Light by taking you out of the darkness, so faithful and true to me you shall remain.

Believe all that I say to you and you will never be disappointed.
Unite yourself with me through faith and consider the good we are to achieve.
Your Creator lives in you, beloved, and because I live, you too shall also live.
My Will must be acknowledged throughout the earth.

Continue to acknowledge me and reveal my zeal.

Amen

Love

Joh 15:5 *"I am the vine; you are the branches. If you remain in me and I in you, you will bear much fruit; apart from me you can do nothing.*

Journey
- 225 -

GLORIFIED

Lean on my shoulder of love and rest in my presence of glory-- you know you can. I urge you, child, not to become unlawful to me, by your deeds of darkness suppressing you, and by your negative thoughts of darkness running through your veins.

I am calling my people home to me.
Go after them, Oh, child... go after them, so that they will no longer be disheartened. Free them from their anxiety and strife.
Let them not slip out of our hands, for they are the enemy's target to strike them any time.
Be a shepherd to them on my behalf.
Give them hope and a future during these dark times of sorrow. Release them from their dungeon-- from their own prison walls of insecurity and fear, that they may rejoice once again and be found in me. Help them know between right and wrong.

Time is ending on every individual, and the curtains are about to be closed. Tell them to seek me early, that they may find me before all is gone and I disappear from their sight.

Do not chase after idols-- be lovers of God, instead.
Call everyone to repentance in order to share my abundance.

You are great in my sight.
Your future is in my hand, for you are redeemed.

Amen

Love

Psa 54:1 **Save me, O God, by your Name; vindicate me by your might.**

Journey
- 226 -

MERCIFUL SAVIOR

Rest, O my child, rest, tell your soul to rest.
Be still and know, that I am, who I said, I am - God.

In righteousness, you shall be upheld, and by the power of my zeal, you shall be restored.

Keep me in mind: The One who calls is victorious.
You will not be defeated nor waste away.
Your Great wealth shall be restored, and for all the years the locusts have eaten, I shall repay double.

Consider the great damage your enemy has caused.
Yes, you are to resist him at all times and on every turn.

Be assured today, that the greater One lives in you, and He is on your side at all times.
From the East, I commission a man to help you, and from the West another to accompany you.

Perfect yourself in me, but not in accordance to the system of the world.
Love must be redeemed by grace.
He who watches over you will keep you safe, so you have nothing to fear.

Amen

Love

2Sa 22:3 my God is my rock, in whom I take refuge, my shield and the horn of my salvation. He is my stronghold, my refuge and my Savior-- from violent people you save me.

Journey
- 227 -

FOREVER I AM

Be determined and run the race with courage.
Be inflamed with the fire of my perfection and burn with zeal.
Step up into a higher realm of my approval without any complaint.
Burn with compassion for the lost.
Burn with my spiritual fervor of Love and never give up on Life.
Master your position and never grow weary.

I took you from the ends of the earth and from its furthest corners
I called you to be mine; my very own possession.

Fear not, you will not be put to shame.
I have already rescued you and will continue to empower you.
I am never too far away. Call and you will find me near.
No harm shall befall you, for I am the One, who protects you.
Nothing shall come near your tent.
You are special… just believe what you hear from me and act on my Word of wisdom.

Be connected to me in spirit and reunite the family of believers to their original form.
Be cautioned: Pay attention to these minor details of your life, and keep a watchful eye on the truth you have come to know.
Reach out to others in love, so that they too, may have a chance to survive in this dark world of sorrow and overwhelming fear.
Your mission is not yet complete, but soon will be.

Amen

Love

Joh 14:15 *"If you love me, keep my commands.*

Journey
- 228 -

I AM YOUR KING, MASTER OF EVERYTHING

Oh, yes, beloved, I have loved you with an everlasting love, and with tender loving kindness drew you near.
I brought you to myself and placed a crown of pure gold upon your head, that you may serve me and in love join me.
Come to me all you who are weary, burdened and troubled, and I will give you rest - Eternal comfort in my presence.
You shall find comfort in my tender arms of love... disaster shall be kept far from you and will not come near you a second time around. You shall laugh at disaster and in me find a place of refuge.
Take my yoke upon you and learn from me, for I am genuine, gentle and humble in heart.
Restrain not from obeying my Will, for I am the One, who takes care of your every need. Hold on to Love, rather than to the things of this world, which burden the mind, body, soul and spirit.

Yes, I have loved you with an everlasting love and with loving kindness drew you to myself.
The King of kings is here, and He Himself is watching over you.

Keep me safe in your tender loving arms, O my God of Love, and sustain me with your bread of life, for to you I turn.

Let my Will be done in you, and through you, child, so we may run the race together and achieve the goal, purposed for eternity.
Let us together accomplish all that needs to be achieved.

Amen

Love

Psa 62:5 **Yes, my soul, find rest in God; my hope comes from him.**

Journey
- 229 -

THE COMFORTER IS HERE

*Splendor and Majesty to you in the highest, O my Eternal One.
You are my Fame and Life Breath. You, Oh, Lord, are the God of the spirits of all mankind, and you live in an honorable place.
On the mountain heights, you dwell and guide many.
You lead them to your shelter of your love and protect them from the storms of life... carrying them from all harm.
I love and adore your holy Name, for you are YOU - My Comforter and Source of strength. The word of your love sustains me, and I am taken by your goodness to us all.*

I love you, O child of mine; you truly are precious to me.
You have touched my core, and now my spirit rests in peace within your heart... in the comforting arms of my love.

Rest and do not be overwhelmed by trouble, for nothing by any means shall come near to harm you or injure you.

Perfection comes from me, for I am the God of all eternity.
Perfect yourself in me, let us hurry together to my chamber of Love-- where there is mercy and forgiveness.
I shall dress you in white and with costly fabric and fine linen you shall be clothed.
I kept you safe, O child, and protected all that is yours.
Journey on and never look back.

Amen

Love

Psa 121:1-2 I lift up my eyes to the mountains-- where does my help come from? My help comes from the LORD, the Maker of heaven and earth.

Journey
- 230 -

DIVINE INTERACTION

Speak to one another in love.
Keep the unity of the spirit kindled through peace.
Develop my skills and grow in character.
Maintain the unity of divine interaction at all times.
I, your Friend am here. Develop character and stature.

Your Sovereign shall no longer allow anything to stand in your way.
Perfect that which needs perfecting, for I shall raise you up to a higher standard in love, and lead you on by my spirit of grace.
You shall not want for anything.
Nothing can nor shall ever take your place, for I, your God, shall watch over your position of glory and keep you sustained.
I will never leave you behind, nor ever neglect you, for I have chosen you before the creation of the world to be my very own.
I am with you, just as I have been for all eternity.

I trust in you, O my Hope, as I lay my supplications before you.

Trust in me further, child, and you will know my deliverance.

Empower my spirit, Oh, Lord my Savior, that I may run with you. Touch my soul by your spirit and renew my mind by grace.

I have given you eternal life, child, now dwell in my love.

Amen

Love

1Ch 4:10 ... *"Oh, that you would bless me and enlarge my territory! Let your hand be with me, and keep me from harm so that I will be free from pain." And God granted his request.*

Journey
- 231 -

DILIGENT HANDS

Rejoice and be glad, for you have been chosen for such a time and task as this.
My Name is mightier than the roar of a lion, louder than thunder and lightning, greater than the storms of life and the waves of the sea, higher than any mountain, and sharper than any double-edged sword.
Sharpen your skills, O you mighty warrior and strengthen your defenses, for the strategies of the enemy are advanced, but the One who lives in you is far greater than the one who is in the world.

I am All in all and through all Everything.

I shall confront them on your behalf, and you shall not lose a fight. No wickedness, defeat, or evil schemes shall ever take you by surprise, for you are the child of the Most High God.

Keep believing, even when it is tough sometimes.
You will overcome every difficulty and situation that may rise up against you.

I have delivered you from the flesh. Why turn back to it?
I am your Savior, Deliverer and Double-Edged Sword - Your Great Reward.
You shall not be forsaken; so let my anointing flow.

Be led by my spirit every step of the way.

Amen

Love

Isa 61:10 *I delight greatly in the LORD; my soul rejoices in my God...*

Journey
- 232 -

BINDING FAITH

The hope of glory is in this place.
Do not waver in faith, for the time draws near.

I have prepared a special place for you in heaven.

Since you have proved faithful, I will now give you nations.
I have done this, so that the world may know that you are my child.
The power is in your hands.
Enjoy your time with me when spending time with my Word.

I will see you through every difficulty, that you may encounter...
this too is for my glory and fame.
Teach little children to worship and honor my Name-- I am their
Savior, Redeemer and Hope.
Do not pay attention to the things of this world, for they are of no
value to you, and will only ruin your thoughts.

There is hope; now cheer up and rule over nations.
I have blessed you with my authority. You will not be condemned.

You, O my precious ordained young king, have not burdened me in
any way, but gained honor and knowledge, instead.
Due to your relationship with me, your fame shall spread among
the nations on account of your beauty displayed in splendor, before
the eyes of all.

Amen

Love

Psa 86:11 Teach me your way, LORD, that I may rely on your faithfulness; give me an undivided heart, that I may fear your Name.

Journey
- 233 -

WORSHIPER OF TRUTH

Be content and live in peace and harmony with me.

Before you were born I knew you. I formed you in the womb and carefully watched over you. I nursed you with my tender care, and with loving kindness satisfied you. I gave you pure milk to drink and solid food to eat. You grew up and developed and became the most beautiful of jewels. I satisfied you with the desires of My heart and gave you the key of victory. I dressed you with my crown of righteousness, and you became my sacred possession, the most beautiful of diamonds - A royal diadem in the hand of your God.

Oh, you, who are highly exalted.
You reflected my inner-outer image and kept my royal command to love your neighbor as yourself. Therefore, you shall now eat from the best of the Land, never to waste away again.

My rewards are with me, and I will distribute them as I please and with whom I am pleased.

Oh, my special Bride. I am calling you home to myself.
Just a touch from heaven.

Redeem yourself in me, child, and you will see greater things.
Be mine just as I am yours, for the One who is in you is greater, than the one who is ruling this world.

Amen

Love

Psa 91:15 *He will call on me, and I will answer him; I will be with him in trouble, I will deliver him and honor him.*

Journey
- 234 -

SKILLED VESSEL

Do you not know, child, that I have come to give Eternal Life to the desperate, dying and needy? I am always near those who worship me in truth, and in my presence they shall find rest.

I will yet fill your mouth with laughter and give you everlasting joy.

Take care of your children and bless the helpless.
Comfort the weary, and challenge the greedy.
Convict the abrupt and arrogant, those mutilators of the flesh who do evil, destroy the weak and never give up until someone falls.
These people do not walk in my truth nor acknowledge my ways.
They live in total denial of my love and accept a bribe for my word.
They speak against the Holy One of Israel and think nothing of it. They are a brood of vipers, good for nothing, manipulators, a sinful nation. Their sin shall testify against them... have nothing to do with such as these.

Keep a watchful eye, and mind your own business.
Come near my house with all your heart and do not sin against me.

I, your God, am Holy, so be holy in all you do.
Worship me in spirit and truth and glorify me in praise.
Open your heart to Wisdom and seek revelational Truth through my Word of Life.

You are blessed with my eternal blessings of love.

Amen

Love

Psa 104:34 **May my meditation be pleasing to him, as I rejoice in the LORD.**

Journey
- 235 -
LABOR NO LONGER

*I lift up my eyes to you, to you whose throne is in heaven.
Where does my help come from? My help comes from my Comforter -
The Creator of all things beautiful, the Maker of everything good.
He will keep me safe in the shelter of his Tabernacle and lift me up
high upon a Rock. He will watch over my soul and bring me safely to
his Chambers - Into his Courtyard, his Inner Sanctuary.
In a dry and weary land, he will wash away my pain, and redeem me
to himself.*

I will direct you to walk in my footsteps of love, and help you follow my ways in the realm of my spirit, O my child.
I shall direct you in my loving ways and watch over you with an eagle's view. No one dares touch you, for you are the apple of my eye, and I am the Giver of life. I shall keep you safe and will not rule over you with a hot iron. I will only revive you to be awakened on my bosom of love. You are redeemed... there is no flaw in you.

Be one with me in body, soul and spirit.
Be determined to walk my walk, that you may live and prosper.
Fight the good fight of the faith, that you may establish ground and be set free from your adversary - The evil one. Be not discouraged.

Set your foundation right and you will be blessed beyond measure. Enjoy your prosperity, for I shall spread a table in the desert for you and satisfy you with love.

Amen

Love

Psa 119:35 **Direct me in the path of your commands, for there I find delight.**

Journey
- 236 -

EVERLASTING SUBMISSION

Assure accuracy as you speak my words of wisdom while benefiting others with Truth, that they too may walk in forgiveness, and rely on me to give them grace.
I have an open door for you to walk in, that no man can ever shut, nor reopen.
You are polished, revealed and made known to all your family. They shall soon come home and know the truth that sets them free.

Keep calm when storms hit other towns, and do not run to another place not your own. Stay exactly where you are now, in the place I have commissioned you - The place of your calling.
Without any hesitation, run the race marked out for you with great diligence, and assure safety to others, that they may run the course of time with you-- away from oppression and evil conditions.
I have restored your faith by giving you hope and a future.
Delight not in evil, overcome it with good, instead, for it has no power over you to seduce, for you are a conqueror, redeemed by faith. Injure not yourself by these present situations overwhelming your feelings. Stay calm and look up to me.
I will deliver you from the charmer.
The fire shall keep burning within your spirit, enlightening your soul with revelational Truth bestowed upon you daily through my Living Word.
Wonder upon wonders shall be released direct from heaven to you.

Amen

Love

Psa 62:5 **Yes, my soul, find rest in God; my hope comes from him.**

Journey
- 237 -

UNSHACKLED BY GRACE

Fan into flame the gift of love given you, child, and do not put out the spirit's fire planted within you.
Hold me close to your heart, for I am holding you closer to mine.

Do you not know, that you are already perfect in my sight, as well as holy? It is not your own righteousness and holiness that I see, but my very own through you, beloved.
O, my precious one, you are the apple of my eye and your name is engraved in the palm of my hand.
Search for me throughout the Scriptures, ask of me in prayer, reach out to me in worship and I will be there, just as I am here right now.
You are my very own possession, holy and pure.
Are you asking, why? Because I love you, and I have made you mine by the power of my eternal sacrifice.

Rescue those who are ready, for the harvest is ripe.
Let those who do right continue to do right, those who are evil continue to do evil, and those who are holy continue to be holy.
The future will not benefit anyone who does not look to me.
I am all and in all, through all everything.
I am on the way to you, and my reward is with me.
I shall give to each person according to what he has done.

You are holy, for I have made you holy.

Amen

Love

Psa 119:154 **Defend my cause and redeem me; preserve my life according to your promise.**

Journey
- 238 -

PERSIST IN LOVE

Did you not make your own choices and decisions without me?
I am glad, that you are now turning back to me.

Turn to me with all your heart and do not take the easy way out downhill - The road to destruction.
Stay away from every wicked thing presented before you, for they serve no purpose, and only harm they bring.

Let us settle scores. Let us forgive to forget.
Can we shake hands as two genuine people agreeing on a business venture?

The time is now: Let us recover the wasted years and the times lost.
I do nothing half-hearted, nor should you!

Be consumed with the fire of my forgiveness, and I will back you up all the way.
Open up and let me into your core being.

Forgive my hidden faults, Oh, God, and assure me salvation.
I do not wish to die, but live a healthy lifestyle with you.
Take over my life, and do with me as you please, as you see fit, for you know what is best for me.

I am with you always, even to the very ends of the earth.
Future benefits, future assurance is yours, Oh, my child of love.

Amen

Love

Col 1:14 in whom we have redemption, the forgiveness of sins.

Journey
- 239 -
LIMITATIONS REMOVED

Your brothers and sisters are crying out to me from everywhere.
Will you support them? Will you show them compassion and
extend kindness or will you choose to condemn them?
Will you cover them with love or will you shatter them?

Warm the hearts of many with the Love of my compassion.
Come to my altar of praise with songs of deliverance.
Remain in my love and abide in my greatness.

Be astonished in what I will do for you next.
You are about to reap a multiple harvest.
Keep holding on to that which is satisfying and real.

My Wisdom shall complete you.
Your success comes from me because I change not.

Those who choose the crooked ways, and lead others astray, will be
punished most severely.
They are treacherous, twice dead, abolished with evil doers.
The punishment of the guilty is most severe.

March on, O my soul... March on.
Tell your soul to march on, for I am close and very near.
Those who choose the small gate to walk on the straight and
narrow, will reap a great reward and find eternal Life thereafter.

Amen

Love

Psa 5:8 **Lead me, LORD, in your righteousness because of my enemies-- make your way straight before me.**

Journey
- 240 -

FAITHFULNESS REWARDED

Thank you, thank you, O Lord, my God, for the touch of heaven upon my life, as well as your love for all. The former days have gone, and the latter is yet to come; only the present remains.
Thank you, that we can come and abide in your loving care, Oh, my Glory, for the Kingdom of heaven rejoices when one sinner enters in.

My mercy is as great as my grace, Oh, child of my womb.
So, choose today who you will serve - Me or money?

I am your Refuge of Comfort and Love. You are kept safe from the flaming arrows and striking darts of the enemy.

I surrender my all to you, Oh, Savior of my being... to you who loved me first. I honor your Name, and pray that your Will is done on earth as it is in heaven.

Indulge not in false humility, child, for it benefits no one.
Give up not, for you have room to move. Live the pure life, the holy life, and hide under the shadow of my wings, O my precious one.

Under the shadow of your wings, I shall abide and be kept safe, safe to soar with the eagles. Your Name, O God, is music to my ear, and rhythm divine to my senses, makes me want to sing, dance and shout, "Hallelujah!"
I rejoice in you and find great delight and pleasure in your kindness.

Amen

Love

2Co 9:11 You will be enriched in every way so that you can be generous on every occasion, and through us your generosity will result in thanksgiving to God.

Journey
- 241 -

HOLD ON TIGHTLY

The stormy weather will not hold you back, for you are covered. Obey my commands willingly and live safely in the realm of love of my command. Endurance is my key of safety.

Your desire is my command, O my loving God, King of my soul.
I shall serve you wholeheartedly and never turn back from you.
My mind shall be set on you and my heart shall glorify you.
I love you with all that I am, and with all that you are to me.
To you belongs all the glory and the praise, for all that I am is yours.
I shall look to no one else, but you.

Continue to look to me, O my beloved, for you shall lack no bread to eat, water to drink, food for thought, nor any joy to please.
Kings and queens shall come to your aid, seeking advice, and you are to give them my Word.
Destroy the schemes of the enemy with his own sword, just as David did to Goliath and Jesus to Satan.

Know that this is the day I have chosen for you, so that all may see my glory revealed through you.
People from everywhere will be drawn to your light.
Fly on high in the midst of all this darkness surrounding you.
Soar like an eagle in the sky above the clouds, far above destruction, corruption and deadly pestilence.

Amen

Love

Job 19:25 **I know that my redeemer lives, and that in the end he will stand on the earth.**

Journey
- 242 -

FOREVER YOURS

Child, the time is coming when you will no longer be able to stand on your own two feet. The day is coming when you will need to be rescued from all that is happening to you and around you.
There are major strongholds ruling the world-- you must learn to free yourself as well as others from their grip.

You will not fall into the enemy's camp, for you are distinguished by grace. These forces of darkness have strategies and are well advanced. But remember: You are above them all, because greater is He who is in you than he who is in the world.
They are strategically forming an alliance against you to pull you down, but you are the head and not the tail.
You shall prosper and they shall be ruined. You will win and they will be lost forever. You will flourish and they will wither and die. You shall increase and they will decrease.
You will be honored and they will be dishonored.
You will live and they will waste away. You will have that knowing and they will be clueless. You will heal and they will become sick.

All this-- is, because I am honored by you.
They will even try to distract, ruin and destroy your life if they can, all because of your love for me. Keep in mind: The One, who is in you, is far greater and much more powerful than all the forces of darkness put together; so be encouraged.

Amen

Love

Rom 15:17 Therefore I glory in Christ Jesus in my service to God.

Journey
- 243 -

THE GOAL OF YOUR DREAMS

Step out, save the world from its immediate state of destruction by love and deep compassion, for I have raised you up for such a time as this.

The conclusion of things are not yet over; so be healed and set free to soar.

The Alpha and the Omega I am.
Your Restorer and Deliverer of souls - I am He.

Accomplish much and much more shall be added unto you.
Keep safe and warm in my loving arms while tending my sheep, for my lambs will rest safely in peace.

My companion is my Friend, O Savior, and you are the Giver of Life.

Endure hardship, O child of my loins, and do not be reluctant to waste time on anyone who is in desperate need of me.
Come to my River of Delight and swim in my Grace of Love.

Deep compassion with tender mercy is of me.

Your future is born of Today.
Run and neglect not my hope within you.

Your hope of tomorrow has just begun.
It is here for you today, for all eternity.

Amen

Love

Psa 126:3 *The LORD has done great things for us, and we are filled with joy.*

Journey
- 244 -

THE WELL IS DEEP

Be gracious to yourself and attend to my Word.
Travel through the Scriptures of my Word and find yourself.
Be ready to go places unheard of before this day.
See the world through my eyes; then you will make better choices and decisions.
Speak the words of my Kingdom, that I may hear and respond.
Obey what I say and you will be refined, rejuvenated and ready to do mighty works.
This is not a temptation, but a depth of insight.

Soak in my presence and be glorified.
You will not find the fulfillment you are searching for by the fixations of this world.
Only by the power of my spirit can you ever be released.
Listen carefully to my words of insight and you will be enlightened.
Challenge yourself and go beyond all measures.
Never give into temptation.
Evil is not of me; free yourself and run.

Your need of me is severe and desperate, yet you continue to refuse what I am offering you - The fullness of all my facets.

The journey of life is amazing if one knows how to live in spirit.

Amen

Love

Isa 1:26 *I will restore your leaders as in days of old, your rulers as at the beginning. Afterward you will be called the City of Righteousness, the Faithful City."*

Journey
- 245 -
PURE THOUGHTS

Since you died to the worthless attractions of this world, why do you act as though you still live for them?
Why be submissive to their rules?
Do you not know I am the Way, the Truth, and the Giver of Life?
You were once living in darkness, but now you are children of light, living in the hope of glory.
You are called by my grace alone, so roam as you please in my resurrection life.
Live in the Light as a child of God, and worry not about tomorrow.
Give me reverence that you may be honored.

The time is now, and the end for a new beginning has just begun.
Throw off everything that hinders and the temptations that linger.
Your struggle is not against human experiences, culture and nations, but against the spiritual forces of evil, against the rulers and authorities in the heavenly realms of this dark age.

So my friends, since you know the Way, continue to be a blessing without ceasing or holding back.

God did not set you apart from birth to lead a simple life, but to have an extraordinary love affair with the Almighty.
He was pleased to reveal his grace in you, so that through you, the multitudes may believe.
Be kind-hearted, and reveal my glory through love.

Amen

Love

Jer 29:13 **You will seek me and find me when you seek me with all your heart.**

Journey
- 246 -
YOUR FUTURE IS BRIGHT

I am the One, who protects you from danger and comforts your heart from sorrow and grief. Will you now listen to me and obey?
Will you repent and not challenge my authority?
Will you stop chasing fantasies and go after that which is Best.
No more wasting time on that which is corrupt, deadly and unyielding?
Will you study and memorize the Scriptures?
Will you complete your journey here on earth for a new beginning?
Will you finish the task appointed?
If yes, come join my choir and sing the Hallelujah song with my angels in heaven.

Rescue me, Oh, Lord, rescue me from my present circumstances, that are controlling my life. Set me free from my prison walls, that I may be released to do your Will. I want to be caught up in the clouds to meet you in the air, and so be with you forever.

The darkness is swallowing up the people of this world, child, but you are to remain faithful, true to the Light.

Escape all that is coming upon society by being pure and sure of your salvation, for your life depends on it.
Destroy sin in the flesh, and you will be called an overcomer.
Heal thyself from every obstacle opposing you and never look back.

Amen

Love

Mat 4:16 *the people living in darkness have seen a great light; on those living in the land of the shadow of death a light has dawned."*

Journey
- 247 -

ANCHOR OF DELIVERANCE

Teach little children the Way of Truth and assure them of my love.
Do not be afraid of what is yet to come upon the earth.

No harm nor danger will come near you.
Your household and children will also be safe and protected from the storms of life that shatter.
You are, my beloved, my beauty on earth and honor of fame.
How can I let myself be defamed?

Distance yourself from evil schemers, negative operators, wicked treacherous-- Those evil doers who practice deceit. They have no support or substance. They are backsliders. They lack confidence and have nothing good to say. Their idea of pleasure is to carouse in broad daylight and sniff you throughout the night. They conjure up ways to pull you down from your high position and rejoice in their evil deeds. They are brutes, risen from the grave. Stay away from such as these conniving mutilators of the flesh, for there is nothing good in them. They are as hot as an iron, hot-tempered arrogant beasts... they defile you. They lift up your skirt in the presence of everyone to bring you shame and think nothing of it. They delight in their own wickedness and encourage others to do the same.
They will be paid back for the evil they have done.
Do not fear their threats... They are slime.

Be comforted - Your redemption draws nigh.

Amen

Love

Psa 37:11 **But the meek will inherit the land and enjoy peace and prosperity.**

Journey
- 248 -

GROW IN WISDOM

I am your Security and burden Relief.

Fear not, the days of grace are not yet completely over.
These are just the beginning of labor pains.
The earth is drowning in its own sorrow; crying out for help and support; retaliating, because the foundations are tilting.

Neglect not my Word which can save you.
Serve me in honor and give me your all in praise.

Your sorrows shall soon end, and your wounds disappear, fade away and heal.

By the praise of your worship, I shall be lifted up from the earth.

Refresh, take time out, and run with the wind of my grace.

Your sores have been cut off from your body... you are now healed.

This is the time for my favor upon your life.
You have labored hard, and this is the gift due you.
You have followed me wholeheartedly, and you will now reap the rewards of your labor.

Listen and heed my instruction without retreat.
Never give up.
Offer your life to the poor, lost and needy, and I shall direct your footsteps in my loving kindness.

Amen

Love

Psa 33:4 *For the word of the LORD is right and true; he is faithful in all he does.*

Journey
- 249 -

POWERFUL YET LOYAL

Consider carefully what you have heard and learned from me, and put it into practice.
Apply your heart to understanding and walk in my ways.
Consider the things shown you and in persistence learn from them.
Fix your gaze upon me without retreat.
I am your Beginning and End, the Alpha and the Omega of your life. I will help you and look after your children. Your every need meet. Even during time of hardship I shall watch over you and continue to provide.

You shall soar on the greatest heights into paradise and on my wings of worship rise.
I shall carry you through the deepest darkness, and you will want for nothing.
Do not fear or dread what they fear or you may just be terrified.
Do not be afraid or you may be weakened by oppression.
Lack not the strength to overcome difficulties.

You shall winnow the mountains and crush them... the wind will pick them up and a gale will surely blow them away.
You shall rejoice in your Creator, for your Maker is great.

The tables have now turned against your enemies.
You shall only rejoice from here on...

Amen

Love

Isa 64:4 Since ancient times no one has heard, no ear has perceived, no eye has seen any God besides you, who acts on behalf of those who wait for him.

Journey
- 250 -

ATTENTION REQUIRED

I am the Vine of your life - You are the branches of my Tree of Hope, and the Father is the Gardener of souls.

The work of God which needs persistence has been entrusted to you.
Do you not realize that He who is with you is not against you?
Do you not also know, that friendship with the world is hatred towards the Almighty?

You, O my people, live an honorable life.
Live to imitate the One, who created you - The Giver of Life.
Partake of my nature and zeal and live a healthy prudent lifestyle.

I am Righteous and Gracious in all that I do.
The Creator is close to the broken-hearted and lifts up all who are bowed down. He is close to those who call on Him, to all who call on Him in truth.

Fan into flames the gifts imparted to you, and consider my ways, put them all into practice, without wavering or giving up.
Trust not the flesh, for you will only be disappointed.
Keep your speech filled with grace and flavored with salt, for you are the salt of the earth.

I am with you always. Do not lose sight of me.

Keep your focus on the mark and constantly give me the praise.

Amen

Love

Psa 67:1 **May God be gracious to us and bless us and make his face shine on us—**

Journey
- 251 -

VITAL SACRIFICE

I am your Friend, do not ignore my invitation.
I, the One, who welcomes you into my eternal glory with arms open wide will rescue you from violence, extend loving kindness to your family and lead you towards righteousness. They shall all dwell in safety and be rescued from the snare set before them by the enemy. There is stormy weather ahead... be cautioned.

Rejoice with those who rejoice and keep to yourself in time of sorrow. There is a Friend, who sees your every need and hears your every whisper. Weep with those who are weeping, confused and are in turmoil. Encourage those who are rejected by the world, and with my loving kindness see them saved, assured and secure.

I am, your Savior, and there is no other.
Believe, lest you be defeated by discouragement.
I am the Alpha and Omega of your life, the Living God, who watches over you day and night.

Whisper in my ear the music of love and I shall comfort your heart from the coming storms, hurricanes and weapons of war, that are heading towards the universe.
Serve me shoulder to shoulder, and live by my honor of grace supporting you.

Amen

Love

Isa 40:28 *Do you not know? Have you not heard? The LORD is the everlasting God, the Creator of the ends of the earth. He will not grow tired or weary, and his understanding no one can fathom.*

Journey
- 252 -

PURIFICATION

Remember, the evil one has been destroyed, O my good, faithful, and obedient child. He has no power over you. He has been stripped naked, completely exposed before all who believe.
No weapon raised against my redemption power shall seize you, for the glory alone is mine.
Lay your fears aside, for they do not exist.
The enemy has no power to destroy you, nor snatch anything away from you.
It is now complete. I have completed it once and for all.

Come, rush into my Kingdom with great speed and finality.
Now... now... now... is the time!

Do not call me, Father, unless you are willing to listen, obey my voice and live by my truth of love, having a Father-son relationship.

I seek truth in the inner parts; honoring those who yield their hearts to me.
Those who are sincere will reap their reward of success in love.
You shall not be burdened by any form of trouble, nor falter during times of distress.
I shall uphold your position and you will not fall.
I am your Teacher of Truth, your Savior in love and Best Friend.
Pure in the making.

Amen

Love

Jer 1:19 They will fight against you but will not overcome you, for I am with you and will rescue you," declares the LORD.

Journey
- 253 -

THE GLORY IS MINE

Grow strong, O you mighty warrior.
I will make you bold and beautiful, firm and tender.
I shall care for you, and train your fingers for battle.

Master your gifts, O precious one.
Stand strong, and fight for your life and the lives of your children.
Nothing by any means shall come against you or harm you.

You are not of this world, nor should you think like it.
Though you live in the world, you are not to be part of it.
Carry not its nature, nor mingle in its deceit - It is an evil practice.
Clothe yourself with my salvation and you will be upheld in victory.
Tighten your belt of truth firmly around your waist.
Take my words seriously and be diligent.
Take to heart what I say to you, and shun away from any form negativity.

I, the Spirit of Love, who lives in you, is great.
Your footsteps shall be protected as you diligently honor my Name, and with sound instruction you will be directed.

Those who seek me early shall find me-- they shall live in my Truth and share my Wisdom, Knowledge and Understanding.

Take courage... you will not be defeated, neglected nor ever be put to shame.

Amen

Love

Pro 28:1 ...*the righteous are as bold as a lion.*

Journey
- 254 -

PRODUCE GOOD FRUIT

The road may have been long and steep, Oh, my child, but now the time is short, shortened... on account of my people.
I need you to know, beloved, that my love shall take you far and through you accomplish much.
You shall thresh the mountains and winnow them.
You shall climb the mountain tops and soar above the hills.
You shall speak and everyone will listen.
You have been enlarged by love and increased by grace.
You are about to receive the break of your life.
I shall enable you to climb higher, and your life will never end.
This is a time of testing for everyone. Hold nothing back from me.
I, Love, Am the answer to all your difficulties.

You have learned the secret of things to come.
You have also learned about life, the world and all that is in it.
You have learned about what causes trouble and persecution.
Even now you are learning much from your days of sorrow.
Those who do not know me are in turmoil, they have no peace--tossing and turning all day, they struggle on their beds all night.

Be comforted... you are not on your own, nor will ever be alone. More and more people these days are feeling the pressure, birth pain, changes and renewal of things to come. Remember: During these times of distress and struggle, you shall shine ever so bright.

Amen

Love

Isa 5:26 He lifts up a banner for the distant nations, he whistles for those at the ends of the earth. Here they come, swiftly and speedily!

Journey
- 255 -

THE FACE REFLECTS THE HEART

Without you realizing, Oh, my child; numerous circumstances have brought you closer to me - To my sacrificial Altar - The cross... where I said, we shall always meet, and where you can find me.
At first, you thought you were by yourself working all alone.
But in all these trials and tribulations, I was right there with you, supporting your every move, watching over your every step.
Come join my banquet-- eat and drink your fill, on my table of love, that you may no longer hunger nor thirst again.
Be not discouraged about a thing-- it is all here for you multiplied.
Nourish your soul with my heavenly food, while waiting for my return, and from my banquet of love, drink to flourish.

How can I agree with you, when your ways are not like my ways, nor your thoughts are like mine. Agree with me, that we might be joined as one and multiply. Agree with my words of Wisdom, that you may know the reality of the truth revealed, in order to understand my depth of insight. Believe and you shall receive all that I am offering you from above-- great treasures, for such a time.
Your peace shall run like a river beside quiet waters.
Keep in mind: Distraction will not overcome you a second time around, nor revert your dedication to me.
You will not go unnoticed, for I am the One, who is beholding you.
Be patient and do the work required by completing the task.

Amen

Love

Psa 19:14 *May these words of my mouth and this meditation of my heart be pleasing in your sight, LORD, my Rock and my Redeemer.*

Journey
- 256 -

EMPOWERED TO LIVE

*O Redeemer of hearts, my persecutors surround me, and I'm in need of your help. Help me, Oh, Lord, help me quickly, during this time of weakness and struggle I ask. I am burdened and weakened by all these troubles; feeling anxious and desperate... Oh, rescue me.
My desires are wasting away, and I feel neglected.
My heart is melting deep within me, and I feel unsupported.
What am I to do... What am I to do... Oh, God of my eternity?*

*Hear me, Oh, Healer, hear me and heal my aching heart from sorrow, anxious thoughts, and horrifying pain. Deliver me from this destruction - Destructive forces surrounding me... trying to confuse me. I have lost all that I could gain and more.
Here I am laying before you, empty and destroyed. Help me I pray.*

*Snakes surround me, a brood of vipers entangle me. But you, O God of my eternity, are the strength of my being, my safety net in time of trouble.
Help me, Lord, for I hear trouble around me.
I am entangled and desire to be released from my prison chains.
To whom shall I go? Who would listen?
To whom shall I escape? Who am I? Where am I?
Should I run away or should I seek your face?
Should I be here or should I be there? Tell me, O Righteous Holy One.
Help my little soul. I am dependent on you!
You are all I have... my Companion and Friend in time of need.*

Amen
Love

Son 7:10 *I belong to my beloved, and his desire is for me.*

Journey
- 257 -

ETERNITY AT HAND

Rejoice in your Maker and in all that He has achieved for you.
Confide in me and release your burdens.
You are not alone.
You are called by grace to be strong in love and steadfast in faith.
I, your Ruler have called you to live the blessed life.
Encourage one another in love and live the Real Life - the Pure Life.

Be not discouraged. I need you to remain faithful and true, without corruption or exposure to the ways of the world.
Keep your eyes pure, fixed on me and your gaze upon my throne of honor, that you may run the race with great perseverance, without retreat, worldly influences and disturbance.
The world in its present state is wasting away... on its way out.
Now that you have been birthed again into my spiritual realm of love, settled in a new environment, and walked into a new system, into a new level of glory-- keep yourself washed, sanctified and purified.
Go and reach the multitudes, my little one.
Preach the message of salvation to all nations. Preach to small and great alike, and I shall confirm my Word with signs and wonders.
You have nothing to fear.
My grace shall accompany your salvation.

Amen

Love

Hos 6:3 **Let us acknowledge the LORD; let us press on to acknowledge him. As surely as the sun rises, he will appear; he will come to us like the winter rains, like the spring.**

Journey
- 258 -

SUBMISSION TO THE CALL

My heart is burning with such great warmth and affection for you, Oh, child of my Kingdom. My compassion is moved to another level. For though you ran with other gods at one point, who are not at all gods, but only idols - You remained mine.
My compassion is aroused, stirred up deep within me, and I am calling you back home to me - To your rightful place of honor.
Return, Oh, child, return to me, from the proud, ruthless and cruel.
Return to your haven - Your place of refuge.
Everyone who disturbs you will be put to shame and confusion.
Those who wage war against you, are also waging war against me.
These people have nothing else better to do than give you a hard time. They are lost sheep, not of my Kingdom.

Listen to the sound of my love... the whisper of my voice within your heart, and call upon my Name.
Arise and shine, for your Light has come. Your King is coming on his bridal horse, coming to sweep his bride off her feet - You.
Rejoice, for your King is coming without delay.
Remember who I am, in the midst of all this storm and waver not.
I am coming to you soon, coming to take you home to be with me forever, O beloved. Look no further.

Redeem the brothers, O Redeemer of souls, that they may see your face and glorify you on that day - the day of redemption.

Amen

Love

Gen 45:20 **Never mind about your belongings, because the best of all Egypt will be yours."**

Journey
- 259 -

BEHOLD MY NAME

Enlarge the place of your tent.
Stretch your tent curtain wide and be developed by grace.
Hold back from me no longer, for I am truly on the way.
Regain strength to recapture the sight of love once again.
Be self-controlled and endure hardship.

Honey is sweet, but too much of it will make you feel sick.

You shall spread to the right and to the left, and conquer cities that are not your own. Your children shall settle in them, and be blessed in the Land of my Promise.
You shall prosper and rejoice in your Maker, for all the wonderful things he has done for you.
I, your God, have spoken and I, shall fulfill all my promises.

Since no one can proclaim the former things: I have declared an oath in my honor-- only you, have I chosen of all the people on the face of the earth. You are my tribe, my very own treasured possession. Declare my likeness to a people who are not yet born, Oh, man of God. You call me Master and rightly so, for that is **what** I am - Your Leader. You can also depend on me, for that is **who** I am - Faithful.
Now that you know **who** I am and **what** I do... be and do likewise.
Run without ceasing, for the time is now!

Amen

Love

Psa 119:133 **Direct my footsteps according to your word; let no sin rule over me.**

Journey
- 260 -

ANGELIC DIVINE

I, your God will make you known to your enemies.
They will not be able to withstand the power you carry.
During time of war, I shall make you strong, and during time of peace, you shall rest your head upon my shoulder of love.
You shall acquire much, and much more shall be added to you.

Reveal me to your family, that they too may see the days ahead and acknowledge my Name.
Speak the truth to them, and no longer hide me away.
They shall turn to me with all their hearts and be established.

Be not afraid, I have taken great delight in you.
Your work will not be overlooked.

You shall take great delight when you see them streaming towards my altar of praise, and your heart will be filled with joy.
You shall grow in honor and overflow with grace.
You shall rise to maturity, become complete, and not lack anything.

Your King of royalty is Faithful, beloved.
You need not lose hope nor your vision of glory.

For your information, I have called you before the creation of the world to be my very own... so rest assured.

Stand still and know that I am your Cornerstone of Blessings.

Amen

Love

Pro 6:22 *When you walk, they will guide you; when you sleep, they will watch over you; when you awake, they will speak to you.*

Journey
- 261 -

WATCH YOUR FOOTSTEPS

Choose to have me first in your life, O child, for my ways are not your ways. In weakness, I shall make you strong.
My Name is a Strong Tower, like my Word that shatters, like a hammer that crushes down the strongholds-- uprooting accusations and resisting opposition.

I am your fortified City during time of war.
Put on the full armor of God, and waver not in your faith.
I shall take you up the mountain and be with you down the valley.

Even though you live in this world, you my friends, are not of this world, nor should you be wasting time on the system of this world... which is coming to nothing.
Do not wage war like the world does.
Your weapons are mighty, bearing supernatural strength, divine power and illuminating presence... blinding the enemy.
I am your Divine Weapon, by the power of my Spirit through faith.
In my Name, all things are possible, accomplished and fulfilled.

Strengthen your heart, by my heart of worship, and do not be weakened by the temptations of this world.
See to it, that you do not miss the Way by walking in the old way.
Give me your all and rest with me eternally.
I am the Light of your inheritance.

Amen

Love

Psa 119:154 *Defend my cause and redeem me; preserve my life according to your promise.*

Journey
- 262 -

PRODUCE GOOD FRUIT

Even I, am He, who comforts you.
Who are you, that you fear mortal men, the sons of men who are but a breath, that you forget God your Strength? Your Maker, who stretched out the heavens and the universe on your behalf, and laid the earth's foundation, sealing it with a kiss... Is your Ultimate.
Why are you in constant terror because of the oppressor, who is bent on destruction? Where is the wrath of that oppressor?
The cowering prisoners shall soon come home. They shall profit in their dungeons and be unshackled from their prison walls.

I am the God of all those who love you.
I do all that I please, at any time I choose.
Who can confront me with wrongdoing? The Lord of all, I Am.
I have put my words in your mouth and covered your shame.
In righteousness, I have set you apart for myself.

Do not put your trust in mortal men, for they are only but dust... fading away to nothing.
Maintain your standards, and make your requests known to me.
I am the Lord, your God, who loves you - Your Redeemer of hearts.
Acknowledge me, and you will be glad you did.
Forget the former things, for new things I now declare to you... before they spring forth, I announce them to you.
Speak of my Kingdom and righteousness to your family, for they are ready to listen, and you will be glad you did.

Amen
Love

Psa 56:11 *in God I trust and am not afraid. What can man do to me?*

Journey
- 263 -

MAKE ME KNOWN

Surrender your all to me, O my son, and reap a harvest of righteousness for your fruitful labor.
I have given you everlasting peace to love and grow.

Offer me the best that you ARE, and your plans will definitely succeed. Bless and you will be blessed, ask and you shall receive, seek and you will find.
Knock on the door of my heart and heaven will open wide.

I have chosen you, O mighty warrior, to do mighty acts in my Name, that would shock the world.
I have brought you close to me, that you may be entangled by Love.
I have known your ways, now come to know mine.
Give me your all, not just a small portion of yourself.
I shall fulfill your desires, wants and needs, for I know them all...
desires that I myself have placed within you.
Seek no one else to fulfill them.

I know all things... nothing is ever hidden from my view.
Never underestimate my power entrusted to you.
I am your Healer, Deliverer, Shepherd, Gentle Lamb and Best Friend.
I shall restore double for all your losses.

Amen

Love

Isa 58:11 The LORD will guide you always; he will satisfy your needs in a sun-scorched land and will strengthen your frame. You will be like a well-watered garden, like a spring whose waters never fail.

Journey
- 264 -

AN IMPORTANT MESSAGE

I believe in you, Oh, my sweet child of Love, I believe in you.
Run and never tire of running the course of life, set out for you since time began.
Never seek the past for help or support, but only recall the lessons learned from mistakes made and apply them well.
I have already wiped away some of these memories from your mind and will continue to do so, for they are not beneficial.

Remember, I am your Friend and intimate Love.
What I desire for you, no man can do for you.
Hold on and let us begin our journey together.

Hold my hand and lead me, Oh, my God and eternal Glory.

O beloved, never wander from the path of Life.
You have received much, and much more shall you be given-- much more is coming your way yet.

Look no further, for your day has just begun.
You have no idea, what I have in store for you-- great blessings stored up for you to receive are beyond imagination.
You shall flourish to move forward.
What I have prepared for you, O my precious one, cannot be measured and will only be given to you and to you alone.

Amen

Love

Isa 40:31 **but those who hope in the LORD will renew their strength. They will soar on wings like eagles; they will run and not grow weary, they will walk and not be faint.**

Journey
- 265 -

BE STRONG TO CARRY ON

Continue to walk with me wholeheartedly, O my precious one.
I am not unjust. I understand your endurance, for the sake of my Name. I love you, O how I love you, child. You belong to me.
Those who touch you, touch the apple of my eye. You are mine, and I am your Great Weapon of Defense. Stand firm in the faith and rule over them. Rule over these circumstances, that are holding you back from moving forward with me. Bold and courageous you shall always be. Remain strong and steadfast in righteousness, and watch your enemies cower before you. They shall all be crushed before you and under your feet lay. I have given you rest from all your enemies, you have nothing to fear or worry about.

Continue to prosper, and do not give up on me nor on yourself.
I am pleased with you, pleased to give you the treasures of heaven.
Since you love righteousness and hate wickedness, I, your God, shall fulfill the desires of your heart, and anoint you with the oil of joy - The sacred oil of my anointing.
Overflow with thanks, and let the fullness of my love reside in you.
Act in accordance to my Will at all times, and never give up.
Continue in what you have learned from me, and became convinced of, without retreat or second thoughts.
I have confidence in you, that you will continue to do the very things shown you on the Mountain... which I have commanded.

Amen

Love

Pro 5:21 **For your ways are in full view of the LORD, and he examines all your paths.**

Journey
- 266 -
THE OLD IS NO MORE

Do not waste any more time on worthless things that do not count in my Kingdom... reconcile yourself to me instead.

I am waiting for your return. Am I to be despised for that?

When you are confronted, face it like a man of faith should. I am your God, your Deliverer and your Protector.

Despise not my Name and corrupt not thy morals.

I am all, in all, and through all everything. Make up your own mind, who you will serve!

Do not allow anyone to manipulate your mind, nor your way of thinking. I am the Way, the Truth and your very Life Breath-- both now and forever more, in every way and at every moment.

Reflect my likeness, that my grace may be evident to all.

In due season, I shall reveal myself to you, and you will know that I am, who I said I am - The great I Am.

Your sins are forgiven on account of my sacrificial blood shed for you on the cross.

No matter what the circumstances are, all is well, all is good, and all shall be restored back to you... double time.

Amen

Love

Psa 33:11 *But the plans of the LORD stand firm forever, the purposes of his heart through all generations.*

Journey
- 267 -

I AM YOUR ALL

Give me your heart, not just your possession, and you will see my deliverance. In my presence, you shall be glorified.

I have conquered death, therefore, you have nothing to worry about. Just be strong and courageous to carry on.
You are my warrior of worship, a true saint of the Most High.

Break any chain that may withhold you from turning to me, and keep running my way... in my direction of safety.

The strongholds that laid you waste, shall no longer oppress you.
The enemy has no hold any longer.
You are free to roam in my Kingdom as you please.
Fear nothing, for it is the, 'I' in you, who makes you whole.
Do not be weak or discouraged, for the destroyer has no hold on you, nor will he be able to touch you a second time around.
I am with you, fighting the biggest battles on your behalf.
You will not be defeated. I have rescued you on many occasions.
Do you now doubt my power or zeal?

I told you, that I am coming soon. Why be uncertain now?
Keep your light shining above water and sink not into deep sleep.
Sing on my altar of praise and confine yourself to me.
Sacrifice yourself on my altar of praise, and continue to be obedient to my Gracious Will.

Amen

Love

Joh 5:21 *For just as the Father raises the dead and gives them life, even so the Son gives life to whom he is pleased to give it.*

Journey
- 268 -

BE NOT AGGRESSIVE

My Kingdom is not like the kingdom of this world, nor like anything you have established for yourself.
Come, rest in me and be assured of your calling.
You are called to free others from bondage, strife, tormenting experiences, resistance and pride.
Complete your journey here on earth, for there is no time to waste.
Keep me as the apple of your eye and your number one priority.
I am about to show upon the earth my heavenly signs of wonder.
So be ready and prepared for action.
The way may be narrow, but my highway is sturdy.

You are not kept in darkness, that these disasters should overtake you by surprise; you knew about them since your conversion.

No longer grieve over my lost sheep, instead, encourage them and help them run to me for shelter, for my redemption draws nigh.
Capture the hearts of many before the deeds of darkness rule over.

Take heart and be not afraid. You are free from anxiety.
Run the course of time marked out for you, with great perseverance, and without any pride, hold on to that which is good.
You shall prosper.
Do not linger behind, nor wait for anyone to come help you along, for I am your help and Great Support.

Amen

Love

Psa 36:7 *How priceless is your unfailing love, O God! People take refuge in the shadow of your wings.*

Journey
- 269 -
RULE OVER YOUR FLESH

Oh, my children, why do you hurt me the way you do?
You gain nothing by resisting me and grieving my Spirit!
Why bring upon yourself the consequences of your guilt, sorrow and shame? Do not be like the rest, who have no shame and know not how to blush.
You say you cannot wait for my return and be home with me, yet you continue to do as you please. When are you ever going to be reunited to me and change your ways?
Renew your way of thinking, that you may be transformed into my likeness. Have a new perspective on life, that you may be transfigured - Changed from the inside-out.

You make plans for yourselves without consulting me... without even thinking of having my Will done in your life.
Why children? Why do you ignore me as you do? Why torture yourselves for no reason? Why distort the Word of God for a profit?

Consider the price paid on the cross to set you free.
Acknowledge my Way of doing things, and repent from willful sins, crime and rebellion, that I may return to you soon.
How long must I wait for you, children, and endure grievous moments that you cause me?
Do you not know that I am interceding for you, my friends?

Let go and soak in my presence.

Amen

Love

Psa 119:103 *How sweet are your words to my taste, sweeter than honey to my mouth!*

Journey
- 270 -
SECURITY IN LOVE

Look to the hills and see where your help comes from.
Your help comes from your Maker, the Creator of heaven and earth. He shall not slumber, nor sleep, nor be out of reach.
Safe in his tender embrace you shall rest and always be.

Even though you had to endure much difficulty, you stood strong, firm and courageous. You did not waver under trial, nor give into temptation. You remained strong, aloof and steadfast.
You conquered and won mighty battles.
You have passed the test of time, trials and temptations.
You are a conqueror, and you shall give my glory to no other.

Apart from loving one another, and doing what is right, nothing else should be more important than me.
Your faith in my Word shall reward you abundantly, for you shall reap a harvest if you do not give up.

The word of your love sustains me, O Creator of hearts, and I am taken by your greatness and goodness to us all.

On your behalf, I shall recover the lost, and everything that has breath... including every loss.
Your Creator is calling you to Himself.

Keep in mind: The purpose of my sacrifice was for you.

Amen

Love

2Co 9:11 You will be enriched in every way so that you can be generous on every occasion, and through us your generosity will result in thanksgiving to God.

Journey
- 271 -
NEGLECT NOT THY MORALS

I am the true way of love and forgiveness.
You shall not be defeated by trouble, for I myself am with you.
I have encouraged you by giving you a hope and a future.

The fire of my love shall burn within you, and turn your enemies away from you, for my flames shall burn their wickedness to ashes. You shall stand strong and mighty, declaring my freedom to every nation.
I have called you for such a time as this-- now act on my Will in the presence of them all. You will not be torn to pieces by them.
I have summoned you by name, charge on and never give up.
I shall comfort you, and you will be comforted over my people.

You will be supported from every angle.
Fear no disaster, for it will not come near you, nor reach you a second time. I have covered you in the palm of my hand, so that others may not see you, but only the 'I,' in you, shall be recognized. To some you shall remain invisible, while to others, you shall be seen to be known by Me - Your Author of life - The great I Am.

You shall not be crowded by trouble, for I have given you another chance to accelerate. The majority are crying out, but I have chosen you, for such a task as this.
Prepare for action and be ready... fully charged and armed.

Amen

Love

Psa 86:17 *Give me a sign of your goodness, that my enemies may see it and be put to shame, for you, LORD, have helped me and comforted me.*

Journey
- 272 -

A DISTINGUISHED LIFE

I have given you many revelations, rewards, as well as special gifts to behold.
Comfort those who are willing and wailing on their sick bed.
Have them run to my arms of love, for I am here for the rescue.

The Crown of Life awaits your arrival.
Draw closer, for my return draws near.
I have promised you many good things which I am about to fulfill.

Be ready and run, before the world topples from its place, and destroys its inhabitants further.
Be not robbed of the Secret Treasure hidden within you.
Guard all that I have entrusted to you... guard them well with the help of my Spirit within you.

My resurrection life will restore, renew and cover all your offenses.

Keep in mind, that your burdens are my burdens, and your tears become my tears of sorrow.
Be restored and uplifted.
Forget the days of old when it was all too hard.

As you progress, prosperity shall overtake you, and many good days ahead you shall see.
The future awaits your arrival.

Amen

Love

Psa 20:4 **May he give you the desire of your heart and make all your plans succeed.**

Journey
- 273 -

UNDYING LOVE

I have freed you from every burden and delighted myself in you.
Do you now wish to leave me behind?
I have helped you climb the mountains and ascend to the heavens.
Do you now wish for me to leave you alone?
I have taken your burdens upon my shoulders and set you free
from the sting of death. Do you now choose to be elsewhere?

You are the apple of my eye, my pleasure and great delight.
Create a new world for yourself from within.
Remember never to forget.
Remember my love lest you forget my grace.

Hallelujah to you, O my Anchoring Hope.
You alone know the thoughts of man and their intentions.
You have never neglected a prayer of mine, nor ever forsaken those
who cry out to you from their core being; from the depth.
I understand, that the righteous is taken away to be spared from evil.
Savior, you are my King; I care very little about what the world is
saying. My interest is in you and all about my future with you.
Thank you for removing every obstacle out of my way, and turning
my thoughts around to suit you.
You are wonderful in Counsel and complete in love.

Remember: Your growth is found in me - Your Maker.
Your constant provision of Grace... I am.

Amen

Love

Job 8:7 **Your beginnings will seem humble, so prosperous will your future be.**

Journey
- 274 -

PREVAILING LOVE

Oh, my children, my children.
Why abuse yourselves in the manner that you do?
You leave the straight and narrow to follow your own natural instinct, desires, greed, lust, the world and all that is in it.
Be careful or you may become enticed and ambushed by it!

Accept Him whose Word is True, and do not go after ill-gotten gain. It is of no value to you and only ruins those who partake of its sorcery.
Lost in the midst of the storms, you say.
Be strengthened by grace, so that you will not fall into the trap set for you by the enemy of souls. He knows your weaknesses and all those who are mine... who have been resurrected by my power.
Rule lest you be ruled by false humility, stumble and fall.
Set yourself above your brother and you will surely fall from your high position.
Count it worthy, that I have come to set you free.
Attend to my word and escape the grip holding you back from coming to me in prayer.
Seek me to live and live to know me.
Pardon your brother who is seeking your forgiveness and let your mercy flow.
I have called you in righteousness. Do you now doubt my ability?

Amen

Love

Psa 119:80 **May I wholeheartedly follow your decrees, that I may not be put to shame.**

Journey
- 275 -

FOREVER SEALED

You, my God, are my Sun and Shield - The Beginning and the End of my life, the Alpha and my Omega, my Start and Finish.
You are eternal, and so we your children, shall live with you eternally.
We were made in your image to partake of your likeness.
You, my God, are perfect in every way and firm in all your decrees.
In accordance to your Word we walk, that we may be made whole and complete, not lacking anything.
Under the shadow of your Tabernacle, we rest and give you praise.

Your Spirit teaches us all things and from the abundance of your storeroom, we are filled. You give us food at the proper time and satisfy the desires of every living thing.

In your presence, we are consumed by integrity.
Your words are sweeter than honey to my lips... tastier than the best of wines to my mouth.
Oh, my Refuge, my Source of Strength.
Humbly I offer myself to you, and my knee I bow before your throne.
I have learned to dance in the midst of all this darkness surrounding me, and troubled times suppressing me because your love sustains me.
Your victory is my strength and Source of support.
Tribulation is to no avail-- it cannot even touch me, for I am yours.

Yes, child, you are my very own and am in love with you.

Amen

Love

Joh 17:10 *All I have is yours, and all you have is mine. And glory has come to me through them.*

Journey
- 276 -

IN DUE SEASON

Hold yourself back from me no longer. I am here to give you Life.
Do not let go of me no matter what you may face tomorrow.
Understand my ways and acknowledge my Name.
Do not dishonor my anointing by your own actions of today and so displease me.
Hold on, hold on and do not let go. Hold on with all your might to what you have in me and I will raise you up in due time.
Those who endure will not pay the penalty, nor fall into disaster, like those who reject my good Will and perfect love for their lives.

Your sweet soul is yearning to be loved and accepted by others.
And why not!
Remember, it is I who gives you the pleasure you seek from above.
Do not look down on yourself because you are young.
It is I, who fills your mouth with laughter, and your heart with joy.
Call on me, your Savior and Entirety.
Turn from anything and everything wicked, so that you are not left on your own accord. Say to them: "Away... away with you, away from me, you evildoers, you filthy rags," and they shall flee far from you. Have nothing to do with the wicked schemes of evil men, nor indulge yourself with magic spells, that hinder your calling of me, for my truth remains.
My return draws near. Keep safe and do not become wasted.

Amen

Love

Job 36:16 "*He is wooing you from the jaws of distress to a spacious place free from restriction, to the comfort of your table laden with choice food.*

Journey
- 277 -

YOU SHALL BE LIFTED UP

Do this, so that you will not commit a crime and live in regret.
Be rescued from the pit of destruction and live by grace.
It is time to change - To be made new.
Reflect on what I am saying... it is not yet over.
You call me Abba Father, yet you treat me offensively as if I was an enemy.
When will you learn to call me, 'Father,' and treat me Holy?
When will you grow up and learn my ways? When will you listen?
You do as you please, then come and complain... asking for help.
Why do you do this to both of us? Why do you chase after fantasies and not Reality? Why commit crime and live in denial?

How long must I chase after you? How long must I endure this severe pain you cause to both of us? How long must I put up with you? Why the separation, friend? Why torment your soul, by grieving my Spirit and so become a useless vessel?
Do you believe you are mine? Because I do.
You need to watch your steps carefully.
Your burdens are not your own; they are also mine.
If they are disturbing you, then they are disturbing me also.
Will you not agree, that this is the time to retreat from the old ways of doing things and come to my aid?
Children, delay not my return, neither, stay in your comfort zone.

Amen

Love

Psa 86:12 *I will praise you, Lord my God, with all my heart; I will glorify your name forever.*

Journey
- 278 -

INCOMING CALLS

Prepare your hearts for action, for the time is now.
Be ready. Through the leading of my presence, you shall defeat the wrong, and turn it around to make it right.
The purpose of my Will is to see you fulfilled.
I shall hold nothing back from you, as long as you are with me in the fullness of my reality... not just in dreams or fantasies.
You shall reach higher ground by my ability, and win over the enemy, by the Sword of my Spirit entrusted to you.
Do not argue about words... it is of no value to you, and only ruins those who listen.
Be comforted to know my reward is with me.
Comfort one another with my love and resist temptation at all times. Rest on my bosom of love and compassion.
Give not yourself away to the enemy.
Acknowledge that you may be acknowledged and bless that you may be blessed.
Touch not my anointed. Resist every kind of evil.
Act on my Will and reap the benefits of the true life.

Learn about **what** I do in order to understand **how** to do, what I do.
Your opinion of me shall change once you see the fruitful results.
You will know **what** to do once you understand **how**.
I am always positive... nothing about me is ever negative.
You can become as good as the 'I' in you, if you choose.

Amen

Love

Psa 63:2 *I have seen you in the sanctuary and beheld your power and your glory.*

Journey
- 279 -

A STATE OF RENEWAL

I am the Bread of Life, he who comes to me, I will never drive away... contrary to what the world does to its own inhabitants.
You will never hunger nor thirst, for the Greater One lives and dwells within you.
Come to me, O little ones, and I shall give you rest in my comfort.
Come you Israelites, come to my loving arms of rest.
I have seen your tears and watched over your ways.
I am willing to rescue you from all your troubles and shame.
I have heard your cry and seen your tears.
I will bless you and not reject you, nor will I ever leave you lonely.

My heart is grieved over my children. Why you ask?
Because their tears are not of me, but only for themselves.
They only wish to receive from me the desires of their own greed.
Can you not see; do you not realize, that my thoughts are not like their thoughts, nor my desires are like theirs?
Definitely, we are not equal. This too is ridiculous.
Why do you burden me with trouble... the troubles you have brought upon yourselves?
You have opened the door to destruction and fallen into a hole.
Care nothing for the world, but only for the One who is living in you - The 'I Am' within.
Comfort yourself in me and thrive to reach my fullness.

Amen

Love

Psa 18:48 **who saves me from my enemies. You exalted me above my foes; from a violent man you rescued me.**

Journey
- 280 -

FORGET THE OLD WAY

Test yourself, so that you may not need to be disciplined.
Humble yourself, so that you do not need to be humbled.
Since you call me 'Father' treat me like One... as a child should.
Discipline yourself and walk in total obedience to me, that you may prosper and live a healthy lifestyle.
Live with me, for I am the Alpha and the Omega.
Seek peace and pursue it, then you will find green pasture.

I have placed your enemies under your feet, never to rise again.
The things of old are not the same as today.
I know all about your troubles and persecutions, the sufferings you had to endure, but worry no longer, for all is over now.
I have come to rescue you, and will always snatch you out of the fire, that would try to kidnap you away from me. The hand of him who destroys and ruin lives shall be cut off-- dare he try again.
I myself am your Deliverer.
No one can touch you without my approval.
You need to persevere and see through my eyes the welcoming presence of my Majesty.
I have approved you into my Kingdom, and the honor is mine. See me as I am. See through my eyes and you will not be deceived.
Your enemies are my enemies. Whoever touches you destroys himself, but to him who shows you kindness, I will surely bless.
Your eternity is with me. Rest assured.

Amen

Love

Pro 10:4 *Lazy hands make for poverty, but diligent hands bring wealth.*

Journey
- 281 -
LEAN ON ME

*I have complete confidence in you, Oh, my Heavenly Savior.
I shall sing and make music to your Name, for your Name is great.*

*Wake up, O my soul! Wake up, rejoice in what God, your God, has done for you. Dance and shout with joy for the Kingdom has come.
People everywhere are telling lies about me, but I will not be defeated, for it is you who looks after me and watches over my ways.
The battle has been won, I therefore, cannot lose.
I shall not be afraid... what can men do to me.
The enemy is crushed under my feet, and I have the victory.
I rest my case before you and rejoice in your love.
Rejoice, O heavens, and see the victory of our glorious King.
Oh, my Strength, how I ache to see you soon.
You are honored, before those who love you, and I, your servant, am content, for what you have done for me on the cross of Calvary.*

*Thank you to you, Father, for with you united forever I stand.
I know nothing can or will ever be able to separate us-- no weapon, sin, death, life, authority or anything else in all creation has any power to separate us from your love.*

*O God of love, you have broken off our chains and redeemed us from death.
My heart yields to your Will, and I am honored in the sight of all.
I shall praise you eternally and in reverence, give you the honor due.*

Amen

Love

Psa 119:16 *I delight in your decrees; I will not neglect your word.*

Journey
- 282 -

CREATIVE JOURNEY

Do not think of yourselves more highly than you ought, rather think of yourself as a humble servant, a true saint of the Most High, an instrument of praise to the glory of his Name, godly and righteous-- a man who correctly handles the word of truth.

Be submissive to my rule of love and excel in my form of grace. I am the one who truly loves you, who meets your every need and gives you everything good.

Do not return to your own ways of doing things, nor be a baby any longer, rather be a man of courage and hold your head up high.

Look not to your past nor to your old way of thinking, for the experiences of your past is now gone, dead and buried, done and dusted. You are to look forward to a new day, to a new beginning, to a brighter future ahead.

Drink from the wells of Yeshua - The well of Salvation, not from your muddied water - The cistern of this world.
Pollute not yourself, rather be purified from all lust.
This sort of pollution and greed is rusty and deadly... it carries poison under its tongue.

The new wine from my press is nourishing... bringing forth vitality. O my beloved, how the old has gone, and the new has just arrived.

Amen

Love

Psa 9:10 *Those who know your name trust in you, for you, LORD, have never forsaken those who seek you.*

Journey
- 283 -

THE KINGDOM COME

There is pleasure in remembering my words - My precious promises spoken to your spirit, during time of loneliness, need, struggle, darkness and grief.
I will never deprive you of anything good.
Stay on the mark, pure and clean-- undefiled by the things of this world, that are injuring your mind and hurting you.

I have not deprived you of anything good, nor allowed you to be led astray by the enemy.
You do not need to turn to idols in order to fulfill your cravings.
Come to me for cover and hide, that you may recover the attacks.
Carry your shield.
I have only prepared the best for you.

When you weep, I weep and when you ache, I also ache.
Your strength comes from me, so continue to be encouraged and never give up.

Apart from loving one another and doing that which is right, nothing should be more important than you loving me.

Glorify my presence in the midst of all this darkness strangling your thoughts of me and release yourself from their entanglement.

All things lost shall be recovered.

Amen

Love

Pro 4:10 **Listen, my son, accept what I say, and the years of your life will be many.**

Journey

- 284 -

MEMORIES OF NOW

Be merciful to me, Oh, God of forgiveness, be merciful to your own child. I have suffered much agony, and am tormented, by those who call themselves your children. They heap abuse on me all day, and never stop foaming up lies about me. I have suffered much stress, and pain from those who are called by your Name. They have become my enemies, and I no longer know what to do.
Save me, save me, O Lord, and stop my aching heart from burning. I am tormented in spirit, and my soul is in constant pain and agony because of them. Let me not fight the enemy in the wrong way, for he is trying to snuff me out through them. I must put a stop to him once and for all... by the power of your spirit, wisdom and knowledge. Our struggle is not against human vessels, flesh and blood, but against the deeds of darkness, the spiritual forces of evil, that come through these destructive charmers of wickedness.

I am on your side, child, on the side of truth. Be not discouraged.
Continue on that path which you have come to know about Me.
Even though at present you are passing through tough times,
struggling with the flesh and are challenged to give in and give up.
Do your best to remain steadfast, unmoved by the destroyer.
Hold back no longer.
I have given you power to resist all, except Me.
The fire is in your hands... go out, heal and be a great blessing.

Amen

Love

Isa 33:17 **Your eyes will see the king in his beauty and view a land that stretches afar.**

Journey
- 285 -
ETERNAL DESTINY

I have come to give you Life - Eternal comfort in my presence.
Fear not, for I am with you.
Do not be afraid; I have redeemed you from the curse.
I have turned the tables around. You need not worry.
You are safe in my arms of grace.
I have instructed my angels to keep watch over your steps, lest you strike your foot against a stone.
I have redeemed you from the curse, so that you may be blessed and not condemned.

No one can snatch you out of my Kingdom, for you are in the palm of my hand.
I have given you eternal life, that you may find comfort in my presence.

Submit, and you will see the Light of Life shining upon your face.
Your Savior is here - He has risen.
He will soon bless you abundantly. Is my language not clear to you?

Learn from me and discover new truths about yourself.
Lean not on your own understanding... gain wisdom instead.

Your future is in the here and now - Established.

Drink from the River of Life - Refresh.

Amen

Love

Pro 7:2 **Keep my commands and you will live; guard my teachings as the apple of your eye.**

Journey
- 286 -

REDEMPTION FOR ALL

Take over my life, Oh, great One, take over, that I may sing your praises and be lifted up.
Take me home to be with you when my job on earth here is done.

Do not lose heart, Oh, my child, do not lose yourself, for the time of my return has arrived.

Oh, God of creation, how I believe in you.
I believe in your Will for my life and it is perfect.

Rejoice, son, be joyful and rejoice.
Let your gentleness be evident to all.
I am your Master Teacher, you shall learn and distribute much.
You shall conceive new gifts and manifest abundant life.
I shall achieve much, and through you accomplish much more.
My words of Love placed in your mouth adds flavor to your lips.

Cover me, O Mighty One, cover me with your beauty divine and everlasting love, that I may lift up my voice, and sing your praises.
Help me never fall, waver or slide back... ever, I pray.

Children, O my children, where are you?
Where have you been all this time? Is my presence not enough?

Lord, I need you to be with me forever, for my eternity with you has been made complete.

Amen

Love

Jer 33:3 'Call to me and I will answer you and tell you great and unsearchable things you do not know.'

Journey
- 287 -

WASH YOURSELF CLEAN

Your beauty is sufficient for me, O sweet Savior, just as your mercy is new every morning.
Hold my hand, O my Leading Teacher, and lead me the way.
Lead me in righteousness on the straight and narrow, that I may cross over the land of sorrow and distress.

Guide my footsteps, so that I will not fall and injure myself.
Keep me safe and sound, resting on your bosom of love.
Help me know you better; help me grow in your ways.
Take me by the hand and teach me your decrees.

Guide me, O my Teacher, that I may never falter in my growth, and mission to serve you. I desire to remain strong, walking in the fear of the Lord all day long. Salvation comes from you, and I am helped. I know the One, who works in me, to will and to act, according to his good pleasure.

Save me, Oh, save me from this burden that I am carrying, and restore me to my rightful place in you.
Save me from this trouble that has come upon me.

I believe, therefore, I have received the fullness of your glory.

Restore the joy of my salvation, that I may live a happy life, and glorify your Name.

Amen

Love

Rev 22:12 *"Look, I am coming soon! My reward is with me, and I will give to each person according to what they have done.*

Journey
- 288 -

THINK STRAIGHT

Search to find yourself in me, beloved, and be comforted.

Be resurrected through my Word and you will be denied nothing.
My Word is true and appealing to all who believe.

Neglect not yourself, while looking after everyone else.
Drink from the River of Life and give me all the praise.

I shall satisfy your thirsty land, that you may become a fully grown tree-- delicate and tender, yet mighty and strong.

Reach your full potential in me, and become a fruitful harvest.
Impart wisdom to others, lest you become a fool yourself.
Elevate yourself from trouble and carry no stress.

The cost paid was worth the price.
Your salvation is in the palm of my hand, and my love is truly sufficient.
I will not promise you anything that I cannot deliver, for I am the God of all. I am able to achieve and accomplish all things on your behalf. But are you willing to receive?
Rejoice, for I shall see you through every difficulty.
Worship the Almighty, and know the truth, that sets the captives free.
Illuminate and shine through my Light in a dark and dying world.

Amen

Love

Heb 6:19 *We have this hope as an anchor for the soul, firm and secure. It enters the inner sanctuary behind the curtain,*

Journey
- 289 -
WALK AWAY FROM FALSE ASSUMPTION

Let my holiness shine through you, child, and reveal my beauty to the world, that they may see the Light of Life; come and be saved.

You are an eagle in a bodily form, and I am your Father Figure of Authority, from whom you have learned much.
I am holy, so you too, be holy.
Love the brothers of the faith, and be kind to your neighbor as well.

I have saved you on many occasions, from the hands of the fowler.
Under my feathers, you shall remain safe.
He cannot snatch you out of my hand.
Rejoice and be glad, for I have set you apart, for such a time as this, for this is like no other time.
You do not belong to your enemy, the evil one, but to me your God.
Behold my beauty and grow in stature.
Capture the hearts of many, by doing the Will of God, who dwells and lives in your heart.

You will no longer be restricted, for you have many more places to go and greater adventures to attend.
I am returning very soon. Do you not perceive it?
I am on my way to you, without anyone's permission.
Glorify me in your body, and reflect my likeness in all your ways of doing things, so that others may see the love you have for me, and run to my altar of praise.

Amen

Love

Ex 33:18 ..."*Now show me your glory.*"

Journey
- 290 -

APPROACH THE KING

It is essential and extremely vital, that you pray.
Pray, and I will heal you, and deliver many others through you.
Give your worries, problems, concerns and troubles over to me,
and I will turn your bitter water sweet.
Do not overshadow your life by greed, rather, pamper yourself, by
the washing of my word, through love and forgiveness instead.
Call on me and you will see miracles take place.
Proclaim to your relatives and friends my Word of love and
perfection, and I shall entrust you with more. Salvation shall then
take them by surprise, and sweep over you like a flood.
Rejoice in Spirit and worship me in Truth.
I have protected you, from your enemies, who hounded you on
every side and tormented you like a storm.
My Will for your life is perfect, and it is now complete.

Take care, lest you fall from your secure position.
Your enemy, the evil one, roars like a lion, lurks like a vulture and
hisses like a snake, seeking someone to devour.
Therefore, watch and pray, that you may not fall into his
temptation, like the rest who have no hope.
Be skillful and focused on the goal.
Never forget, that I am with you always and forever more.
Continue, and never give up on me, nor ever turn away from me.

Amen

Love

2Ti 4:18 The Lord will rescue me from every evil attack and will bring me safely to his heavenly kingdom. To him be glory for ever and ever. Amen.

Journey
- 291 -

NEVER LOOK BACK

Grieve not my Holy Spirit, friends, for I took you out of the world and brought you unto myself, into the Land of the Living, where there is green pasture to enjoy.
Offer your thanksgiving on my altar of praise.
Be weary of these wolves who are surrounding you, these imposters who are attacking the world and all that is in it.
Always be on your guard and never neglect your calling, nor your submission to Me. Keep your defenses strong.

Alert yourself daily. Watch and pray.
Take my Word with you everywhere you go, for my Word will give you life and be with you no matter where you are.
Always be where I am and where my Word takes you.

You shall never falter nor fail.

Speak my promises and prophecies into the air, into the atmosphere of your life and the environment will be changed, transformed into directive submission.
Call on me and betray not thy soul nor confidence.
I shall make a way for you in the wilderness, that you may drink fresh water and be supplied.

Master your gifts and remember my promises made to you.

Amen

Love

Rev 3:5 The one who is victorious will, like them, be dressed in white. I will never blot out the name of that person from the book of life, but will acknowledge that name before my Father and his angels.

Journey
- 292 -

THE FRUIT OF LOVE

The Fruit of Love is forbidden, they say.
How wrong they are, my child, O how wrong they are... only if they knew the deep secrets of things.
See things as they really are from now on, child, that you may not be deceived by the charmer, that ancient serpent of old.
See things through my Word, that you may not be deceived by the temptations of this world, presenting delights... remember karma.

Share your secrets, deep secrets with me, beloved, confess them all. I love you deeply. If you are unsure of how much, then share in my suffering, and you will understand the pain endured on the cross. Are you still in doubt? Then, remind yourself of your past dreary days and compare them to your present, Oh, how you have advanced. Since those days - Sale of the century, everything has been sold. Even now the whole world is selling itself cheaply; without a second thought or consideration of Me - The Good I Am.

Resist every temptation facing you, and flee from every kind of evil. You are victorious, therefore, the battle of the end times will not stand a chance against you.
You, O my children, have been purchased by the precious price paid on the Cross - The blood of the Lamb.
Keep your head up, and know, that your name is written in the Book of Life.

Amen

Love

Psa 51:13 Then I will teach transgressors your ways, so that sinners will turn back to you.

Journey
- 293 -

FRUITFUL HARVEST

My Comfort, during time of worry and concern, is that your promise sustains me. I need you, O Heavenly Guide, how I need you.
I need your wisdom to guide me, and your righteousness to lead me.

Comfort my heart in your love, that I may rejoice in your glory.
You shield me from the storms of life, that I may learn to take cover under your wings of love and safety.
You give me the key of victory and I am secure.

As you know, child, I am your Safety Guide, who channels you in the right direction, so that you do not miss the mark.
Yes, I am your Comfort, Support Stream of love, and Source of Strength.
Learn from the experiences of others and do not follow their path of wrongdoing.
Learn for yourself, what is right and wrong, and lean not on your own understanding. You need to learn what to do, when you are faced with situations, that are bigger than yourself.

Inquire of me every step of the way and on all occasions.
I will support you. The answers are within you.
All you need to do is discover the Me in you, to find out who you really are in me.
The time has neither been lost, robbed, or taken from you.

Amen

Love

Psa 28:8 The LORD is the strength of his people, a fortress of salvation for his anointed one.

Journey
- 294 -

PERSECUTION RESISTED

May the King of glory bless you with confidence.
May you be blessed all the days of your life.

Do not be discouraged, just serve the True Living God with pure intentions, sincerity of heart, in love and adoration.

Keep in mind, that without holiness no one will see my face of glory shining through.
Speed my return by your actions of Truth.

Help me, Oh, God of Love, and comfort my weary soul from trouble; from these disasters, that are surrounding my environment. Help me grow under your care, under your wings of love and deep compassion. I love you, God, I truly do. Help me not be aggressive, but rather humble. Help me be true and loving, depending totally on you.

My Name is great.
Do not forget to be obedient to my Will through faith.

I have set you free to worship me.
Now complete your mission through the vision shown you.

Act on that which is best and you will be exalted.
Perfect yourself in love, and be ready to soar on the highest heights.

I shall look after your every need without retreat.

Amen

Love

Heb 11:33 who through faith conquered kingdoms, administered justice, and gained what was promised; who shut the mouths of lions,

Journey
- 295 -

THE CONQUEROR IS NEAR

O my great Shepherd, you are gentle and humble. My soul finds rest in your promises. You have taught me much, and much more I desire to give back to you in return for all your goodness.
Savior, you are awesome, sufficient in all your works.
I thank you for your welcoming grace.

Ride with me, Oh, my child of glory, ride on, and let us fly on high.
Even in the wilderness, you shall find rest for your soul.
Cross over from the old way of living to the new.
Lean not on your own ability, but on my sufficient grace instead.
Establish yourself in my Kingdom, and secure your destiny in the realm of love. Intrigue shall no longer be your downfall. You have truly passed the test of time and crossed over from death to life.
You have made the right decision of leaving those things behind.
No longer stumble over yourself.
Take hold of my Word and run with my revelation of truth.
Hold on to what you have in me and nothing shall be robbed, stolen or lost from you.
Do not slow down, for we have much to accomplish and finalize.
The end has come upon everyone, and we need to awaken the people of the earth to safety.
We need to be saving lives without any hesitation.

Amen

Love

Isa 46:13 *I am bringing my righteousness near, it is not far away; and my salvation will not be delayed. I will grant salvation to Zion, my splendor to Israel.*

Journey
- 296 -

THE ENLIGHTENED WORD

May destruction never touch you Oh, my people, my faithful ones. Be ready, and prepare yourselves, for this is your final journey, because you are now living in the end times. Be sealed in my redemption of grace, before the darkness sweeps over the earth. People everywhere must learn to hear my truth, in order to escape the corruption of this world and all that is about to come upon it.
The world is losing sight of the future, but you are not.
Keep believing, keep marching during times of battle, keep reaching your highest goals, and I will move you to a better place. Rescue the world from its immediate state, by my spoken Truth in love. Redeem them from their ways, that they may escape all that is coming upon the entire world.
The world and its temptations shall pass away, but the man who does my Will, shall stand strong and firm, steadfast and established with me forever.

You are covered with the blood of Life. Journey on...
You have my protection-- sheltered from the storms of life.
I shall bind you to me, and you will be bound forever in my presence - In the Kingdom of Love by choice.
You are not of this world, but of my Kingdom.
You belong to no man, but Me.
I am pleased with you, for you are my very own.

Amen

Love

Psa 119:109 **Though I constantly take my life in my hands, I will not forget your law.**

Journey
- 297 -
SOURCE OF ACTION

Love never ending is what I desire from you, Oh, Lord of my life.

Flourish in the Land of the living by abiding in me.
Walk in the righteousness of my love and you will prosper.

Your beauty is divine, and I desire to walk in your way of truth, Oh, God of the living.

Seek me, child, and live in the Land of the Living; where there is no sorrow nor grief.
Your brothers who desire the same things are unable to reach my glory, but because you have touched the tip of my Scepter; I welcome you into my realm of love.

Lay your requests before me, that I may heed your voice, and obey your commands, Oh, God my Father.

Oh, my child, you know the requirements of the Law. Why query my judgment and question my words? Why doubt my love?

Holy Savior, may I be captured, that I may be raptured.
Gracious One, you have seen my life. Do you approve?

My soul is enraptured by you. May I never leave your place of safety.
May I always be entangled with you and never become untangled.
I faint in adoration of you, O my God.
Through thick and thin I am yours forever... betrothed for all eternity.

Amen

Love

Psa 74:12 *But God is my King from long ago; he brings salvation on the earth.*

Journey
- 298 -

CREATIVE MIND

Rise up, O you mighty warrior and stand strong in battle.
Be not discouraged, for you shall live in my presence.
Fret not; for you shall not lose the battle of the Almighty.
Glory to our Maker - The King eternal.
Rest, O you mighty warrior, rest in the shadow of the Almighty.
Do not wage war against your brother, just defend yourself in spirit.
Mix not the spiritual with the non-spiritual.

Your weapon is not of metal and steal, but of power and might.
You are the head not the tail.
Do not be hindered by the crowd who maligns the word of God for money.
They speak against you and with teeth full of poison spit out lies.
Have no care in the world, for I am with you.
Praise your Maker, who is Me, and continue to be thankful all day, everywhere and in every way.
Rest, Oh, you mighty warrior, rest while in great battle, for you will not be defeated.
This is the day your Creator has made; rest and enjoy the Field of Love. Rejoice, for my warriors are gathering together to be united with you in spirit.
Your shield will not be broken nor damaged, but will remain honorable, intact, in its place, splendorous beyond measure.

Amen

Love

Job 14:5 *A person's days are determined; you have decreed the number of his months and have set limits he cannot exceed.*

Journey
- 299 -

MY FULFILLED PURPOSE

Hold me close to your heart and never let go.
I am your All, in this world of sadness, grief and sorrow.
Do not hold on to anything, that has no value, so that you may survive the deadly experiences most are suffering.
Accept correction from my mouth, and you will heal the sick and be enlightened to do wonders.
Hold to nothing of this world, for nothing really carries any weight, except for my resurrection power.
Put salve on your eyes to view the world differently.
Accept correction before the day dawns.

I will not quieten the rivers for you, nor calm the raging sea on your behalf, for you must put into practice, all that I have taught you and shown you. I have trained you and empowered you, now act on what you know.
I have given you the courage to stand firm and strong.
Bold, you shall always remain faithful.
The One who dwells in you, Is greater, than the one, who is destroying lives.
Rely on your Anchor of hope who stabilizes you.
Weigh your options carefully and consider who you are to follow.
Choose carefully, for I myself, am your Source of Life.
The time is short, but the journey remains the same.

Amen

Love

Rom 14:18 **because anyone who serves Christ in this way is pleasing to God and receives human approval.**

Journey

- 300 -

TAKE A STAND

I am all, in all, and through all everything.
I do not change like shifting shadows.

Behold my glory and compassion.
Worry not about tomorrow, nor about your children, for I am taking good care of them both.
Keep climbing higher, above the mountains and raging seas.
Grow not weary of my Word which is solid for you.
Finally, keep your weapon of armor on at all times.
Stand firm and do not neglect what I have shown you.
Hand in hand we walk on water and cross over on dry sand to reach the Promised Land.
Let the music play and your voice resound.
The future has just begun.
Follow me and do not be disillusioned by trouble.
Keep the fire burning within you through and through...

Your brothers and sisters are crying out to me from everywhere. Will you support them? Will you reveal me to them and extend kindness? Will you show them my love and watch over them? Will you lift them up or condemn them?

Follow me and do not be disillusioned by this world's system of horror.

Amen

Love

1Jn 1:2 *The life appeared; we have seen it and testify to it, and we proclaim to you the eternal life, which was with the Father and has appeared to us.*

Journey
- 301 -

HONOR & MAJESTY

O my warrior of Love, you surely have courage.
I exalted you to the highest place of royalty, and you proved loyal.
I entrusted you with little, and you proved faithful.
I gave you my solemn oath, and you did not relent.
I gave you favor, and you flourished.
I moved you close to my side and you abided.

You, O my special child, are pure in my eyes.
I shall always see you as one perfect in me.
You shall continue to shine throughout the universe... bringing joy to the nations.

I love you as you are.
I would only request one thing, that you mingle with your own kind.
Let the dead bury their own, but you come and follow me - The Rider of the white horse.
View the earth from afar... from where I am.

The snake which I caused you to trample on, is no longer lingering beneath your feet... it has been destroyed, vanished, gone forever.

You will not be subdued by the enemy, for I am your Creator.

The joy is yours, for it is set before you.

Amen

Love

Psa 106:2 **Who can proclaim the mighty acts of the LORD or fully declare his praise?**

Journey
- 302 -

HEAVEN IS OPEN

I am on my way, beloved, on my way to you soon.
Delay not my revival on earth.
Hurry me up by your deeds of action and support.
Draw me near by your valiant faith and courage.
Drift not away from me, nor from my direction of truth, son.

I am not driven by fear, nor by the storms, that entangle your thoughts, but rather by faith and faith alone.

You can do all things through me who gives you strength and ability, as you well know.
Be strong and courageous, for I shall enlighten your being with my presence.
I have chosen you to serve me always.
Do not let your guard down. I am your refuge.

The hills shall shatter before you, and the high mountains melt like wax. With your own eyes, you will see the magnificence of the King in all His glory, and be entranced by his presence.
I shall remove the bad from you and fill you with the good--exchange death for life, and sadness for joy.
I shall add a few more years to your life, and you will prosper greatly. Nothing is ever too hard, difficult or impossible for me to do for you.

Amen

Love

Psa 5:7 But I, by your great love, can come into your house; in reverence I bow down toward your holy temple.

Journey
- 303 -

THE STORY OF US

Father, I am so lonely, empty and burdened, desiring to have someone special in my life. Help me find that just one right person who is suitable for me and my future. Lead me to them or them to me, Oh gracious One. Will you show me how and where to look?
Guide me, Oh, my guiding Light, that I may be a blessing to them.
Help me also be ready I ask... thank you!

Let us move up to a higher place, beloved, up the mountain in love, where we can commune better.
Let us find a peaceful place, where you will feel my gentle breeze upon your skin, hear my voice and act upon my Will.
I will move you to follow me, for this is a delicate matter.
Make room for me in your heart first, then you will know how to love and receive love. Spend time in my presence; then you will know how to live in peace and harmony with someone else.
Become fulfilled in me first, to be enriched to fulfill your duty with another. Be enriched in me first, to fulfill your destiny and become complete with the love of your life. Commit to me first, in order to understand what commitment is, and how to be devoted to someone else in love.
I am willing to set you free, but what will you do at the end?
Love is the answer to all things, as you well know!
You are not restricted... you have plenty of room to move.

Amen

Love

Psa 107:30 *They were glad when it grew calm, and he guided them to their desired haven.*

Journey
- 304 -
LIMITED TIME

May your Will be done in my life, Oh, Lord, that I may serve you wholeheartedly and be responsive to your call.
May your grace continue to spread in my life.

Why don't you, child, why don't you obey my Will and walk in all my ways?
My glory must first be revealed, and my compassion released.

God of Comfort, hold me close to feel your heartbeat of compassion drawing me closer.

How can I neglect my creation, Oh, child-- all those I have formed and made for my glory? Surely I can not!
You are my treasure, my very precious possession.

Forever I shall be singing your praises, Oh my King, forever and ever.

Yes, O my loved one, I have given you the wisdom and the ability to know what to do in all circumstances. Now do what you know best!

Get yourself and everyone around you ready, that they too may know what to do, prosper and live.
Continue to stand firm in your faith, O mighty warrior of worship, that you may be caught up with me in the cloud.

Master your gifts and always remember my promises.

Amen

Love

Psa 132:18 *I will clothe his enemies with shame, but his head will be adorned with a radiant crown."*

Journey
- 305 -

THE REAL LIFE

Help me, Oh, my Support, help me, for you know the rest of the story. I am renewed but also fragile, in desperate need of your touch; in need of your wisdom to support me, and your discretion to watch over me, your discernment to uphold me and your grace to rescue me.

I am fighting the good fight of the faith, but to no avail. I remain aloof... far from your truth. Keep me safe and heal my broken heart. I am broken, revive me, Oh, Lord.

You are my love song during the night and my rising sun throughout the day. My sweet aroma is of your making, O my precious Delight. I need to be transformed, transfigured in your glory to live your life of love in the realm of your spirit.
I seek you, but don't seem to find you! Where are you?

I am right here beside you, holding your hand, beautiful one, crying with you.
When you cry, I also cry... your tears become my tears of sadness, and when you are joyful, I, too am elated.

Run wild in love and concern yourself not with much.
I am here to support you.

I can only give to others what I myself, have received from you... love and compassion. Oh, my Lord, show me your glory!

Amen

Love

Psa 68:6 **God sets the lonely in families, he leads out the prisoners with singing; but the rebellious live in a sun-scorched land.**

Journey
- 306 -

NO MORE TEARS

Accuse not your brother nor anyone else falsely.
Those who accuse you will be judged, but if you accuse, your discipline shall be severe. No pointing of the finger now.

Do away with slander, accusation and gossip of the tongue.
Do to others as I have done and forgive as I have forgiven you.
Run with freedom.
Hold on to the reality of things, not the imaginary things of this condemned world.
Watch and pray, for salvation for every nation is at hand.
Know my Will and act upon my truth revealed to you, for my statutes are beneficial to everyone in this dark and dying world.
Do away with sorrow and despair, for your Source of Life is here.
Sing songs of joy, peace and harmony, rather than songs of grief and disturbance.

I am watching over you. Fear no man.
I am the Comforter of hearts.
Be not disturbed by trouble, nor about what the media is saying or not saying. Look only to me, for I am your Good News, not the daily bad news.

Keep focused and do not lose hope.
The glory is mine and mine alone. The Comforter is here!

Amen

Love

Psa 25:15 **My eyes are ever on the LORD, for only he will release my feet from the snare.**

Journey
- 307 -

DETERMINED FAITH

The joy of Love is your strength, O beloved child.
Do not be easily deceived by false conception, that the Day of my return has come.
Do not believe the world nor anything of the world.
Face it in love, move on and mind your own business.

There are false brothers who are trying to throw you into confusion. You are not to believe a word they say.

Your salvation is sealed and eternally guaranteed.
You have nothing to worry about.

You have gained access by the blood of my Covenant.
You have gained all these treasures in which you are now living.

Do not isolate yourself from the environment, but associate with the right people, instead.
Disaster after disaster shall follow... but will never come near you, nor touch your family.
Turn your ear to me and not away from me.
Inquire of me without any reservation, and I will hear your plea and respond to your every request.

Keeping you safe and sound in my love is my number one priority.
Behold me; I am your Glory and Revealer of truth.

Amen

Love

Isa 38:3 *"Remember, LORD, how I have walked before you faithfully and with wholehearted devotion and have done what is good in your eyes."...*

Journey
- 308 -

BE CAREFUL LEST YOU FALL

Rejoice and be glad, for I have chosen you.
I have brought you out of the darkness and into the Light, that you may benefit and walk in my field of love.

Sing my praises and rejoice in my presence.

The commands given you, by the power of my spirit through Scripture reading are for your wellbeing.

You are my ministering angel, my minister of love, to every tribe, nation and person.

Your confidence comes from me.
Now complete the task placed before you.

Your broken heart of sorrow I shall heal, and your love for people shall increase.
Be a blessing and fear nothing; fear nothing and be a great blessing.
Redeem all things lost, by entering into my Covenant of Love.

I shall bring you relief, and your heart shall rest.
There shall be no more tears, nor sorrow, nor pain.

No longer wander about like a lost sheep in the wilderness, for you serve a great God.
The desert is no longer for you.

Amen

Love

Psa 27:3 **Though an army besiege me, my heart will not fear; though war break out against me, even then I will be confident.**

Journey
- 309 -
POSITION YOURSELF

Continue in the way you have chosen, beloved, and I shall support you every step of the way.
Acknowledge my Name, and I will exalt you among the crowd.
I am pleased with you, pleased with the work of your hands... it is of my spirit. Continue to be accomplished and determined.
Keep me in full view and you will reach your full destiny.
Keep up the good work, and live in the realm of my spirit.
You shall build and succeed, and dust in your hands shall turn into gold.
Your security comes from me, and I am about to anoint you afresh.
Since you are precious and honored in my sight and because I love you... your enemies I shall give in exchange for your life.
Even those who despise you, shall surrender to you, and serve you.

Be anxious for nothing.
I am about to fulfill your every dream and bring every desire to pass. The vision of tomorrow from my heavenly realm of glory is about to be fulfilled in you, and through you to the world.
You dreamed the dreams and saw the visions; now you are about to receive all that is yours-- so indulge. I shall do this to no other person, and before the eyes of all, so that I may be glorified.
Be completely humble and courteous, and rejoice, for it is all coming to pass... even now, it is falling into place.

Amen

Love

Psa 85:12 **The LORD will indeed give what is good, and our land will yield its harvest.**

Journey
- 310 -

REPENT TO BE REDEEMED

Sing and make music in your heart. Rejoice, for your Creator lives.
Disturb not my anointing.
Heal the sick, deliver the needy and convict the guilty.
Hold yourself back not from me.

I am able to do exceedingly more than you can ever ask or imagine.
Just as I have done for you, so now, you too, go and do likewise--
deliver, set free, acknowledge, establish, build up, birth life, rescue
and comfort, for by the power of my Spirit, you can do all things.

I will give you the energy and provision to accomplish your mission.
Go forth without wavering, doubting or fearing.
Nothing, absolutely nothing, can or will ever be too difficult for you
to demonstrate, accomplish and fulfill.

I am the One, who is living among you and also in you.
You now have it all. Go and walk on water.
In my Name, you shall accomplish much and will not live in regret.

Time is of the essence, and your faith has now multiplied.
You are now pregnant with many sons and daughters.
You will soon give birth and call each one by name.

Enhance yourself with me and your youth will be renewed forever.

Amen

Love

Psa 119:73 *Your hands made me and formed me; give me understanding to learn your commands.*

Journey
- 311 -

STRONG YET TENDER

Do not be slow to act, Oh, my child, for the future draws near.
I have called you in righteousness.

I know you tremble at the thought of my Word, so the enemy has no hold on you.
The fear of the Lord is in you because my love has consumed you.

Understand this, child: The day I gave birth to you, was the day I gave life to you. Keep in mind: That I am He, who existed way before you were formed, and way before the world was created.

Be tender in prayer, yet very bold towards your enemy - The evil conniving one.
Be true to your word by keeping to your vows.

I am extending time for you here on earth.
Call on me and you will have a breakthrough with great speed and finality. Hold on to my promises... let them not depart from you.

Child, Oh, my child, I desire to bless you more than you could ever ask or imagine... beyond all your dreams come true.

Oh, my eternal King, how faithful you are to your Word.

Be anxious for nothing, child. I am about to give you nations.
Rest and be assured - Rest and be rested.

Amen

Love

Jer 18:4 *But the pot he was shaping from the clay was marred in his hands; so the potter formed it into another pot, shaping it as seemed best to him.*

Journey
- 312 -
ACKNOWLEDGED TRUTH

Be pleasing to me in every way and settle not in your own comfort zone, Oh, my precious child.
I have loved you with an undying love and clothed you in righteousness. I have established you in my Will, and snatched you out by my salvation of hope, bestowed on you so graciously.
Take note and listen to my Word daily.
There is no more time. Judgment has reached its climax.
I am about to close the door on this masquerade - The world and its falsehood.
Imitate that which is good and leave the ways of the world behind. Close the door on everything, that hinders, and the sin, that is so entrapping. Escape all danger entrapments, the corruption of this world caused by greed and evil desires.
Run for your life into my arms of love.
Hold me close to your heart, son, so that you may never fall or injure yourself.
The end times are forthcoming, but you will not be hindered.
Those days are coming with great speed and finality.

Acknowledge my Will, and always be ready and dressed in white.
In the spirit realm is where the action is.
Devour no one... except my Word of Life in Spirit.
I am with you always.

Amen

Love

Isa 40:5 *And the glory of the LORD will be revealed, and all people will see it together. For the mouth of the LORD has spoken."*

Journey
- 313 -

HERE COMES YOUR VICTORY

Savior, I am crying out to you for help. Help me, Oh, Lord, help me, I ask. I am in desperate need of your touch and deep compassion, for none is given.
I need you to capture my heart and change me to suit you.
I desire not to be displeasing to you, nor live in arrogance towards your Holy Word. Instead, I desire and choose to be clean, pure and holy in your sight. I want to make others feel better about themselves, so help me achieve your purpose to accomplish my goal.
This is your mission, O my God of glory, before it is mine.

O my Comforter, I cry out to you on behalf of all who are in need. Help them, bless them, find them and lead them, that they may grow to know you. Oh, my Creator, I call out to you in honor and praise. Keep reminding me of all the good, that is coming my way.

I desire to see a change in my life for the better.
I will not just see a change, but also a total transformation from start to finish coming from you.
You have my heart in the palm of your hand.
I trust in you, therefore, I will not be neglected nor deceived, for you will be guiding me on this remarkable journey of Love.

Escape the corruption of this world, Oh, my child, for it is not for you to partake of its immorality and crime.

Amen

Love

Tit 3:14 Our people must learn to devote themselves to doing what is good, in order to provide for urgent needs and not live unproductive lives.

Journey
- 314 -

MEMORIAL TIMES

O God of love, I need your help and am desperate for your touch. Teach me how to love you, need you, and want you in every way. Help... help... is the word from me to you today.

Call on me, O loved one, and you will be touched by mercy.
Call upon my Name and you will be reached by grace.
Teach others the Way of Life and they will be changed forever, never to be the same.
Oh, child, I will not send you to your graveyard as some have suggested, but will only release you from your bondage and chains.

You call me, 'Abba Father,' and rightfully so, for this is who I am.
Grow in love as I have trained you, and walk in the way chosen especially for you.
Direct your footsteps and follow my decrees as you walk in submission to my Law of forgiveness. Walk in response to my petition and requirements, and you will be blessed.
These requirements set before you, are sealed, for your goodness.

I will solve every problem, that you may face today.
Keep reminding yourself of this: I do not wait for things to take place... I make them happen.

I, the Creator and Savior of the world am He - God of love.

Amen

Love

Psa 10:14 But you, God, see the trouble of the afflicted; you consider their grief and take it in hand. The victims commit themselves to you; you are the helper of the fatherless.

Journey
- 315 -

MY PURPOSED DESTINY

God of heaven, help me see your goodness to me, know your love and forgive, as you have forgiven me.
Deliver me from my anxious thoughts and obscurities.
I seem to enjoy doing more harm than good.
Free me, Oh, free me... please, Oh, free me, I plead.

Test your servant and see, if there is any fault in me, and purify my heart to serve you wholeheartedly. Do all that you need to do.
Deliver me from this burden, that is holding me back from you.
I am, your beloved child.
Free me from my corruptive ways - Self-destruction, I pray.
I only seem to hurt myself, when I pay for those who have done me wrong.
Every good thing comes from you, and I am blessed to have you in my heart. All I have accomplished has been done through you, but every negative encounter has been my own wrongdoing and fault.

O Master Teacher, I have learned one thing that is true-- there is no real joy in deception, falsehood, wrong intentions and lies.
There is no accuracy when moved by animal instinct, feelings and raw emotions. To you, I surrender.

Beloved, you are mine of old; since the beginning of time.
Show yourself strong and neglect not thy calling.

Amen

Love

Psa 86:11 **Teach me your way, LORD, that I may rely on your faithfulness; give me an undivided heart, that I may fear your name.**

Journey
- 316 -

BE SUBMISSIVE

Cause no harm to anyone, child, rather keep your eyes fixed on the goal, focus firmly on winning the prize set before you.
I, the Son, was sent to reassure the world the love the Father has for everyone; but the world has become corrupt - Worthless.
The world does not know the right from wrong, left from right, black from white, light from darkness, nor love from deception.

Child, search to find who I am, not just for what I can do for you. Search to discover my Will for your life, before the world becomes more lost and confused.
Defend everyone with my weapon of Love, and weep bitterly over the lost. Show compassion.

Your journey is not yet completely over - It has just begun.

Since there is no other way to enter heaven except through Love, why don't you flee the evil desires of youth, that you may really be comforted in my Kingdom of Support?
Turn to me with all your heart and let your desires come to pass. Be submissive, that you may become a blessing.

I shall shower you with my superb blessings, and not neglect you of your calling. You are forgiven by the precious blood of my Covenant. Now let your actions agree with my Word.
Run with arms open wide into my love and be faultless.

Amen

Love

Psa 71:4 Deliver me, my God, from the hand of the wicked, from the grasp of those who are evil and cruel.

Journey
- 317 -

TURN NOT AWAY FROM ME

Consider me, consider the cost, that I myself paid for you, that you may survive every experience known to man.

Why despise the days of humble beginnings? Why not glorify me? Why delight yourself in the old, rather than, embrace the new? Why look back rather than forward? Why give the enemy a foothold, the upper hand to snake through? Why? Why, child?

Remove every obstacle that is holding you back from moving forward with me. Allow nothing to restrain you from loving me.

Do not cry over yourself and say, "Oh, woe me, poor me."
I am the One interceding for you, have nothing to worry about.

Look at your friends; where are they all now!
Keep your sanity and walk with your head held high.
I will reward you handsomely.
I watch over you day and night. Be not miserable.

This is the time for everyone to be seeking me.
Look for me, and you will find me standing at the door of your heart. Your sin is not more powerful than my love.
Capture me while you still can.
My grace is sufficient when you call Me - Abba Father.
I shall bless you eternally. Run with perseverance, for I am yours.

Amen

Love

Rev 2:26 *To the one who is victorious and does my will to the end, I will give authority over the nations--*

Journey
- 318 -

COURTESY EMPHASIZED

I love those who love me, and those who have no interest to gather with me will scatter. I am the great Shepherd.
My sheep listen to my voice, and I lead them out of slaughter.
My sheep listen to no other voice, but mine.
Did you understand all this?
If yes, then shout, "Hallelujah! Amen... glory to God in the highest."
Listen and take heed, my precious lambs, before the sun turns to blood and the moon topples from its place.
Listen, before the cold grows colder, and the night becomes darker.
My hands made everything beautiful in its time, but now it is ruined, destroyed by mankind.

Help me, O my God of love, help me walk in obedience to your commands. Help me reach you, and be one with you in spirit and truth, Oh, God of Love, for I desire you.
May my journey with you be one of grace.
May I never do you wrong and bring complications upon my life.
May I always be pleasing in your sight.
I shall never lose hope, for you are my Hope and Destiny.
Spare me, Oh, spare my life from my own hands.
Truly I am, my worst enemy.
I desire to submit and be true to you... help me!

O my child of Love, I have not been absent.
Touch my heart and you will feel my presence, for I am right here.

Amen
Love

Psa 51:18 **May it please you to prosper Zion, to build up the walls of Jerusalem**

Journey
- 319 -

REVERE MY NAME

I have been watching over your life, for many years now.
I have never left you behind nor ever neglected you.
Why make your own choices without consulting me?
Have I not shown you the way?
Have I not given you confidence to move forward?
What crime have I done, that you desert me and go your own way?
Do you need me to force your hand to do what is right? That I would never do, for I desire your willing heart and submission.

I have seen your struggles and watched over your ways, so that you would not lose confidence. Why treat me as an enemy?
Why sow wickedness and so reap disillusionment?
Why reap the consequences of your guilt, Oh, my child?
Why waver in faith and no longer look forward to a new beginning? Have I not always taken good care of you?
Have I not looked after your wellbeing and giving you good health and assurance? Why separate yourself now and no longer speak to me about your issues?

Return, O my precious one, return to your rightful place of inheritance.

I shall restore double for all your losses, and continue to bless you even more.

Amen

Love

Pro 24:14 **Know also that wisdom is like honey for you: If you find it, there is a future hope for you, and your hope will not be cut off.**

Journey
- 320 -
REVERSE THE CYCLE

Disaster will not come to you a second time around, child.
Those who kill, steal, murder and destroy will be held accountable.
Keep your distance and walk away from it all.
Disturb not yourself with all these troubles. Cherish the moments we share together, and rest your weary soul upon my heart of love.
Purify yourself in Me, and maintain the Resurrected Life.
Share my love with the world, for they too are in need of my special touch upon their lives.
Dwell not on past experiences long gone, rather, save yourself the agony of remembrance as well as trauma.

I have released you from the snare of death.
You shall no longer be targeted or misled.
I will not share you with anyone, nor should you.
I shall not give you worldly wisdom, but only heavenly treasures will I impart to you. I will even calm the storms on your behalf, if you were to ask me. I shall do nothing out of order, but only fulfill my promises, and so prove to be Faithful, Loyal and True.

I am who I am.
Reveal my image by reflecting my likeness.
Empower yourself through my Word, that you may be glorified.
Whisper my Name and I shall hear.
Shout my praises and I will answer.

Amen

Love

1Jn 1:9 If we confess our sins, he is faithful and just and will forgive us our sins and purify us from all unrighteousness.

Journey
- 321 -

BEYOND IMAGINATION

Do not love the world or anything in the world, child, for those who love the world are not of me.
Be consecrated, set apart to live the Life of Love.
Delight yourself in me and dwell in safety.
Be not concerned. I am your Friend.
Be alert and never give up, for your future is nearly here.
Be wise towards outsiders, stand your ground and carry yourself with dignity.
Turn your heart from darkness into the light.

My heart is with you, and my eyes are watching over you.
Everything I have is yours, and all that you are is mine.

You shall be seated with me on my throne of grace and not be burdened by trouble.
Take hold of me and run before I return.
I am your future.
The Will of your heavenly Father must be accomplished.

I have set you apart for such a time as this.
Move in the direction of my purpose and you will be fulfilled.
My purpose must be established in you.
Practice hospitality.
You are fully grown - Fully mature.

Amen

Love

Isa 26:12 *LORD, you establish peace for us; all that we have accomplished you have done for us.*

Journey
- 322 -

MONEY GIVEN BACK

My Holy Spirit shall restore you back to life, and in me, you will discover your identity-- The real you, The 'I' in you.

You shall weigh your options carefully, and recognize the difference between your old life, and the life you are now living, between your past circumstances and your present blessings.

I am your True God of old, who truly loves you.
I have compassion on all.

Call on me during time of uncertainty, and I will shower you with my grace upon grace.

Your body, soul and spirit, shall be healed from wasted years of sorrow and mistakes made.
You shall no longer live on your own, for I will be providing you with a comforting partner.
You shall manifest Love everywhere you go, for you did not know me then, but you sure do now.

Look up and access your gifts.
You shall call and find me - Reach out and touch me.

My spirit shall lead you and my favor shall comfort you.
My eyes are always upon you, child. Find rest for your soul.

Peace and protection to you my people.

Amen

Love

Psa 119:160 **All your words are true; all your righteous laws are eternal.**

Journey
- 323 -

THE FORMER IS GONE

I shall sustain you by the power of my hand.

Serve me with all your heart and reach the greatest heights in Love.
The depth you desire is available, enter without retreat.
Welcome to my Throne Room.

My weapon of forgiveness is in your heart.

Recharge yourself with my affection of grace and be empowered.
No one is able to snatch you out of my hand.
You are completely mine.
Those who belong to me, trust me.
My house is an open door to all.
I shall satisfy the need with all that is good.
From the fruit of your labor, you shall inherit a blessing.

I will be with you always, and you shall be encouraged.
I shall cause your heart to chase after me and you to follow.

You shall never be in lack.
Learn, consider and ponder on my statutes.
Never doubt your calling, for you shall counsel many.
Welcome my presence of grace, and restore the times lost between us - You and I.
I, your Comforter, am your burden Relief and Satisfier.

Amen

Love

Isa 29:19 *Once more the humble will rejoice in the LORD; the needy will rejoice in the Holy One of Israel.*

Journey
- 324 -

UNIVERSAL LOVE

In my everlasting arms is where you belong.
Rest and you will recognize my accomplishments on your behalf.

Beloved child, the consequence of not listening to my Word is not to be taken lightly.
Take heed, lest you fall into a trap of temptation.

I am your Comforter, Supporter and Greatest Friend.
I will not condemn anyone who believes, but those who choose their own path of wickedness and turn their back to me, will find no rest for their weary soul and lose heart.
Those who do not accept my resurrection power will not see the light of Day.
Those who refuse their destiny with me... will not be allowed to enter my Throne nor receive my kingly anointing.
I am merciful.
You need not ask whether I am gracious too, for that is who I am.

You have not called upon me for favor, nor asked me for anything.
Ask and it shall be given you.
At the proper time, you shall receive all the promises made.

Do all that you hear me say, and gain the victory over your life.
You are strong.
Do not misuse your freedom for ill-gotten pleasure... grow in your salvation instead.

Amen

Love

Psa 119:96 **To all perfection I see a limit, but your commands are boundless.**

Journey
- 325 -

YOU ARE VICTORIOUS

I am truly the Alpha and the Omega.
Keep reminding yourself of this one truth, and you will never be disappointed. My Word is True till the very end.
The One who calls you is Faithful.
He will dress your wounds with soothing oil for healing.
My righteousness draws near with great speed and finality.
Your future is safe in the palm of my hand.
During time of trouble, I am near.
Depart not from my words of Life, for I am the One, who takes care of your every need.
Consider the cost paid on the cross for your salvation.
Moments away from me makes all the difference, so be careful of turning away.
Be careful: You are seeking my hand and not my face.
Why desert me as you do, and then ask me for favors?
I shall show you my face, not just my hand, if you were to ask me.
What wrong have your forefathers found in me, that you neglect me as you do and think nothing of it? Answer me! Is my Love not enough for you? Are you not satisfied, that you treat me this way?

Watch your steps carefully, that you may not miss the Mark of Life.
Falter not in time of need, for I am with you, to see you through every difficulty facing you.

Amen

Love

Psa 21:2 **You have granted him his heart's desire and have not withheld the request of his lips.**

Journey
- 326 -

WALLOW NOT IN SORROW

Rescue the needy, strengthen the weary and fight the good fight of the faith.

You will never be put to shame no matter what comes your way.

Those who think they are something when they are nothing, shall come to a horrible end. They are nothing but wind driven by a storm. They shall be counted with the wicked.

You are pure in thought and deed, for I have forgiven your past illegal experiences, that shattered lives and brought you disturbance.
I have created you in my image and reformed you in my nature. In the image of God, you have been sealed and marked as one truly holy.
Now go and wash others with the same blood of the Lamb - The blood of Life, that gives the victory to all who believe.

Strengthen your weak arms and feeble knees; make level paths for your feet and move in one direction.
Do not be hasty nor lazy, rather move forward by the power of my spirit enabling you, and be not reluctant towards those who want to move forward with you.
Feed the multitudes by the power of my spirit bestowed upon you so freely, and release them from agony.
Those who are in sorrow ought to pray, so that they may be set free.

Amen

Love

Psa 119:64 *The earth is filled with your love, LORD; teach me your decrees.*

Journey
- 327 -
A WILLING HEART

Oh, child, son of my loins, why suffer the consequences of your guilt, son, by going your own way? Why turn your back on me, and neglect the word of truth? Why disturb me and feel so guilty? Why? Have I been a burden to you? Have I ever stood in your way? Have I not always given you a choice to make in the presence of all my angels? Have I not said, "choose me, choose Life and live? Choose Life not death, O my precious one, for this is your destiny."

Why try to capture the hearts of many while refusing me? Why disturb your future by choosing your own way and make plans without me? Why separate yourself from me, child? Why bow to idols when they are of no use to anyone? Why, child? Answer me! Do not disregard what I am telling you... draw closer to me instead.
Why manifest evil behavior rather than good?
Why torment yourself by rebelling against my Will?
Why take my place of judgment? Do you not see? Do you not understand the ways of God? Will you not learn a lesson and submit? Do you not perceive what I have already accomplished for you? Do you not know, that I am on the way from heaven?
Why suffer and rebel against my truth?
Circumstances are insignificant; rebellion is death, and anger destroys. Is that what you want?
Oh, my people, wake up from your slumber before it is too late.

Amen

Love

Psa 91:16 **With long life I will satisfy him and show him my salvation."**

Journey
- 328 -

COMMIT TO LOVE

All shall come to you bearing gifts.
You shall point every man to God Almighty.
They shall soar on the highest point in Love, and be astonished by the work of my hands which I have provided.
Look not to the left nor to the right. Keep your focus on your Maker, for with open arms I have welcomed you.

Pure thoughts are the right motives.
Have the right intentions and you will keep the enemy underfoot.

I took you by the hand and moved you ever so close; now take hold of my hand, that you may not waver in faith.
I shall strengthen you and not neglect you. I shall support you and help you. I shall provide water to quench your thirst, and food to nourish your soul. Your children, too, will be blessed.

Search for me, that you may discover who you are in me.
Come to know the 'I' in you and you will be changed, transformed forever eternally. In the Light of Life, you shall be recognized.
The Word of Truth is where you shall always find Me.

I shall deliver you from every attack set against you, accusation, murmur and strife. You shall look to me and be rescued.
I shall deliver you in the sight of all, for the victory is mine.
You are supported by grace.
Enlighten yourself.

Amen

Love

Isa 32:8 **But the noble make noble plans, and by noble deeds they stand.**

Journey
- 329 -
RESIST NOT MY WILL

Accept knowledge from my mouth and walk in my fullness.
You are not on your own, I am right here beside you, working to see you through.

Yes, many are suffering for the sake of my Name, child, and many more will be persecuted.
Grow up in your salvation and walk in the footsteps of my spirit.
Be aware of evil - the negative schemes of the enemy.
Be not fooled by him, rather be vigilant, unmoved by trouble and circumstances instead.
Be willing to learn my Way of Love and develop in character.
My Way is not your way, nor my spiritual words are your everyday natural earthly words.
Do not give up on your mission which is your calling, for much more is yet to be done-- places to go and new people to meet.

My purposes are very different than the plans you have made for yourself. Rescue yourself from this present dominion.

Who will you follow, my Way or your way, my Kingdom, or your valley of destruction? Choose today, who you will follow.
Oh, my anointed servant, I have blessed you with my peace.
Why corrupt yourself further when I am right here?

Amen

Love

2Co 3:18 *And we all, who with unveiled faces contemplate the Lord's glory, are being transformed into his image with ever-increasing glory, which comes from the Lord, who is the Spirit.*

Journey
- 330 -
PURE FORM

Turn not to your past for help or support, nor to your future for mercy, but only lean on me and turn your face.

My Kingdom is not of this world, nor is your weapon of warfare.

Walk in the path that I have chosen for you, that you may be lifted up in due season.
Fight the good fight of the faith to finish the race, and win the crown promised to those who love me.

I have spoken clearly, and therefore, revealed my thoughts to you. Nothing can or will ever hold you back from me.
I shall deny you nothing, and nations you shall subdue in my Name.
May you also be brought to complete unity, so that the world may see, know and believe, that you are mine, and that my love is greater than all.

I shall declare your Name and exalt your greatness to every nation, Oh, God my Lord of all creation. May every nation, bow before your throne and acknowledge that your Name is Holy.
I desire for my worship and praise of you to penetrate every nation.

Give me yourself completely, child, that you may receive my inheritance-- sealed just for you.

Amen

Love

Psa 143:10 **Teach me to do your will, for you are my God; may your good Spirit lead me on level ground.**

Journey
- 331 -
HEAR MY CALL

How can I leave you lonely, Oh, child? How can I treat you like an outcast? Oh, no... not you, beloved... not you, my saint.
I have loved you completely, and am committed to watch over you.
I am your God, the Maker of the Universe.
Complete your mission to fulfill your vision.
I love you eternally. Come to know my Will in your life.
Confess your sorrows, and I will heal your soul from agony, suffering and pain.

Your eyes are so delightful, and you are so tender, Oh, my beautiful one, my dove, my innocent and blameless one.
Your beauty is beyond description and gentle is your touch.
You touched me with your purity of heart, and reached my very core being.
Dance and sleep comfortably in my loving arms of peace, O my delicate flower.
Maintain your standard of living, beloved, no matter what anyone may say about you, for you are mine, acknowledged by name.
You are sanctified and sealed in my Kingdom.
Yes, my queen, my holy one, you are the one I love.
Ask me for anything and I shall supply and deliver.
I shall even give you the full measure of my double anointing here and now... even multiple blessings shall come upon you all at once.

Amen

Love

Psa 28:8 The LORD is the strength of his people, a fortress of salvation for his anointed one.

Journey
- 332 -

THE LOVE WE SHARE

"Help O God," you say, yet you do as you please, without helping anyone who is in need. I have heard your cries for self, but not once ever seeing you shed a tear for me. You claim to know me, but by your actions are constantly denying me the pleasure of your love. Repent and do the things you used to do, lest you fall on the side road and lose your way forever.

I have given you the Key to victory - The Treasures of Life.
What are you doing about them?
Walk in Wisdom, lest you forget tomorrow and what it may bring.
Learn to forgive, and unlock every door made possible.
You will be set free, healed and restored from all your anxieties.
I have watched your ways and seen the inclination of your heart.
You prefer your past to your destined future.
You lean more towards your appetite of past experiences,
than growing out of the old. You prefer to keep your present circumstances unresolved than do something about them.
You retreat from me and speak about others falsely.
When will you ever learn to help others effectively?

My heart aches every time I see you betraying your own soul, and led astray by self-denial, child. Do you not understand this?
Do you think I am blind to it all? Refuse me not.
Why do you do these things, the things that ought not be done?
Why? When you yourself know better?

Amen

Psa 119:131 **I open my mouth and pant, longing for your commands**

Journey
- 333 -

SPIRITUAL AWAKENING

Teach me patience, O Lord of my life, and help me persevere.
Oh, my Creator of hearts, I desire to be one with you in spirit, reach my fullness and walk in your footsteps of love.
Speak that I may acknowledge your Word and obey your Truth.
Help me understand that which is best for me.
Feed me your Word, that I may understand your Will.
Give me knowledge, that I may rest in your glory.
I am like a thirsty land, that never says enough to your goodness, O Lord of my life, but asks for more of you, my Savior King-- pleading and desiring more of your affection and tender mercy.
Stretch me further in faith, that I may rest on your mountain of love.
May I always be submissive to your commands, and worship you wholeheartedly.
I shall always be dressed in white and be committed to serving you.
God, you have seen my heart towards you and approved of my ways.
You have held me since my youth and I am grateful.
O King of my being, you have been true to your Word.
You have always been there, even from the first day I was created.
You have set me free to soar like an eagle.
I am so grateful, O my Heavenly Being, Creator and Best Friend.
My very all belongs to you.
All that I have achieved comes from your loving hands.

O my child, you are the apple of my eye. Neglect me not.

Amen

Love

Psa 119:66 **Teach me knowledge and good judgment, for I trust your commands.**

Journey
- 334 -

DESTINED FOR GREATNESS

Consider your ways, Oh, Child of Love, while reaching out to others, and you will blossom to the very end.
I will exalt you before all who despise you, and you shall shine throughout the Universe.
Teach little children to pray in my Name.
Teach them to obey my statutes and live a Life of Love.
Be an example, a model of glory, that the eyes of all may see my acts of righteousness and be blessed.
You are kind, but when helping others, you need to be cautious of how much time you give.

Watch your life carefully and neglect not your calling.
Watch your steps carefully and maintain contact with me in spirit.

I have been watching over my word to see it fulfilled in your life. Glory to me, your Savior, who has never left you stranded nor ever rejected you. Why? Well, how can I watch you be lead astray and do nothing about it?
How can I neglect those whom I have chosen for my glory?

Be eager to go everywhere I send you, and destroy not my work, for the sake of food. My Kingdom does not depend on food, water or clothing, but on living in total obedience to my plan for your life.

My return shall bring you benefits.

Amen

Love

Job 36:4 *Be assured that my words are not false; one who has perfect knowledge is with you.*

Journey
- 335 -

LIVE MY LIFE OF LOVE

From this day on I shall bless you twice as much.
I am about to restore a double portion of my anointing to you, and your household... Your children shall benefit just as much.

Be not reluctant to receive my double anointing, for I shall restore comfort to you and you will be comforted.

Enjoy all that I have given you, and all that I am about to give you.
I have much more to give you, much more than you can even now handle or comprehend.
I have kept quiet for a long time, but those days are now over.
All is coming to fruition.
I am about to confront your enemies and put them to shame, by building you up. I shall tower you on high and keep him underfoot.

You remained faithful even when all seemed lost.
You are redeemed - Rest assured.

Even without assurance of your future, you remained faithful and believing. You also endured much, for the sake of Love.
I have been watching, and I am about to reward you handsomely.
Your rewards will not be revoked.
I will make you famous like the stars in the universe, and your fame will spread among the nations. You shall see it with your eyes and eat the best from the Land – The fruit of your harvest is ripe.

Amen

Love

Psa 12:7 **You, LORD, will keep the needy safe and will protect us forever from the wicked,**

Journey
- 336 -
COMPLETE YOUR JOURNEY

I am with you to redeem all those who are lost.
I have redeemed you from the valley of decision by taking you unto myself from the valley of death and destruction.
You shall have no friction. You shall not give your control over to these people who are hovering over you, ready to attack.
Burden yourself with them no longer. They are lost fools.

Having lost all sensitivity, they indulge in every kind of wickedness and think nothing of it. With their tongue they promise freedom, but their hearts are far from me. They are deceived by the enemy who fools them with deceit-- consuming their hearts with false hope, assumption and delusion. They have no direction, no stability, no home to call their own. They shall waste away and vanish forever. Only ruin and distress awaits them.
Unwilling to live the Good Life, they have chosen their own path of unrighteousness leading them downhill. They live in self-denial and boast about the good old days and all that tomorrow will bring. They serve the dead, rather than the Living. Empowered by greed, they wander the streets... murmuring all day, they become more and more depraved. Unknown of what the future holds, they dream on about tomorrow, which never comes. They live in a fantasy land, and waste away to nothing. Charm is their only avenue, their only way out. Have nothing to do with such as these.

Forgive to forget and wait for my return. I am your All.

Amen

Love

Psa 11:5 *The Lord examines the righteous...*

Journey
- 337 -

SHINE FORTH

*Oh, King of my Heart, you are the Center of my life, the Source of all that is good and wonderful. I am yours and to your Will, I surrender.
Earnestly I seek your face.
My soul thirsts for your love, and in your Word I put my trust.
Savior of my soul, Redeemer of my spirit, to you I call.*

*Oh, my Ancient of Days, to you I give my all.
You have rescued me from the pit of hell, destruction and injury.
My heart belongs to you. My life is in the palm of your hand.
I seek you to live, and in the Scriptures, I look for you.*

*I adore you, and in excitement bow before your throne.
Out of the depth of my being, I sing your praises.
Your mighty acts are revealed, and I am thankful.*

*I speak of your love all day long and seek your face all night.
I bring bread to the hungry and am moved by your deep compassion.
I rejoice in your love and forgiveness.
You water the thirsty land of my soul, and I am satisfied.
I consider your decrees and obey your commands.*

*I am moved and accomplished by grace.
In you and in you alone, I put my trust.*

Your glory is my sunshine, your salvation is my hope, your Word is my faith and your joy is my strength.

Amen

Love

Ps 11:7 **For the LORD is righteous, he loves justice; the upright will see his face.**

Journey
- 338 -

AWAKEN THY SOUL

Take me back into your Sanctuary, O my God of love, to the place where I belong, for in your sweet loving kindness and gentle arms is where I truly belong. Hold me close to you, Oh, my gentle Shepherd. Cradle me; have mercy on me and spare my life by your tender embrace.

I am holding you very close to my heart, child.
Now do likewise with your children, family and loved ones.

Teach me, O Master Teacher, to learn your ways, that I may obey your voice. Hold on to me and never let go.
May I love you eternally by clinging to your Word, to your Name, to your wonders and to my salvation in total holiness.
May I never waver in faith, nor neglect your precious promises, that you once shared with me in confidence.
Let nothing, absolutely nothing, take me away from you, O my Heart.

Oh, Mighty One, you are my reality, my dream come true.
I desire to reflect your likeness and holiness in a dead and dying world. I desire to be pleasing to you every step of the way.
With every step, may my heart beat as one with yours.
May I never be afflicted by sorrow, nor by any tear of discouragement.
May I walk in the fullness of your love, fearless and in full assurance of faith. I praise you for I am your worshiper.

Rejoice, you are a spoiled child of mine. My return shall not linger.

Amen

Love

Psa 119:162 **I rejoice in your promise like one who finds great spoil.**

Journey
- 339 -
TIME TO RUN

Give me your all, Oh, child of my Kingdom, and be set free.
Grow tall in my love and be established.

You are unable to achieve on your own all that you desire.
You shall not fall from your high position, for I have enabled you to stand strong on the Solid Rock Eternal.
On the greatest heights of glory, you shall remain steadfast.
You shall not be moved from your calling, for you are standing strong and firm in your faith.

All things are made possible in my Name.
I shall breathe life into your situation and resurrect you.
Do not be overcome with doubt, fear and confusion, for my promises are always yes and Amen. Be rescued from the snare.
You shall move mountains in my Name, for I have gone ahead of you to prepare the way.
Do not lose hope over this issue enlarged on your body, for you must walk by faith and not by sight.
Lose no sleep over these issues burdening your mind, for I shall see you through. Be not burdened, for I have resolved your situation.
I have set you free from all concerns.
Nothing nor anyone has any hold on you.

What man can do, I do better, for I am the Builder of everything.
What I can achieve for you, is far greater than all.

Amen

Love

Psa 118:32 *It is God who arms me with strength and keeps my way secure.*

Journey
- 340 -

BE NOT MANIPULATED

Let no one take you captive through hollow and deceptive philosophy, that helps no one.
Be not led astray by witchcraft, nor be enticed by any form of teaching presenting itself as real... created, formed and applied by men. Anything that does not come from the Truth is false.
Stay away from everything that hinders, and the sin that so easily entangles-- enticing the soul.
Comfort yourself in me and you will find rest.
Follow my teaching by obeying my commands.
Accept my Will and you will not be burdened by trouble.

You are now too advanced for your enemy - The evil one.
You shall no longer be enticed by him, for he cannot reach you nor touch you. You are ahead of him in knowledge and learning.
You have exceeded all-- beyond all limitations.

The time will come when each man's work will be tested by fire.
He who is with me will be blessed, but he who does not gather with me will stray.
The hearts of everyone will also be tested by the fire of my spirit.
Testing will come and go and pass away, but my Word remains true and the same forever.
I declare to you today, that you are eternally mine.
You have a future, for I have sworn you in by my honor of grace.

Amen

Love

Psa 92:12 *The righteous will flourish like a palm tree, they will grow like a cedar of Lebanon;*

Journey
- 341 -

A SPACIOUS PLACE

You sure have won my favor, child, for you are perfect in my eyes.
Be comforted, you will no longer be restricted.

I am not unjust. I will never forget your work and the love you have shown me as you have helped everyone, everywhere and continue to bless them. Show the same diligence till my return.
By loving everyone, you are showering them with grace.
Be diligent till the very end and I will rescue you from trouble.
Keep doing what you know best, for my favor rests on you.
I shall continue to prosper you.
You shall not be harmed, for I am your Existence.
You shall not be held back from moving forward.
I shall bless the work of your hands.

The time is coming when you will be changed, transformed into my likeness. You shall worry no longer, for I have taken over.

I have given you Wisdom to follow... now, move forward with me, and be drenched in my presence. You shall gain knowledge and understanding as you learn my ways and walk in my footsteps.

Your honor is my delight, O Heavenly Protector, just as your love is my satisfaction.

Child, you are my heart and my very own possession in the making of perfection. I have declared-- You are mine.

Amen

Love

Son 8:7 **Many waters cannot quench love; rivers cannot sweep it away...**

Journey
- 342 -

MOVE FORWARD

Do not waver, doubt nor fear anything, Oh, my child of love.
Keep your eyes on the goal, instead, fixed and focused thoroughly on Me - The Author and Perfecter of your faith.
No longer be a wanderer upon the earth, for the future is near and forthcoming.
Stay in your calling and you shall find Everlasting Love.

Eager I am to comfort you, Oh, honorable one, to ride over your mistakes and give you hope and a future.
You are secure in the arms of Love.

Do not lift a finger against a fellow believer, nor judge anyone wrongly.
I know, Oh, my child, I do know your fears, and your concerns lay open before me. Your many worries shall soon fade away.
There is a solution to every problem... you do not need to face and solve them all by yourself. I am here, alive and well, helping you through and watching over your wellbeing.

Do you not feel my heartbeat longing to be touched by you?

I desire to give you a new journey, a new start, a new beginning.
No longer give into old habits, fleshly desires, and cycles of damaging patterns, that bring you shame and do you no good.
Control the flesh by renewing your mind in spirit.
Keep the image of my love alive and dwell in safety.

Amen

Love

Jer 8:18 **You who are my Comforter in sorrow, my heart is faint within me.**

Journey
- 343 -

MUTUAL UNDERSTANDING

Yes, child, I in you and you in me, is the perfect harmony.
Together we shall ride on the wind of the dawn - The glorious white horse.
Keep pressing through, moving forward.
You shall not regret a thing.

I have given you my weapon to fight the enemy with, not your brother. My weapon is to be used for the advantage of my Kingdom, not to destroy one another.
The Sword of my Perfect Love rests in your heart.
Fight, for the victory is yours. Fight the beast who is called the prince of this world, for his time has come to an end.
Shortly without delay, he shall perish to no return.

You are not limited nor restricted to anything anyone may say or think about you, but only to your way of thinking will you be answerable, revealed and bound. Be careful not to boast, and think of yourself more highly than you ought.

Since the time is coming to an end, shall you be seeking wonderful things for yourself? Seek them not, for the time draws near.
Be careful of watering-down my word and turning it into a whitewash object.
I am Holy, so you too be holy in accordance to my Way.

Amen

Love

Zec 2:5 *And I myself will be a wall of fire around it,' declares the LORD, 'and I will be its glory within.'*

Journey
- 344 -

GONE WITH THE WIND

Why are you deserting me, child, as if I don't even exist, as if there is no room for me in your heart?
Am I a burden to you, that you disregard my Word of splendor and desert me? Am I only a God in heaven and not the God of your existence? Why torment yourself by separating yourself from me? Why waste your energy elsewhere? Why comfort all, but me?

I have made you sacred. Why defile yourself with idols?
I have washed you clean. Why corrupt yourself?
Why run away and live a life of prostitution?
Why neglect that which is best for you, and go after so-called gods, that do no one any good? Why? What is my crime? Answer me!

I have brought you up in my loving care and tenderness.
Do you now want to deny me?
You became a precious diamond in my hands, but then corrupted yourself with idol living and so brought me shame.
Why blame me, for your wrongdoing and corruption?

It is time to make a firm decision.
Return to your Sanctuary of Love - Your sacred place of honor.
Look to me, but never away from me.

I will not hesitate to bring you back to myself.
I need you to listen in order for me to respond.
In my loving arms is where you truly belong.

Amen

Love

Psa 88:1 *LORD, you are the God who saves me; day and night I cry out to you.*

Journey
- 345 -

OVERCOMING WARRIOR

You are so dear to me, child. Listen to my heart beating as one with you, and be consumed by my fire of love through baptism.
Stray not from your calling, for you are safe in my loving arms.
I will not neglect you. Live a life of love built on faith.
Stay pure and protected while you are in this tent of the body.

I have given you the victory to sing my praises.
Sing my love songs of praise and take back what the enemy has stolen from you. Be submissive and honorable, and you will be rescued from the deepest darkness confronting you.
I have given you authority-- now trample on those snakes and scorpions opposing you. I will build you up and not tear you down.
You shall overcome every difficulty known to man.
Your time of harvest will surely come, and you will no longer be wasting time on all those who are cold in heart.
Those who do not take heed of my Word will perish, and those who are not willing to listen to my truth, and be awakened by my grace, will pay the penalty ever so severely. They shall waste away and come to nothing. Driven by storms they will also be reduced to ashes.
You will not be defeated, for your Crown of Righteousness has been established.
Even in negative situations you shall flourish and be noticed.

Amen

Love

Luk 6:19 **and the people all tried to touch him, because power was coming from him and healing them all.**

Journey
- 346 -

WEALTHY LIVING

Your Sovereignty comes from me. You no longer need to look back. I am the Alpha and the Omega, the Start and the Finish of your life.

You have nothing to fret or worry about.
I myself, am in control of your destiny.
Follow my voice, direction, love, supplication and way of living.
Rest for your soul you will find.
Who do you have in heaven apart from me to rely on?
I, the One, who calls you, am He in the making of your life.
Consider my return to earth - It is of great worth.

I am on my way to you, and my reward is definitely with me.
Are you ready for the return of your King?
Are you dressed appropriately for the Wedding Supper?
Are you clothed with my garment of salvation?
Are you on the move with my spirit?
Have you made yourself ready, or are you just waiting around for something to happen?
If you are just stringing along, then be careful, for there are dangers out there, beyond your own strength and abilities to handle!

Watch your steps carefully or you may just become ambushed.
The time is now.
Watch and pray, for I am your healing Balm.

Amen

Love

Joh 18:21 **Why question me? Ask those who heard me. Surely they know what I said.**

Journey
- 347 -

FREE TO SOAR

People these days are lost more than ever... tossing and turning, worried and confused, struggling and suffering, hurting and being uncertain. Fearful commotion and doubt everywhere. From the East to the West, North and South; all in confusion and strife.

People everywhere are so lost and wondering why.
They have no idea anymore of who they are, where they from or going... all losing hope.
They are in constant agony, looking for the truth in the midst of all this darkness, wailing in turmoil, seeking comfort from it all.
Truth has vanished from the streets... it is nowhere to be seen, hidden from sight.

Listen, my children, stay close to Me - Your Maker.
The One close to you in soul and spirit is very near.
Despise not the days of small beginnings, but master your gifts instead. I am your Father, your heavenly Light of Inheritance.
Those things must first take place before my return.
Despite all these persecutions, know your God exists and that you will be richly rewarded for your good deeds.

You shall not stand on trial, nor any hair on your head be touched.
Your King is on the way; therefore, there shall be no more delays.
I am calling you home to myself... come home to me.
Come away with me on my white horse.

Amen

Love

Psa 33:21 *In him our hearts rejoice, for we trust in his holy name.*

Journey
- 348 -

HEED DISCIPLINE

Rebellion is a crime and an unspeakable act.
Those in the habit of lying are not of me, nor do they know me.
Advise the guilty to repent, so they may not reap the consequences of their guilt. Speak truth to them, that they may repent and be made whole.
Hide not the Truth from anyone... it benefits no one to keep quiet.
Your works will be shown for what it is, for the fire of my spirit shall reveal the truth of all things.
You shall be blessed, for you have proved faithful.
Many will flock to you and gather to hear my Word of Truth.
Sit in amazement and be astonished, for all I have done for you.
Allow them to ask you any questions they may choose, and I myself will answer them by my spirit through you.
You shall not falter.

Open wide your mouth and I will fill it-- The Treasure of Life spoken out loud. I shall guide your heart to say what needs to be said at the time, and many will flock to you and be led on the straight and narrow. Pray that they may not falter nor fall.

Disregard that which is not beneficial for you, and keep running the race of time to which you were called.
You shall prosper and be a blessing.
Prosperity shall chase you and overtake you in an instant.

Amen

Love

Pro 28:19 Those who work their land will have abundant food, but those who chase fantasies will have their fill of poverty.

Journey
- 349 -

LOOK TO NO MAN

Look to me and I will save you from all these disasters, tortures and mutilations injuring your flesh.
Look to no one else for help but me. You only need me for support. Depend not on your own strength, for I am here, responding to your every prayer. Receive all that I have for you.

Turn not to anyone during time of trouble, for I myself am here.

I am the One who protects you. Even from death you shall be saved. My Word of Wisdom shall enlighten you, my Sword of Love shall empower you, and my depth of compassion shall support you.

Be wise and act on that knowing which you have received from me. Keep my belt of truth buckled tightly around your waist, and hold securely to my shield of faith. The breastplate of righteousness should always be in place, and your feet constantly fitted with readiness that comes from the gospel of peace.
I am your Prince of Peace. Misplace not your helmet of salvation. Touch my hand, feel my side, and know who I am.
Yield to my commands and you will be astonished by the results. You will not be neglected.
Avoid not my command which enlightens your spirit and helps you submit to my rule of action in love.

Amen

Love

Joh 4:23 Yet a time is coming and has now come when the true worshipers will worship the Father in the Spirit and in truth, for they are the kind of worshipers the Father seeks.

Journey

- 350 -

TO YOU I CALL

Help me, Father, help me, O God... help me.
Thank you for all your goodness, for who you are, my Alpha and Omega, my First and Last.

I lift up my soul to you, to you whose throne is in heaven.
I surrender my all to your love, to you, O my Heavenly, I surrender.
Help me be in need of your love; help me not rely on my own strength and so fail. Help me desire your glory and aim for perfection.
Help me serve you in accordance to your commands, that I may know the difference and choose to do what is right.

I love you with all my heart, but it is not enough.
I offer my body, soul and spirit to you completely, for in you I am made complete. I do not wish to waver in faith towards you.
Help me listen and obey.

Turn to me and not away from me, child.
I am not angry nor frustrated with you, just sad.
You are learning lessons the hard way, in a land not your own.

I myself am completing the work I began in you, and you are about to see it fulfilled.
See through my eyes - The eyes of my spirit and the door of revelation will open wide for you.
Walk in the truth you know, so that my revelations can carry you through.

Amen

Love

Ecc 11:7 **Light is sweet, and it pleases the eyes to see the sun.**

Journey
- 351 -

LEARN TO LOVE THYSELF

Holy am I, child, holy.
I am the One you are to worship and glorify.
Rejoice in my loving kindness, lest you be weakened by trauma, for this horrific state of society, is overruling the world by its destructive forces.
Serve me wholeheartedly, lest you be limited in your way of thinking.
I am God - The Fullness of everything.

Walk in the footsteps of Grace, before you become overwhelmed by trouble, sadness and devastation.
Do not linger behind and so grieve my spirit.
Declare my good news to all who are willing to listen, and walk in the fullness of the truth yourself.
Fulfill your calling.
Do not misuse the authority given you and so become proud.

I have given you authority to trample on snakes and scorpions, not tread on people and lives. So, be wise and show yourself a man.

Shudder not before your enemy, for then you won't stand a chance.
Honor me with your life as well as with your finances, so that you may prosper beyond measure.
I have blessed you abundantly. Why stop now!

Amen

Love

Job 24:22 **But God drags away the mighty by his power; though they become established, they have no assurance of life.**

Journey
- 352 -

FROM THE HIGHEST POINT

Keep safe by hiding in my refuge of Love.
I shall prosper you, and you shall grow strong, mighty and ready to face any difficulty.
I have come to give you a prosperous abundant life.
Look up, and see me standing there, ready to receive you.
Grieve nor more, for your future is bright.

The Temple of the Living God - His body, the Church, has been broken down, damaged, looking desperate and destroyed.
But in these last days the tables will be turned, and what once was, shall no longer be, and what was not, shall now manifest into existence.
This is the last second of the last minute of the Hour.
The church shall arise to a new horizon, new level, new height of glory-- all shall be restored. What once looked broken down and defeated, shall only be exalted - Lifted up in glory.
What lays waste now shall only become fortified before the many.

You, my child, shall reach your highest potential.
This is your time. Come home with me.

You shall rise again and take a stand.
Your Weapon - The glory of God is powerful, ready in full force.
Stand strong in battle, Oh, you mighty warrior, and rise to a new height. Raise your sword and be lifted up.

Amen

Love

Mat 22:33 **When the crowds heard this, they were astonished at his teaching.**

Journey
- 353 -

RESTORATION IS YOURS

The time for my appearance has arrived, and I shall see you in heaven soon.
Turn not to the left nor to the right, but remain in your calling, for this is where you truly belong. I am your Glory.
You will no longer be defiled by your so-called best friends.
I will see to it, that you do not walk in their corruption.

I have beheld you since your youth and considered all your ways.
When you were young and negligent, I supported you, and when you were neglected I came to your aid.
Wolves surrounded you, but I never neglected you.
I kept you safe from their attacks, vicious bites, and slander.
What they have done against you was really done against themselves and me.

I have forgiven your rebellion. You shall no longer be guilty of any crime. I am with you to carry you through.
I have taken away your guilt, and with justice delivered you.
Heed my voice, seek my advice and listen to my appeal.
I am your Righteous Judge without any fault nor blame.
Just as I give grace to the humble, so I also oppose the proud.

Be glad, that you have been forgiven from all your iniquities and past mistakes. I am your eternal God.

Amen

Love

Psa 83:18 **Let them know that you, whose name is the LORD-- that you alone are the Most High over all the earth.**

Journey

- 354 -

ANCHOR OF HOPE

I love you, child.
You surely have obeyed my perfect Will and passed the test.
Even under the most severe trials, you did not waver, give up or lose sight of me. More than that, you did not bow your knee to the enemy and therefore, made me proud.

I am Faithful, and you have kept yourself blameless by the power of my Spirit at work in you. You have acknowledged that without me, you are nothing and freely offered yourself to me.
You kept my word no matter what the situation.
Even under heavy duty trials, severe conditions and circumstances, you kept on giving. You remained strong and steadfast.
So now you shall eat the best from the Land, that is flowing with milk and honey.

Run by faith till the end and complete the race.
Keep up your courage and the great work you are achieving.

What you once endured, you will no longer face again, for I am about to renew all things and bring amazing new adventures into your life.

Enjoy the new life given you, the new start, a new beginning.
Renewed by fame.

Amen

Love

Rev 12:14 The woman was given the two wings of a great eagle, so that she might fly to the place prepared for her in the wilderness, where she would be taken care of for a time, times and half a time, out of the serpent's reach.

Journey
- 355 -

FULFILL YOUR PURPOSE

Choose today who you will serve, follow and obey.
To whom will you turn during these days of trouble and disaster?
The world is in catastrophe, in a deep catastrophic state.
Choose today, who you will serve!

Your forefathers left the path of righteousness, and no longer followed my way of life. They turned away from obeying my commandments and deserted my laws and decrees which I said, would give them life.
Will you follow their destructive forces?
Will you submit and obey or just walk away!
Will you neglect your calling and your future, to no avail?
How would that benefit anyone! How will that serve you!
Will you follow their leading and so be misled?
Will you follow their example and think nothing of it?

They refused to listen to my counsel and so suffered the consequences of their guilt.
They followed worthless idols and became worthless themselves.
They wandered in deserts like refuse and wasted away like rejects.
Do you wish to become one like them, an object of scorn?
Do you want to suffer the guilt of your own sin, child?

Rebuke the guilty and defend the fatherless.

Amen

Love

Jer 30:21 ...*I will bring him near and he will come close to me-- for who is he who will devote himself to be close to me?' declares the LORD.*

Journey
- 356 -

PASS THE TEST OF TIME

Be determined to know the truth set before you, the mystery, that has long been hidden, but now revealed to God's holy people-- apostles, prophets, teachers and evangelists...
Be courageous and know the truth, that sets the captives free from sin, sicknesses, crippling finances and fear of death.
The enemy has taken these people captive to do his will. Be careful, lest you be enticed and ensnared. Watch your steps carefully.

I am the great I Am. I will always be the head of nations.
I Am, and there is no other. I Am Existence.

Reach my fullness, and you will never abort nor miscarry.
Be determined to walk in my ways.
Rest in my arms of comfort and follow my rule of love.
Maintain a good healthy attitude.
Waver not, lest you be burdened by trouble.
Keep my flames of compassion alive... burning within.
The greatest desire of love is Me.
Call others into my Kingdom, that they too may come to know me and gain knowledge. Help them be free from all their troubled waters, ways of destruction, burdens and persecutions.

I am the God who sees all things. Nothing is hidden from my sight.
Be strong and courageous.

Amen

Love

Joh 14:13 **And I will do whatever you ask in my name, so that the Father may be glorified in the Son.**

Journey
- 357 -
CONSULT ME

Only truth you shall find in me, and only through obedience shall you reach perfection.
Despise not the days of small beginnings; for little by little, you will prosper and get there. Start one step at a time, precept upon precept, then from glory to glory you shall rise. Start not from the top of the ladder, but take the first steps necessary - Step by step.

Remember this very truth: I exalt those who are humble in heart and contrite in spirit, but those who exalt themselves-- I humble. Everyone who loves his life will lose it, while everyone who hates his life in this world, for my sake will find it eternally. Again, everyone who wants to be first must be the very least, just as the greatest of all, should be the most humble of all. You must first be a humble servant to become an anointed king. In order to be entrusted with much, you must first prove faithful with the little.

Act on what I say and you will never be put to shame.
Consider nothing more than my love for you.
Let your number one priority be love-- Scripture reading, prayer, meditation and my Will done in your life.
All these virtues are important to your spiritual growth-- survival, entire being, as well as to your physical health.

Your One and Only - Me.

Amen

Love

Pro 11:25 *A generous person will prosper; whoever refreshes others will be refreshed.*

Journey
- 358 -

REDEEMING MISSION

*Set me free... Oh, my Holy God, set me free.
I can no longer take what is happening to me. I am so very tired, worn out, burdened and angry to the point of giving up. I can no longer take what is transpiring in my life, no longer, Oh, my Savior. I need a place of rest and comfort. No more grief and confusion.*

*Help me be released from all this mess confusing me.
I have suffered much already. Why must I go through the valley of the shadow of death... this terror of sadness and madness, that others are causing me? Must I take it? Must I carry their fault and confusion? Why am I so desperate for an answer? Why am I so unsettled, so unlisted from everyone's book? Why the past as well as the present?*

Child, O my child, look up I am here.
Why are you suffering in this way? Why do you question my resurrection and disregard my power that is so at work and effective in your life? I will never leave nor forsake you.
Why dress your wounds with temporary relief?
You clothe your hurts and pains with immediate fixations, that do you no good. You lean more towards your comfort zone than on me. Have you considered my path of Life, that leads to heaven?

Listen and pray... your merciful loving God is calling you home to himself. Be not discouraged.

Amen

Love

Isa 62:5 As a young man marries a young woman, so will your Builder marry you; as a bridegroom rejoices over his bride, so will your God rejoice over you.

Journey
- 359 -

HEAVEN APPROACHES

I created and formed you for my glory.
You shall have no other God, but Me.
Serve me in the fullness of my love and you shall see the future of your fame.

Awaken me by love, Oh, God, awaken me.

Your future is very near, child, very much at hand.
Glorify me and you will find my presence waiting, ready to receive you. Illuminating the room of your life.
You shall keep yourself obedient to my Word of Truth in action.

Enlarge the place of your territory, and roam freely in the midst of all this darkness surrounding you.
I shall never leave you stranded, wavering or consumed by any false fire. The heat of my love shall sustain you and glorify the place of my presence.
You are to look up to me and never look down on yourself.
Bathe in my presence.
Take on my fullness and recover all things lost.
You are more than capable of handling any stronghold, that would try to consume you.
Take up my shield of faith and the Sword of my Spirit in your hand, to win the war of victory, for truly you are victorious.

Amen

Love

Psa 145:4 **One generation commends your works to another; they tell of your mighty acts.**

Journey
- 360 -

CONTINUE IN WHAT YOU KNOW

I am your joy and your everlasting peace.
Keep going, continue your course of action and walk in the truth you know. Burden yourself no longer with past experiences, that do you no good-- those deadly experiences, that you brought upon yourself, as well as those of others.
Complete the mission appointed to you till the finish line... you will be glad you did.

Have your way with me, Oh, King of my heart.
I seek your face in all I do. I love your Word; it is my life and joy.
My peace comes from you, and I am overjoyed.
Hold me close to your heart and never let go. Never allow me to slip away from you, for my true calling, my home of security is You.

Son of man, I have given you authority to destroy kingdoms.
Go ahead and trample on snakes and scorpions.
Overcome every power, ruler and authority, that provokes the Name of your God and sets itself up against you.
Destroy the wicked schemes of the enemy without any hesitation.

Why are you not fulfilling your divine purpose?
Nothing by any means shall ever harm you. Do not rejoice, because these spirits submit to you, rejoice however that your name is written upon my heart and sealed in heaven with me.

Amen

Love

Isa 48:21 *They did not thirst when he led them through the deserts; he made water flow for them from the rock; he split the rock and water gushed out.*

Journey
- 361 -

YOU ARE MISSED

Your Eternity is calling you home.
Be prepared and ready, for the greatest battle of the end time is coming over the whole world.
This is the last and final call. Your journey on earth is nearly over.
You have reached the final stages for a new beginning.
The world is ending, and so are those who are of it.
Your journey here on earth will not last much longer.
Only the strong and the meek will survive.

You have covered all avenues.
You are now ready for a new beginning. Tower on high.
You need not change, nor be anyone else, than who you really are in me.
You are exactly how I have ordained and intended for you to be.
You are already here in the now. Let the journey begin to continue.

Walk in prosperity and you shall advance more quickly.
My spirit shall accomplish all that is necessary for you.
Many more things shall take place and much more shall happen.

Are you ready? Are you soaring on my wings of worship, that you may prosper in every area of your life?
I am about to move you very quickly and thrust you to where you belong. You shall reach your highest place of honor.

Amen

Love

Psa 140:7 **Sovereign LORD, my strong deliverer, you shield my head in the day of battle.**

Journey
- 362 -

BE CAREFUL

Obey my precious Word by putting it into practice.
Why don't you, child, before the darkness overshadows your view,
and robs you from knowledge, wisdom and understanding?

I am your sincere Friend and your God of compassion.
I, who loves you, am He.
Draw yourself to that which is right and avoid the wrong.
Serve me in all humility.
You are on your way home to be with me.
I spread the corner of my garment over you and covered your nakedness. You became mine and accelerated.
I washed you with the water of my word, and you were purified in righteousness.
I made a covenant with you and you reached your fullness in me.
I shall never leave you, nor ever forsake you... my promise remains.
My love for you is greater than all.

Before you were created, I claimed you for myself.
I set you apart in the womb to win nations.
You grew up and developed and became mine.
I breathed life into you, and you were reborn of my Spirit.

You shall prosper in all you do.
Keep knocking on the door of my heart for revelational truth.
I have claimed you for myself - You are now mine.

Amen

Love

Psa 43:3 **Glorify the Lord with me; let us exalt his name together.**

Journey
- 363 -

BE NOT AFRAID

Glory, glory... arise and shine.
You are wiser now than when you first believed.

Recover the journey of old while there is still time.
Purify yourself during these hard times of affliction.
Come to me with all your heart, for the results will benefit.
Shine, that everyone may see my Light and be comforted from these storms and hardships.
I tell you the truth-- I will not take you anywhere you choose not to be, but will only guide you in the direction best chosen for you.
Follow my leading. By the hand, I shall lead you and by my spirit direct your every step.
Remove every obstacle, that stands in your way.
Keep corrupt talk far away from your mouth.
Do not entertain evil, nor any negative thoughts into your heart and mind, for then destruction will overwhelm you.

The darkness will not separate us, but will only empower us to be knitted together tightly - United deeply.
The night is nearly over and the Day is almost here, so purify yourself before the day dawns.

Keep faith without wavering, love without hating, good without evil, and hope without any distraction.
Rejoice for the Power of Love has rescued you.

Amen

Love

Psa 103:2 **Praise the LORD, my soul, and forget not all his benefits-**

Journey
- 364 -
ASSURANCE IS SECURITY

Allow my Will to be done daily in your life, child.

If you obey my commands, you will be known as one truly faithful.
I shall send you all the help needed, and you will be supported.

Acknowledge me by faith, and I will do wonders never seen before.
Today, I will astonish you with great wonders unknown to man.

Keep going, run the course of time.
Hear the thunder and lightning; the sound of my coming rain--
coming to awaken the people of the earth. The wild storms are coming to take over the land of nations who refuse to repent.
Everyone will run for cover, but you will stand still and know that I am the great I Am.

I shall take care of your every need, so that the needs of others may also be met through you.

While the world is falling apart, you will be standing strong.
While the world is going backwards, you shall be moving forward.
The wonders of my blessings shall remain upon you.
While the world grows poorly, you will increase richly.
The world shall lose, but you will certainly always win.

Greatness you shall inherit and walk in supplication of my love.
No one will be able to take advantage of you.

Amen

Love

1Pe 1:9 for you are receiving the end result of your faith, the salvation of your souls.

Journey
- 365 -

I SHALL WARM YOUR HEART

I have enabled you to reach many nations. Why stop now? Nor your time nor the world is yet over to retreat from your calling. Walk in the direction best chosen for you - The path of my eternal Life, which is open for you.
My Name is Great and is a Strong Tower.
You shall marvel at what I have in store for you.
The harvest is plentiful, but my workers are just very few.
Bring others in, that they may be saved from their calamities.
I have shown you that which is best for you, child.
Why creep and crawl under? Why not rather be lifted up in glory?
I have called you to rule over nations.
Now show them my power and reveal my zeal.

Why entangle yourself with that which is not important?
Why run the race without a Shepherd to watch over you?
Answer me! Tell me why, if you can.
You say one thing and act on another. Why walk in rebellion?
Why not settle down in just one place and love me?
I shall exalt those who are lowly in spirit, and your family will ascend to be with me in heaven.
Your future is assured and secure.
Rule over your enemies.
You shall not fear the troubles of tomorrow, for you are victorious.

Amen

Love

Job 33:28 **God has delivered me from going down to the pit, and I shall live to** *enjoy the light of life.'*

Journey
- 366 -

CHANGE YOUR APPROACH

Sing me a new song and touch me in spirit.
Sing me a love song and make my praises known.

I love those who love me and those who hate me shall drift away, never to be seen again.

Destroy not thy soul by following the flesh.
Death is creeping up on everyone.
Close the door while you still can on these hurricanes, that you may survive the blow.
Apply the blood of my Life and rescue the children.
Listen to all that I am saying and you will be safe.
Take nothing for granted.
Flee from every wicked temptation that destroys.
I urge you to avoid every evil encounter.
Remove yourself from everything that hinders, from everything that kidnaps soul to destroy spirit.
Be careful not to deprive yourself from Good.
Do not wear yourself out on my account in these last days, for I am in control and in charge of your life.
You shall not be burdened by anything.

Restrict not thyself by the troubles of this world.
Maintain your stand.

Amen

Love

1Co 11:19 **No doubt there have to be differences among you to show which of you have God's approval.**

Journey
- 367 -
A NEW START

You Are Now

Mine

Isa 65:17 *"See, I will create new heavens and a new earth. The former things will not be remembered, nor will they come to mind.*

Your Journey

Your Journey

Your Journey

Your Journey

> "The End
> For
> A New
> Beginning

Check out our range of exciting and motivational new **Beyond Woman**® books, inspirational music, irresistible fragrance and selection of empowering products!

www.mybeyondwoman.com
facebook.com/BeyondWoman
facebook.com/MyBeyondWoman
facebook.com/AuthorLinaM
twitter.com/BeyondWoman
twitter.com/MyBeyondWoman

ROYAL DIADEM
PUBLISHING
HOUSE

www.ingramcontent.com/pod-product-compliance
Lightning Source LLC
Chambersburg PA
CBHW080406300426
44113CB00015B/2418